WHAT THEY'RE SAYING ABOUT
VEGAN BITE BY BITE
Transition Guide to a Plant-Based Diet

"*Vegan Bite by Bite* will help many people live healthier, more vibrant and energetic lives. And it will also help them to align their lives with their compassion. If you read this book and heed its message, your life will be richer and better for it."

— JOHN ROBBINS, AUTHOR OF *DIET FOR A NEW AMERICA*, *THE FOOD REVOLUTION*, AND *HEALTHY AT 100*

"I believe that Marilyn Peterson's work should be taken to heart, and that one should think about what she says. Marilyn is touching on things that are worth investigating and worth living. Everyone she serves will receive a blessing and the knowledge to make their family and their bodies healthier. Marilyn has a sincere desire to produce the best there is in nutrition. I feel that her work is the finest I have come across. She's a master at what she does!"

— DR. BERNARD JENSEN, (MARCH 25, 1908–FEBRUARY 22, 2001) PHD CLINICAL NUTRITION, CHIROPRACTOR, AND THE AUTHOR OF NUMEROUS BOOKS AND ARTICLES ON HEALTH AND HEALING

"Vegan Bite by Bite is a terrific resource to travel the road to a healthy diet. Marilyn has written a masterpiece of information allowing the readers to save their own lives. Vegan Bite by Bite is all the information you need to make the transition from where you are, to where you should be, in human health."

— HOWARD F. LYMAN, AUTHOR, *MAD COWBOY AND NO MORE BULL!*

"As a masterful chef and passionate guide to healthier food and lifestyle choices, Marilyn Peterson is at her best in Vegan Bite by Bite.

With joyous enthusiasm, practical advice, and enlightening examples from many contributors, Marilyn makes the transition to a plant-based diet exciting, logical, spiritually rewarding—and even fun and delicious! She lets you know you are not alone on this powerful journey to a health-enhancing, non-violent diet and lifestyle—and she gives you sound strategies to help you succeed, even if you 'slip' along the way.

"Let 'Guide Marilyn' in Vegan Bite by Bite escort you—and cheer you on—as you progress to an eating style that will help create health and balance in your body, as well as promote harmony with the living world around you. I recommend it most highly!"

—MICHAEL KLAPER, MD, AUTHOR, *VEGAN NUTRITION: PURE AND SIMPLE*

"One of the most oft-asked questions of a surprisingly large and growing number of people adopting the plant-based diet is: 'How do I do it?' A recent survey of the general public in Australia suggested that at least 40% of the respondents were interested in giving this dietary lifestyle a try but they simply wanted to know how. Marilyn Peterson does it in her book, *Vegan Bite by Bite,* in a very personal way that I believe many people will find appealing."

—T. COLIN CAMPBELL, PhD AUTHOR, *THE CHINA STUDY,* DIRECTOR OF THE CHINA PROJECT, NUTRITIONAL BIOCHEMISTRY PROFESSOR (EMERITUS), CORNELL UNIVERSITY

VEGAN BITE
BY BITE

VEGAN BITE BY BITE

A RECIPE FOR *TRANSITION*

With a *COOKBOOK* AS ONE OF THE INGREDIENTS

Marilyn Peterson

3 Ton Tomato Press — Los Angeles

VEGAN BITE BY BITE — A Recipe for Transition

For information about this title or to order other books and/or electronic media, contact the publisher:

3 Ton Tomato Press
4353 W. 5th Street
Los Angeles, CA 90020
threetontomatopress@me.com

The registered trademarks in this book are the sole property of their respective owners.

ISBN Paperback: 978-0-9824130-0-5
ISBN E-Book: 978-0-9824130-1-2

Printed in the United States of America

Author: Marilyn Peterson
Executive Editor: Charise Diamond
Interview Editors: Lila Wallace, Nicolette Marais, Mark Viergutz
Research Editor: R. Casey Lawrence, MD
Cover Design: Charise Diamond (idea), 1106 Design (creation)
Illustrations: Charise Diamond
Color food styled photos available at www.veganbitebybite.com
Photographer Chapter 5: Wendel Peterson
Interior Book Design: 1106 Design
3 Ton Tomato Photo: Matt Cheek
Book Photo: "Retro Forks" sculptures ©Karen & Tony Barone, ©MMIX
Photographer: Catherine Jardine
Location: Orbit-In, Palm Springs, CA

Disclaimer

This book has been written based on the personal experiences and information compiled by the author. It was designed to provide information only and it is sold with the understanding that the author is not engaged in rendering medical advice.

This educational book is not intended to substitute for any medical or nutritional information or advice. If you have any concerns please consult your physician or health care provider. If you are consulting, or have consulted with a physician, dietician or nutritionist, continue to do so if you are using any of these recipes and information for health reasons of any kind.

As is the Nature of all consumer products, many new ones are introduced to the market while others are discontinued or their ingredients changed. Every effort has been made to ensure that the products recommended in this book are not only available but also suitable for vegans. However; due to the fact that we have no control over their formulas, you are urged to always read the labels and check the nutritional content to confirm that the products meet your lifestyle standards.

Dedication

This book is dedicated to the unseen hand that guides us all, the hand that feeds us, the Spirit that nourishes our spirits, and to my husband, Wendel, whose loving generosity, and support made this book possible.

To my nutrition mentors, Dr. Bernard Jensen, Dr. Pierre Pannetier and Dr. Paavo Airola, great icons in the field of nutrition, for influencing my work toward vegetarianism.

To my parents, who gave me the determination to survive and overcome, and laid the foundation for life's lessons.

To my Spiritual Masters, Charan Singh and Gurinder Singh who taught me about the law of karma and gave me the kingdom keys as a gift. I am eternally grateful!

To my children: Stacy and Stewart, their spouses Mitchell and Julie, and my grandchildren: Rachel, Jordan and Ryan; this is my loving legacy to you.

Setting The Table — Of Contents

Foreword
Neal Barnard, MD

You know you've wanted to eat better. Perhaps your doctor or health professional has recommended some non-animal dietary changes for you but you don't know where to begin. In the following pages, you will be blown away at how easy the transition to healthy eating can be. Marilyn guides you step by step on how to prepare yourself, your family, your pantry and kitchen for plant-based meals.

Once past the introductory chapters you will discover shopping and ingredient lists, brand-name guides, and well-crafted menus and recipes that are easy to follow. She shares stories from doctors, celebrities, authors, individuals and families who have made the switch. She will answer all your questions and gently walk you through everything you need to know.

The transition is outlined in two stages; with introductory foods such as mock meats to make it easier up front, followed by a wide variety of whole foods later on. For those who have already begun the journey toward health, this guide will support you in learning how to eat even healthier, with a focus on simple, whole foods. After you read this thorough but light-hearted handbook, you will be inspired to clear your plate of everything that doesn't belong there.

Our research at the Physicians Committee for Responsible Medicine has shown that by switching to a plant-based diet and eliminating unhealthy saturated fats and cholesterol that come from animal products, you can maintain a healthy weight, prevent chronic disease and feel great. In fact, our research shows that a vegan diet can reverse type 2 diabetes, tackle cholesterol problems, and conquer long-standing weight challenges. Now that's something to chew on!

The *side effects* of a vegan diet are excellent. This is a great book for doctors and patients to have as a guide to disease prevention and health promotion. If you are ready to try this diet out, here's what we recommend; don't just dip your toe in the swimming pool. Don't be tentative. Instead, dive right in. If this way of eating is new to you, we suggest that you set aside at least three weeks to take it for a test drive.

Without exception, the people who chose this change felt healthier, lighter, and more energized. They find — and you will find, too — that this is a prescription to live by.

As the pages turn, may you enjoy all the helpful, healthy hints that Marilyn has waiting for you inside this wonderful guide and may you also enjoy all the health benefits of good nutrition, bite by bite!

—Neal Barnard, MD
Founder/President of Physicians Committee for Responsible Medicine
Author of:

- ✧ *Breaking the Food Seduction*
- ✧ *Dr. Neal Barnard's Program for Reversing Diabetes: The Scientifically Proven System for Reversing Diabetes Without Drugs*

Acknowledgments

As a self-taught chef, I started learning the computer at the same time I started writing this book. I didn't grow up in the high-tech age. My grandchildren, Rachel and Jordan may have known more about the computer than I did.

In the beginning stages of working on this book, and with no budget to hire computer, editorial and research assistance, I had the idea to post vegan consultations, cooking and raw food classes on Craigslist in exchange for the help I needed.

The response was overwhelming! As a result of advertising for researchers, interviewers, recipe testers, and an administrator, the phone was ringing off the hook with people wanting to learn about veganism!

It was amazing to realize how many people were eager to contribute to the book project, mainly because of their interest in learning how to transition to a vegan lifestyle and improve their health. Some were interested in animal rights issues or the environment while others had a great fascination for the chapter on karma. Various subjects appealed to each individual. Most wanted to learn a variety of ways to prepare delicious, healthy dishes. Some were interested in consultation and how to shop, while others wanted to learn about the book process. Some were in humdrum jobs and wanted to be involved with a creative process. An awesome array of talents and expertise came on board. Because of their gifts, this book has come to fruition. I value every intern/student and your contribution. This book could never have been written without the support of everyone who gave of their time and talents, from the kitchen elves to the computer geniuses.

Thank you all, starting with Charise Diamond, a *talented* gem whose research and editorial/writing majesty eloquently polished this book into shape, as a jeweler polishes a delicate stone to bring out all of its brilliant facets, for your expert counsel, manuscript guidance, and your gifted illustrations. Your storytelling magic contributed greatly to the book. Nicolette Marais *generously* contributed her journalistic talents; organizing my original written materials, interviewing and typing research. Martha Theus, for guiding and encouraging the book toward publication. Elisa Morimoto, Nataly Bryce and Nicolette Marais, whose administrative capabilities organized our team. Mark Viergutz, for his *generous* contribution of *extraordinary* artistic talent as food photographer. Craig Thornton, Anna Varnell and Mark Viergutz for assisting me with the food styling for photography. Matt Cheek for photography for the 3 Ton Tomato book cover. Zel Allen, Jeff Nelson, Barbara Gallen and Caryle Katz, "big thanks" for all your support.

Students/Interns — Johnson & Wales Nutrition/Culinary University, Kathy Riley and Rudy Hermanawan, who helped document recipes. Recipe testers, Adrienne Lee, and Joseph Waller, who inspired me in the kitchen offering his creativity. Patrice Fisher, Tia Campbell, Teri Hicks and Phoebe White, for your unconditional support however it was needed. Gwenn Marie and Sita White helped with the original book outline.

Marina Tumas, Tatum Adair, Nana Stark, Nicholas Mendoza, Stephani Cook, Scott Shell, Catheryn Brockett, Vanessa Hidalgo and Matt Cheek for your research contributions. Eva Stefunak for research and technical guidance. Lila Wallace for research, interview editing and manuscript guidance. Bob Schmidt for website research. Marina Tumas for References research. Doug Drory, Preeti Dhiman, Amit Uttamchandani, Bart Goldman, Eleanor Brownn, Levon Goganian and Apple Computer techies, for computer technical expertise. Brian von Dedenroth, Mark Viergutz, Nicolette Marais and Vanessa Hidalgo for taping interviews. Arthur Comstock (former trial lawyer) for his expert legal knowledge in answering my many questions.

To those of you who gave the interviews; thank you for giving your generous time and answering research questions. I would like to express my gratefulness to Dr. Neal Barnard, John Robbins, Howard Lyman, Dr. Michael Klaper and Dr. T. Colin Campbell. Special thanks to Dr. Joel Fuhrman, Dr. John McDougall, Dr. T. Colin Campbell, Dr. Neal Barnard and Jill Eckart for your research contributions. And, to those of you who contributed quotes for the book, a big thank you for your valuable knowledge. Last, but not least, ALL of my friends and family, for cheering me on when I was stuck in the trenches! You are all co-authors!

I am grateful for the integrity of 1106 Design. Working with Michele, Ronda and Diane has been a tutorial, professional delight and blessing! Thank you!

Wishing you, my readers, the blessings of good health!

Introduction

"Transition to a plant-based diet is like eating a three-ton tomato.
How do you eat a three-ton tomato? Bite by bite!"
                                    —*Swami Vegananda*

This book is a *recipe for transition;* a *cookbook* is one of the main ingredients. The purpose of this book is to assist the reader with information and recipes to transition from an animal- and dairy-based diet to a plant-based diet. This is only the beginning of a journey toward the ultimate healthy diet.

I want to begin this book by talking about beginnings. The origin of this book came out of a search for information about my own transition and expanded in the years to follow as I shared those discoveries. I have been working with friends and clients, coaching them through the transition, gathering more information and positive proof as I go along. Now, I am taking my years of experience, since 1966, and simplifying it in writing so that the reader gets right away what it took me a long time to understand and incorporate into my life.

I have written *Vegan Bite by Bite* with the voice of a personal coach. I want you to feel that I am in the kitchen and food market with you, holding your hand, so to speak, as you walk through your own transition step by step, bite by bite.

The first three chapters will take you from the exploration of transition ideas and philosophy into preparation and action. I have also included a collection of interviews given by vegan celebrities, doctors, authors, students/interns and restaurateurs; stories of their own personal experiences and perspectives. My own journey is entertainingly described, and then there are resources and reading recommendations at the back of the book to take you further than you may ever want to go.

SO, WHY VEGAN?

What has brought your interest and attention far enough to pick up this book? Is it based upon one of the following?

- ✧ Doctor's recommendation — Instructed by a physician to make dietary changes
- ✧ Compassion for animals — "Ahimsa" philosophy: non-harm to animals
- ✧ Chronic or life-threatening illness — self or loved one
- ✧ Lactose intolerance, allergies to dairy products
- ✧ Need for more energy — feeling fatigued, depressed
- ✧ "Green," sustainable, ecological living
- ✧ Weight loss
- ✧ Preventative maintenance
- ✧ Fear of harm from animal foods — based on other books/articles or media scare
- ✧ Aspire to vegan examples; friends/folks who have made it and look/feel great
- ✧ Desire to raise healthy children/family
- ✧ Longevity

AFTER "WHY?" COMES "HOW?"

Grasping the rationale behind adopting a plant-based diet and actually doing it may be two different things. Whatever circumstance has brought you to this point; it is clear you want to make a transition but important questions keep popping up:

- ✧ Where do I start?
- ✧ What do I need to know?
- ✧ What can I eat and what do I have to give up?
- ✧ Will I feel deprived and/or hungry all the time?
- ✧ Can I find tasty, adequate substitutes?
- ✧ How complicated and time-consuming is this?
- ✧ Will I feel socially awkward?

THE CORE OF THE TRANSITION IS INTERNAL

It begins with your own decision, becomes a commitment and then a plan of action. There is work and play, fun and struggle, setbacks and progress. Personal efforts to improve will undoubtedly influence those around you, with or without you putting any attention on that. We teach by example. Your greatest strength will come not from trying to change others but from being true to your own passage. If this is a family transition or a buddy/team effort, communication, in addition to this book, will be the backbone. It is still essential for each person to keep an internal focal point before and during the process of linking up with others.

Cut this out and glue it to your forehead:

> **SETBACKS ARE PROGRESS IN DISGUISE**
>
> WITH THE END RESULTS
>
> IN YOUR FAVOR AND FLAVOR

A Transition Definition:

"Transition is the process of letting go of the way things used to be and then taking hold of the way they subsequently become."
— WILLIAM BRIDGES — *THE WAY OF TRANSITION*

"Nothing will benefit human health and increase the chances for survival of life on Earth as much as the evolution to a vegetarian diet."
— ALBERT EINSTEIN

"Let food be thy medicine and medicine be thy food."
— *HIPPOCRATES*

"The American people need to know the truth. They need to know what we have uncovered in our research. People need to know why we are unnecessarily sick, why too many of us die early despite the billions spent on research. The irony is that the solution is simple and inexpensive. The answer to the American health crisis is the food that each of us chooses to put in our mouths each day. It's as simple as that.

"…So what is my prescription for good health? In short, it is about the multiple health benefits of consuming plant-based foods, and the largely unappreciated health dangers of consuming animal-based foods, including all types of meat, dairy and eggs."

FROM *THE CHINA STUDY* BY T. COLIN CAMPBELL, PhD,
DIRECTOR OF THE CHINA PROJECT JACOB GOULD SCHURMAN[1]
PROFESSOR EMERITUS OF NUTRITIONAL BIOCHEMISTRY, CORNELL UNIVERSITY

---

[1] Jacob Gould Schurman is the name of a former and distinguished president of Cornell in the late 1800s–early 1900s. Donors gave money in his honor to establish 6 (endowed) professorships at Cornell. One of these was awarded to T. Colin Campbell in the 1980s.

*J*ust as a large tree begins with a tiny seed, we begin with a small step. The transition centers on the kitchen, but ripples out into lifestyle.

Imagine a neighborhood plagued by a gang of vandals who have no respect for residents or property. What a relief when the gang no longer comes around. When no longer threatened, the neighbors clean up their streets and houses, pick up litter and haul away the trash. Once the debris has been cleared, they begin to beautify the neighborhood by whitewashing fences, painting over graffiti, planting flowers and restoring buildings. This analogy reflects the process that often takes place when the body is no longer being overwhelmed with toxins, and starts to detox from transitioning to a plant-based diet.

Backed up toxins in the body, which often cause irritability, pain or dysfunction, are eliminated as pure foods flush out the system, increasing energy and immunity. How does this affect lifestyle? Simply put, feeling good translates to lighter and brighter everything. This is my snapshot overview.

BACK TO THE GARDEN

The emotional poisons of my childhood colored my consciousness and led me to rebellion but the path back to Nature, to the promise of healing, was always there. Because I was raised on natural methods from birth, this "Garden of Eden" was my heritage, a path to walk in life. After the hypoglycemic collapse I began to see and travel that path.[2] I knew that health was in that garden and if I visited it and followed the laws of Nature, I would reap the benefits.

---

[2] The story relating to the hypoglycemic collapse can be found on pages 265 to 268.

ONCE PAST THE GATE, the transition itself will carry you along. Rely on *VEGAN BITE BY BITE* for support and explore other resources listed here whenever you feel the need. Here is a plan, with mouth-watering recipes and tips, on how to make the transition that may well improve health and, consequently, your quality of life.

DIFFERENT DEFINITIONS OF "VEGETARIAN"

The term vegetarian is distinguished from the term vegan by the fact that vegans eat only plant-based foods. A loose definition of vegetarian can include dairy products (lacto-vegetarian) and sometimes eggs (ovo-vegetarian or lacto-ovo-vegetarian). Within the vegan world are different models also. It is important to be specific about the type of vegan/vegetarian diet that is considered to be health supporting.

> "Those who consume a high volume of a variety of unrefined plant foods generate the statistics that are most impressive."
> —Joel Fuhrman, MD

I am in agreement with Dr. Fuhrman. His emphasis is often on the word "unrefined," meaning fresh produce and whole foods like beans and lentils. There is an art and knowledge to being a *healthy* vegan as opposed to one who eats a high amount of refined foods, fats and sugars, even if they are all plant-based. Discuss the vegan diet with your physician or dietician to verify a personalized *healthy* plan for you and your family.

> "If vegetarians eat vegetables, what do humanitarians eat?"
> —Swami Vegananda

THE INCREDIBLE LIGHTNESS OF BEING VEGAN

The idea of animal products as food can be discussed from many different angles, most of them practical and grounded. There have been many well-researched books written on the subject of abstaining from animals-as-food. Although the focus of this book is the transition itself, I would like to list the rewards you are likely to encounter as a result of your efforts in making this change. The positive paybacks can be summed up as follows:[3]

1. Improved Health and Energy
   a. Weight Loss — "We know that eating a low-fat, low-protein diet high in complex carbohydrates from fruits and vegetables will help you lose weight."[4]
   b. Turn Off Cancer — Meat and dairy promote cancer growth; fruits and vegetables hinder it. "We were finding that high protein intake, in excess of the amount needed for growth, promotes cancer after initiation... But the cancer promoting factor in this case was cow's milk protein..."[5]
   c. Reverse Heart Disease — In Dr. Dean Ornish's research study, published in 1990, 82% (of research subjects) who switched to a low-fat, vegetarian diet, along with exercise and stress management, reversed their heart disease.[i]
   d. Improve and/or Reverse Diabetes — Research has shown that type 2 diabetes can improve or even disappear and type 1 diabetes insulin intake can be reduced to the smallest possible dose through a change in diet. The problems it causes — heart disease, blindness, kidney disease, and amputations — are much less likely to occur.[ii]
   e. Reduce Blood Pressure — In research studies, a combination of diet changes and exercise can bring down blood pressure enough that most people can reduce or even stop their medications.[iii]
   f. Un-lax — With the increased fiber and the absence of intestine-clogging foods, eliminations will be more balanced. Toss the laxatives.
   g. Stronger Bones — Animal protein leaches calcium from the bones and sends it through the kidneys, to be lost in the urine.[iv]
   h. Reduced Menstrual Symptoms — Breaking a meat/dairy habit reduces menstrual symptoms because hormones are better balanced.[v]
   i. Safer from Food-Borne Illnesses
      i. Salmonella
      ii. E. coli
   All food-poisoning bacteria originate in livestock feces. Plants do not have digestive tracts. Therefore, plants, if found to be contaminated, are tainted with manure (fertilizers or close-proximity livestock) or poor

---

[3] Barnard, MD, Neal, *Breaking the Food Seduction*, Chapter 12 — A summary of motivators for changing to and sticking with a healthy (vegan) diet. Additional notes from various sources.
[4] Campbell, PhD, T.C, *The China Study*, Chapter 4 — Lessons from China, "Diet and Body Size."
[5] Campbell, PhD, T.C, *The China Study*, Chapter 3 — Turning Off Cancer, "Not All Proteins Are Alike."

food-handlers' hygiene.[vi] "There are 75 million cases of food poisoning, and 5,000 of these are fatal. The USDA reports that 70% of food poisoning is caused by contaminated animal flesh."[6]

2. Longevity — "Vegetarians live years longer than their meat-eating counterparts."[vii] "The most consistent finding in the nutritional literature throughout every epidemiological study is that as fruit and vegetable consumption increases in the diet, chronic diseases and premature deaths decrease."[7]

3. Better Quality of Life — Health, at any age, is a major factor in quality of life.

4. Financial Advantages — Vegetables are cheaper than meat, yes, and you can save thousands of dollars in prescription costs, hospital and doctor bills. The direct medical costs attributable to meat consumption in the United States, in 1995, were $61 billion.[viii]

5. Reduced Environmental Pollution — It would take numerous pages to do justice to such a huge subject.
   a. Rain forests that took hundreds of years to grow are being decimated to produce cattle-grazing land.
   b. The urine and feces from livestock yards and pastures are seeping into and polluting the ground water and contaminating produce fields irrigated with this water or fertilized with livestock manure.
   c. Livestock-produced methane gas contributes to air pollution.

6. Increased Energy — "The evidence regarding increased energy levels was supported by an enormous amount of anecdotal evidence I have encountered over the years; people have more energy when they eat well. This synergy between nutrition and physical activity is extremely important, and is evidence that these two parts of life are not isolated from each other."[8]

7. Being Kind to Animals — This is often the main reason people become vegan. Animal rights and Veganism are almost synonymous.

Enjoy the journey. There are tools beyond this book, including my website, *www.veganbitebybite.com* with links to resources and information.

"Animals are my friends... and I don't eat my friends."
—George Bernard Shaw

---

6 Theus, Martha *"Throwin' Down Vegetarian Style"*, p. 15.
7 Fuhrman, Joel, MD, *Eat to Live*, Chapter 5 — Are You Dying to Lose Weight? p. 106.
8 Campbell, PhD, TC, *The China Study*, Chapter 11, Eating Right, Principle #8 — All parts are interconnected, p. 239.

"It isn't about how long you live, it is about
how you feel as long as you live!"
—Swami Vegananda

AUTHOR'S NOTE:

"A journey of a thousand miles
must begin with a single step."
—Lao Tzu

While writing this book, I have come to realize that whatever
amount of animal and dairy products can be given up, it is
a good thing, and that whatever the readers do to this end
is a wonderful beginning to their transition. One sets his foot
upon a path from where he is at the time. There is no need
to negate all the footsteps that led to that point. Every step
moves one closer to the desired goal. We each do what we
are ready for according to our own journey's map.

Marilyn Peterson

Endnotes

i   Ornish D, SE Brown, LW Schwerwitz, et al. *Can lifestyle changes reverse coronary heart disease?* Lancet 1990;336:129–133

ii Nicholson AS, M Sklar, ND Barnard, S Gore, R Sullivan, S Browning. *Toward improved management of NIDDM: a randomized controlled, pilot intervention using a low-fat, vegetarian diet.* Prev Med 1999;29:87–91

iii Lindahl O, L Lindwall, A Spangberg, PA Ockerman. *A vegan regimen with reduced medication in the treatment of hypertension.* Br J Nutr 1984;52:11–20

iv Reddy ST, CY Wang, K Sakhaee, L Brinkley, CY Pak. *Effect of low-carbohydrate high-protein diets on acid-base balance, stone-forming propensity, and calcium metabolism.* Am J Kidney Dis 2002;40:265–74

v   Barnard ND, AR Scialli, P Bertron, D Hurlock, K Edmonds, I Talev. *Effectiveness of a low-fat, vegetarian diet in altering serum lipids in healthy premenopausal women.* Am J Cardiol 2000;85:969–72

vi Barnard ND, *Breaking the Food Seduction*, p. 143

vii Fraser GE, DJ Shavlik. *Ten years of life: is it a matter of choice?* Arch Intern Med 2001;161:1645–52

viii Barnard ND, A Nicholson, JL Howard, *The medical costs attributable to meat consumption.* Prev Med 1995;24:646–55

Chapter One
Transition: A Basic Overview

WHY THE TRANSITION?

Why do I recommend the transition from a meat and dairy-based diet to a plant-based diet? There are three main reasons:

1. Physical Health
2. Spiritual Health
3. Environmental Health

I have seen in others and experienced firsthand the positive benefits of a vegan diet. To withhold the foods that are causing harm to the body and redirect the diet to health-supportive foods is the goal of this transition. As the diet becomes lighter, the body becomes lighter and, not surprisingly, abstaining from animal foods also lightens the spirit by easing the karmic load one incurs by killing — or being part of the supply-and-demand chain that causes killing. The transformation that takes place in a person is an absolute wonder and it is built on such a simple foundation. Most of my clients/students will choose to go deeper into the transition because of the way they feel — having greater energy and radiance.

"A diet based on animal foods is a primary driving force
behind the most serious environmental problems we face."
—The World Peace Diet, *Will Tuttle*

1

WHAT DO EXPERTS SAY?

How do animal and dairy[1] foods affect our health? It is thoroughly documented that animal-based food products contribute to any number of health problems; they contain saturated (animal) fats, cholesterol, casein[2] and an array of chemicals and toxins. This book is about making the transition. If you would like concrete evidence on the benefits of becoming vegan and the detriments of animal-based foods, I highly recommend the following authors as trustworthy resources:

- ✧ Howard Lyman — *Mad Cowboy* and *No More Bull!*
- ✧ John Robbins — *Diet For A New America* and *The Food Revolution*
- ✧ T. Colin Campbell, PhD — *The China Study*
- ✧ Neal Barnard, MD — *Breaking the Food Seduction* + many more
- ✧ Joel Fuhrman, MD — *Eat to Live, Disease-Proof Your Child* + more

These stand out as favorites in my own library and I have provided a recommended reading list with a brief synopsis of these and other books at the end of this book. In Chapter Three, "Truth or Consequences — Meat Ain't Neat and Dairy is Scary" I have gone into greater detail on the subject of meat, the protein myth and important facts about dairy.

> "A vegan lifestyle makes the difference
> between heaven and HELLth."
> —*Swami Vegananda*

KARMA

I personally find the karmic aspect of diet to be highly relevant because it addresses the ethical perspective of the transition. I marvel at the phenomenon that, as we remove ourselves from the chain of supply and demand that causes animal suffering, we experience relief in our own suffering. Above and beyond this "Golden Rule" boomerang effect on our physical health, however, there is another point of view, that of spiritual evolution. As I travel my own spiritual path and examine the teachings of mystics from different times and cultures as well, I find a voice threaded through them that speaks to me personally. This is a voice that would have me abstain from

---

[1] Although animal foods are the main focus here, scientists are discovering new health threats from over-processed dairy foods as well as the casein in all dairy products. See Chapter Three for in-depth coverage on animal and dairy foods.

[2] T. Colin Campbell, PhD — *The China Study* — In discussing the kind of education being taught by the dairy industry, Dr. Campbell says: "Obviously neither kids nor their parents are learning about how milk has been linked to Type 1 diabetes, prostate cancer, osteoporosis, multiple sclerosis or other autoimmune diseases, and how casein, the main protein in dairy foods, has been shown to experimentally promote cancer and increase blood cholesterol and atherosclerotic plaque."

taking animal life for the sake of my palate, for it has been scientifically proven that we do not need animal foods for protein.[3] So, in all good conscience, how can I add that karmic debt to my load without harming my spiritual progress?

WHEN YOU COME TO A FORK IN THE ROAD

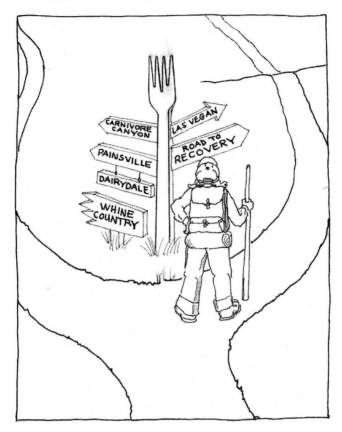

THE TRANSITION DECISION

This may not come all at once and may not be black and white. It can come gradually with several restarts or it can be overnight. Even though the old ways die hard and new ways come and go, if the goals are positive, at some point there will be enough fire and momentum to carry you through the doubts and failed attempts. Every struggle is part of the success.

A PERSONAL TRANSITION DECISION

Everyone has his own transition story, reasons, and stages. Often it is suffering that brings our attention to the need for change. Even suffering can be a gift if it is teaching us something we need to know; this may be the only way to finally get the lesson. My own transition decision came at a time when I was suffering great loss and

---

[3]   See Chapter Three's discussion on "the protein myth."

heartache. In the midst of personal agony, I had gone to a party at a friend's house and was in the kitchen by myself when I opened the refrigerator in search of a beverage. Suddenly I saw plastic-wrapped packages of meat, animals cut up and surrounded by their own blood. The visual effect hit me like a sledgehammer. The sensitivity of my own suffering at that time forced me to relate to the suffering of those slaughtered animals. Before I closed the refrigerator door I knew I was to become vegetarian. That single, dynamic moment's experience swept through my mind and changed it forever, without logic or reasoning. The intensity of that experience is still with me and has been the motivating force in my work all these years. The next steps were already laid out before me. Meat, chicken and fish immediately fell away and eggs/dairy were later eliminated as I gained more knowledge and experience in transitioning.

TRANSITION REVISITED

I have been a vegetarian since 1966 and a vegan since 1981. Having successfully completed these first two transitions years ago, the process of writing this book was to be based on history. The transition once again became fully alive for me, however, when I decided to *experience* the change from vegan to RAW vegan. This recent transition in my own life helped me review the initial vegan transition. The transition dance steps are similar no matter what tune the orchestra is playing; a meat-to-plant transition is basically the same as a vegan-to-raw-vegan transition.

The first steps are based on research and trying it out from time to time. Then, at some point, the moment of truth arrives and you know you are ready for the transition.

- ✧ A 100% commitment is made
- ✧ Preparation steps include: self, family, friends and environment
- ✧ Launch
- ✧ Learn as you go

EXPERIENCE IS THE BEST TEACHER

Over the years, both in my own personal experience and through coaching others in their transition, I have found the best ways to help people start a new way of living and eating. I feel optimistic that people can renovate their diet/lifestyle with positive and lasting results.

Whatever your reason for making this transition, welcome! My primary intention in this book is to make the transition as easy as possible for you. Once you have this basic, introductory knowledge, the timing and style of your first few steps are up to you. I do, however, advise you to stay on this diet long enough for your taste buds to get re-educated and for your body to feel the change. A three-week trial is considered minimum and six weeks or more is ideal.

"Change is inevitable, except from a vending machine."
—Robert C. Gallagher

DEVIOUS DIVERSIONS

Revisiting the transition process forced me to relive the intriguing tango that the mind and senses go through. Like most people, I experienced that what we call *comfort* foods can soon become *discomfort* foods. We are repeatedly taken in by seductive foods while the body is saying "STOP!" The wily mind, living only for the moment, focuses on the pleasure of taste, with a flickering thought on the side of being able to "get away with it." However, there is some kind of internal "Diet Cop" that keeps pulling us over and issuing a warning ticket. Have you experienced that it is not really a surprise when you're busted by your body and have to serve time with aches and pains?

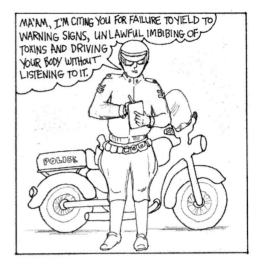

DRIVING IN REVERSE

No matter what kind of transition, there are passages they all have in common. Imagine yourself off to a good start, commitment flags flying in the warm, sunny breeze and you're feeling fabulous.

What is it about feeling good that inspires us to put everything in reverse?

Maybe we're just not used to feeling good. We may find ourselves eating "just a little" of the taboo foods.

Of course we are "ration-a-lying," finding worthy excuses such as:

- ✧ "I am unique, the rules don't apply to me."
- ✧ "I can get away with 'just one.'"
- ✧ "It won't hurt anything."

> "The transition doesn't take willpower. It takes won't power!"
> —Swami Vegananda

At this point, truly honest observation discloses the mind's tricks. There is a feeling of physical discomfort, a diminished energy level is observed, perhaps fatigue sets in more dramatically and one is forced to admit that the body is clearly sending a message that it feels better on vegan foods. In the initial vegan transition, noticing this difference may take awhile. You usually have to be on the vegan side of the fence for at least three weeks before a reintroduction of the old foods will cause a red flag to wave.

WHO'S COACHING WHOM?

On the bright side, there is a point in the transition where all the initial groundwork and effort is translated into "body language," i.e., the body begins to understand and take over the work while *your* work shifts to simply listening to the body. It's a common experience that as the body becomes cleaner and more familiar with receiving wholesome foods, *it* tells you it's preferences. Not only do you get back on track but your progress increases effortlessly. For example, I noticed I had gone from eating 80% raw to 90% raw without really thinking about it. I realized that my body was coaching me. The same shift occurs in the animal-to-plant transition. Watch for it.

LEARNING CURVES — HOW DO WE CHANGE OUR EATING PATTERNS?

Breaking old food habits and starting new ones can be daunting to say the least. With this quest for new health and energy, there are a few dietary adjustments along the way but with a personal commitment on the reader's part plus help and guidance from reliable sources, this can be done. Once the initial transition has taken place, modifications continue at an easy pace until one arrives at a place once thought all but impossible. Then from the successful end of the transition, the traveler can look back and congratulate himself on the changes made. It may even be surprising to discover that the old, cherished foods no longer appeal to the newly educated palate.

How, specifically, do we alter strong and familiar food patterns? The key is simplicity; we do it one step at a time, making adjustments and renewing the journey as we go. Favorite foods of the past are replaced and/or recreated with vegan ingredients rather than being lost or denied. Instead of "mistakes" made, there are lessons learned. One of the initial challenges, which we will address in a later chapter, is how to make the transition when we are not skilled at creating the new delicious dishes needed to take the place of the old familiar meals.[4]

There are discoveries to be made, some common to all and some unique to the individual. Here is something I've observed: once the body adapts to pure food and cleans out the old toxins, it seems to become more sensitive and doesn't allow us as much margin to abuse ourselves in the same old ways.

INVESTMENT = HEALTHY PROFIT

Yes, there is some study, research and learning that go into changing one's dietary lifestyle. If it is going to give you a better quality of life, however, and act as preventative maintenance, it has its payoff. Anyone considering making an investment for the first time — in the stock market for example — will also want to invest time learning the different aspects of it so as to increase the chances of a profit. With this transition our efforts eventually pay off by showing a *healthy* profit.

---

[4] See interview with Pam Popper, page 223.

A TYPICAL TRANSITION EXAMPLE

Shauna, Josh and their five-year-old daughter went through the change to a vegan diet easily, feeling satisfied in ways they had never experienced before. They told me that they didn't miss some of the foods they were used to because the foods that they were now eating were similar enough. The differences they commented on were:

1) The food felt more nutritious and tasted amazingly flavorful.

2) They were eating less in quantity, due to the increased nutritional value of the food, yet feeling completely satisfied.

3) They also noticed a remarkable difference in their elimination, which they said, "gave them more energy."

4) They slept more easily and peacefully.

During their transition, Shauna and Josh decided to give a party to introduce all of their friends and clients to their new food lifestyle. It was a major hit; people thanked them for the new information on staying healthy, complimented them on how fabulous they were looking and how delicious the food tasted. Example is always the best teacher.

A TRANSITION CONSULTATION HISTORY

This client, age 28, had suffered from headaches for 15 years and intense migraine headaches every day for the last two years. When I came over to consult with her, she greeted me from behind dark sunglasses with body language that was the picture of exhaustion; she had been unable to sleep because of headaches. Even though it was a bright, sunshiny day, all windows in her house were covered with drawn blinds and drapes. There wasn't a lot of light in this client's life or energy to have much of a life, other than her suffering. I was not surprised to find that she ate meat and dairy and was only eliminating every few days. It was a surprise to her when I said the body ideally should be eliminating after every meal.

For this client my recommendations were, first and foremost, to eliminate all animal products including dairy. Because she had so little energy and I had not only energy but also time, I expanded my consultation to include the extra services of shopping and food preparation. To keep things simple, she ate several small portions daily of fresh fruits and vegetables, including vegetable juices, to support cleansing. Starchy and high-protein foods were put on hold until elimination improved.

I repeatedly encouraged her with the idea that she would be able to open the blinds and go out into the sunshine without sunglasses and have a life. In the beginning, she didn't believe any of this was possible, including the idea of eliminating after every meal.

These are the results I was informed of, during the month we worked together:

✧ She had only one headache during the entire month.

✧ She began eliminating after every meal. She believed this was a miracle, although I assured her that it is only a natural process of eating the correct foods for the body.

- ✧ She began sleeping at night.
- ✧ She developed the energy to begin working out at a gym.
- ✧ The blinds and drapes were opened and the sunglasses became an outdoor wardrobe item.
- ✧ She was able to bring sunshine into her life.
- ✧ Her medical doctor and I were both happy with her results.

STAGES — A BRIEF OVERVIEW

The transition is divided into two stages just as a loose way of spelling it out. This is only a rough guideline and the reader is free to choose recipes from any stage at any time. There are no time requirements either; stay or move on at your own pace. This is your transition program, so make friends with it. Your body will naturally adjust according to various factors such as climate, how you feel and your personal taste preferences. Be patient; all will be refined with time.

STAGE ONE: LOVE AT FIRST BITE

In Stage One, the big leap is leaving all meats behind and looking ahead to meals without dairy or eggs. Just about anything else goes as we adjust to this change. Once this is mastered, we can refine the process and make further changes. As the palate and body adjust, it becomes easier to fold in more health-building choices and eliminate non-supportive elements.

STAGE TWO: GET THEE BEHIND ME, SEITAN![5]

Whole foods become predominant in this stage and processed foods fall away. Fresh, organic fruits and vegetables are more abundant. Add some more raw food recipes to your menus.

BEYOND THE BEGINNING

Increasing the percentage of raw food is a healthy choice. Raw foods have an abundance of enzymes and health-supportive nutrients that are often destroyed or eliminated when the food is cooked and/or processed.

MORE ON RAW FOODS

Originally, I started to include an additional "Stage Three," a transition to raw foods, but the transition to raw foods is not a required part of becoming vegan. I do however believe, and I repeat it often, that integrating a *variety* of raw foods into the diet is a great help in maintaining a healthy lifestyle. Many people are challenged with the raw foods lifestyle, especially in cold weather. Therefore, including lightly

---

[5] Seitan, pronounced Say-tan, is the protein part of wheat which is *processed* and made into meat substitute foods.

steamed vegetables and cooked grains is a good balance as you continue to refine your diet.

TRANSITION PREPARATION

All change, in some way, requires training. If you are starting a new job for example, someone may "show you the ropes," including some understanding of the business and how it has been done before. Learning how to operate new equipment or work with materials you're not familiar with might be another aspect of this adjustment. No one expects you to learn everything at one time in the beginning. You will probably just get an overview of the job. So, during the transition be easy with yourself, knowing that you're doing the very best that you can do. Like a new job, there will be a certain learning curve or probationary period, yet once you begin to get the hang of it; you will be amazed at how simple it is and you will create a system that works best for you. Before you know it your boss may be congratulating you on your efficiency and supporting that praise with a raise. It's the same with the transition; in the beginning you're just getting an overview of how the transition works and how to prepare for it with internal/external arrangements. Internal preparation is the first priority and then it can ripple outward.

It is necessary to take time to review the materials, particularly in these first three chapters, re-reading until you "get it" enough to feel confident about taking the initial steps. As you get started and follow the guidance given in the following chapters, you will quickly become familiar with such basics as how to design your own menus, create your own shopping list and get into the label-reading habit.

SELF-PREPARATION

A BIT OF HISTORY

Prepare by writing down the foods you have been eating during the past week. (No fudging; no pun intended.) This is for your own reflection. This exercise documents your eating habits in black and white, often increasing awareness of past patterns and supporting a deeper commitment to the transition. You may also want to make a list of your all-time favorite foods; menus and recipes that have been with you until now. This will come in handy when you're creating your new menus. Familiar foods from the past with vegan substitutes are one of the best ways to ease into the transition.

WHAT IS YOUR VISION?

Write about what you intend to accomplish as if it has already happened. See yourself slender if your goal is to lose weight. Visualize yourself as healthy, pain-free, and energetic, having a positive relationship with food. Create affirmations to strengthen your vision.

SELF SABOTAGE

At some point, self sabotage may be part of the picture. We are creatures of habit with strong social/emotional connections to food. Dr. Neal Barnard, in his book *Breaking the Food Seduction,* uses medical research to explain food addictions and emotional eating. He also explains how simple food choices can help restore health.

BECOME YOUR OWN INTERNAL CHAMPION

You are at the core of this transition and must learn to radiate confidence in your choices and intervene on your own behalf. Be on your own team; be determined to win.

© Illustration by permission of Charise Diamond

PREPARING YOUR FAMILY AND FRIENDS

COMMUNICATION IS THE KEY

Let those closest to you know what you're doing. Ask for support; start with those whom you most often share meals with. Present this in a positive light. That's why it is important to get it clear within yourself first; so that your authentic enthusiasm radiates out from your center. If your immediate household members and old friends

> "No one saves us but ourselves. No one can and no one may. We ourselves must walk the path."
> —*Buddha*

don't share your vegan commitment, this may call for additional strategy and diplomacy as part of your preparation. It is also quite likely that new *vegan* friends are just around the corner.

RESISTANCE AT POINT-BLANK RANGE

Often, when people around you are made aware of a change like this one, they can't imagine eating this way, and yet, something tells them it is good so they may feel pulled in two directions at once. If they are not ready or willing to make a change, they may try to negate yours with all sorts of logic, put-downs, temptations or teasing. Being prepared for this may help you understand others, while steadfastly supporting yourself. Look at it this way; no one else is going to do your suffering for you. You are choosing your own health conditions. Let them see your radiant results.

> "Doctors need to learn to make 'kitchen calls' with aprons
> on — so patients won't need to make office calls!"
> —*Swami Vegananda*

PREPARING YOUR ENVIRONMENT

KITCHEN TRANSITION

In this preparation step, you will begin to learn label reading, clear out all foods that do not qualify as vegan and (optional) all foods that are not health-supportive. A list of what to toss and what to keep, and why, is provided in Chapter Four, "What to Stash and What to Trash." There are also a few kitchen tools you may want to consider adding as you go. Check out Chapter Five.

SHOPPING

Chapter Four helps in detail with shopping. It includes list-making, planning, getting familiar with new foods, new stores and actually has a written tour of a supermarket and a natural foods store.

READY, SET, GLOW!

After the decision to replace animal and dairy products in the diet, the most important thing is to START.

The three most important things about starting are:

1. KEEP IT SIMPLE: The decision itself is a big step. Keep the decision in focus and don't get lost in the details.
2. STAY AS CLOSE TO YOUR OLD, FAMILIAR FOODS AS POSSIBLE: Keep the *idea* of familiar foods for the first week or two and substitute plant-based foods wherever necessary to keep the vegan commitment. For example: if you are used to having bacon and eggs for breakfast, try scrambled tofu and a mock-meat such as vegan sausage, soy-based Canadian bacon or a

veggie-based "fake" bacon. Have a slice of toast with a healthy margarine[6] instead of butter.

3. MINIMIZE "NEWNESS" IN THE KITCHEN: Don't make every meal from a challenging new recipe. Although a six-week menu plan is included in Chapter Five, it is also intended to serve as a *suggested* menu guide, which can also be followed in part. When you shop, especially in the beginning of your transition, I would like you to select some already prepared foods. Your time is best used for the main adjustment, rather than learning how to prepare new foods. Natural foods stores stock vegan soups, entrées, salads and desserts already prepared that will help make this transition simple and gradual.

SHOPPING TIPS

Because many foods are being replaced with healthier, new ingredients, it may be best to phone ahead to a store to make certain that the store you have been shopping at carries the new ingredients, so that you are not "running around" looking for these new items. Many of the ingredients used in the recipe section, Chapter Six, can almost always be found at a natural foods store. If natural foods stores are not located in your area, many ingredients can be ordered online. If these ingredients cannot be found, then use the closest substitute you can. For instance, if a recipe calls for Liquid Aminos and you cannot locate this ingredient, use soy sauce in its place. Remember that the recipe may have to be adjusted due to the saltiness of the product.

LAUNCH (and lunch) WHEN READY

Assorted thoughts/tips on the adjustment period and what to expect as you ease into the transition…

NICE AND EASY DOES IT

Wherever there is change, our emotional/psychological processes become involved. This is a very important aspect of the transition to work with. There is mental preparation to be considered here. The main thing is to do whatever it takes to eliminate anxiety, relax and ease into the change. Ask as many questions and do as much research as it takes for you to feel *comfortable*. The transition includes all the time you take to prepare for it. A friend of mine, speaking of fasting, once said, "It isn't just the fast I actually do, it's all the times I didn't do the fast and all the time I spent preparing for the fast I did eventually do."

---

[6] Look for margarine with a short list of ingredients, without hydrogenated oils, low in salt, and no casein or powdered milk. We use the brand Earth Balance at our house. It is also referred to as vegan butter.

ATTITUDE IS EVERYTHING

Ease into following the transition:

- ✧ Be grateful for this newfound awareness.
- ✧ Give yourself credit for following your value system.
- ✧ Be gentle with yourself.
- ✧ Rest assured that you are on the path to improved health.

LEAVE OVERWHELM OUT

When beginning the transition, in Stage One, the only two important things are: 1) to avoid animal and dairy, and 2) to make a start, even if it is not perfect. It is a major accomplishment to complete the first week with no animal or dairy. Your body will start loving you in a greater way because of these elementary food choices. The transition is not about an instant, across-the-board, dietary makeover. After the initial big shift to plant-based foods, it is a process of eliminating and replacing one food or ingredient at a time. We learn substitutes first so we don't feel deprived and out on a limb. In addition, find and insert new things that you like as you go. Foods of lesser quality will gradually drop away as they are replaced, and then those replacements will later be replaced by something even better, and so on.

THINKING OUTSIDE THE CEMENT BLOCK

We are raised with the influences of a Standard American Diet (SAD) and educated on the "Four Basic Food Groups." This is a huge cement-like block of programming for the mind to unravel and rethink in preparation for change. We have to re-educate ourselves based on what so many prominent authors/doctors are saying today about nutrition. Their books, statements and teachings are backed by solid, scientific medical research.

TASTE IS THE MAIN THING

In my experience, the average person choosing to eliminate meat and dairy from his diet is skeptical about whether or not the vegan diet will satisfy him and wonders if he will wind up feeling deprived. I like to assure people that the only thing they will be deprived of is their misery! Fortunately, there is a curiosity about what the new foods will taste like and taste is the main feature in my transition program. Bite after bite, clients are pleasantly surprised about how delicious the food tastes, and their interests are heightened when an amazing variety of ingredients are introduced.

TASTE BUDDIES

Taste buds are conditioned. With powerful flavors, such as sugar or salt, after the original stimulation they will crave stronger and stronger amounts. A person who is used to high amounts of highly stimulating flavors will have difficulty appreciating more subtle flavors. A person accustomed to salty foods (meat is salty) or foods/beverages high in sugar, will insist that carrots and lettuce, for example, are dreadfully flat and boring.

GOOD NEWS! TIME IS ON OUR SIDE

"Taste buds have a memory of about three weeks."[7] When you make a distinct dietary shift, the taste buds will continue to crave the flavors they are used to for a period of a few days or even weeks. Gradually, however, they will stop screaming for the over-stimulating cuisine, quiet down, and begin to enjoy garden fare. After a few weeks, the old, dominating tastes will seem like overload. Taste buds will rebel against the way you used to eat.

> Example: If you give up sugar and sweets for a while, when you go back to sugar it will seem like too much, like a shock at first.

A CLIENT'S EXPERIENCE

A client was having some challenges with weight loss. She was eating the traditional Standard American Diet (SAD) plus her freezer was full of cartons of ice cream. When I start with a new client, I go through their kitchen pantry and refrigerator and empty "junk foods." She was perfectly willing to allow the pantry change, but she pleaded with me to leave her ice cream. I told her that I would leave the ice cream for as long as she wanted; this was her program, and she got to choose the way she wanted to feel.

I later asked my client for feedback about how the food tasted. Below are her responses:

>   Week one — "It is all right."
>   Week two — "The food is good."
>   Week three — "The food is awesome!"

---

[7]   *Breaking the Food Seduction* — Neal Barnard, MD.

This was the same basic food being prepared for her, but *her* taste buds were changing from week to week, as her body was becoming cleaner. This is an example of how the taste buds adjust to new and different foods. By the way, after week two, she asked me to take the ice cream out of her freezer. Once the body starts getting cleaner, the rich, sugary foods lose their appeal. Getting rid of favorite cravings, no longer seems like a sacrifice. The healthier food will taste more delicious as the body rids itself of poisons and becomes cleaner inside.

HAVING FUN

In the beginning of this transition you may or may not be able to put a gourmet meal on the table all the time, but rather than cursing the darkness, light a candle and make it a "camping trip"! It may not have all of the dining comforts you are used to, but "roughing it" during this initial start, can be a fun experience, if you make it one. The fun is in our attitude.

STRICTLY SPEAKING

Don't be too strict. The important thing is to be happy. Food is associated with pleasure. Being rigid about rules can take all the fun out of eating. Do your best and leave the rest.

LIFESTYLE

This is not just a change in food choices. Gradually, as you go along, explore this whole new vegan cuisine world. Research your resources. What and who is out there in Vegan-land? Create a vegan lifestyle; go to a vegan potluck or restaurant. Hang out with others who are practicing the same lifestyle. If you are eating food with a higher vibration, this will ultimately affect your quality of life and your personal philosophy. Get in touch with your "Source." When you feel good about yourself, when you are in touch, you will automatically make healthier choices.

BEYOND FOOD

Too many times people rely entirely on nutrition. A holistic (WHOLE-istic) perspective is important. Some other areas of support for this transition might be:

- ✧ Exercise, yoga, meditation
- ✧ Relaxation, playtime and laughter
- ✧ Sauna or Spa
- ✧ Body work: Massage, Shiatsu, Acupuncture, etc.
- ✧ Extra cleansing (detoxifying)

SUPPLEMENTATION

Vitamin B12 is a *necessary* supplement for **ALL** vegans. Check your natural foods stores for the sublingual vitamin B12 supplement and follow directions on the container. Many fortified breakfast cereals and soy milk, as well as meat substitutes now contain fortified vitamin B12 (check ingredient labels). B12 injections are another way to combat deficiencies, if recommended by your medical doctor.

In an article "Vitamin B12 in the Vegan Diet" by Reed Mangels, PhD, RD she states "Although recommendations for vitamin B12 are very small, a vitamin B12 deficiency is a very serious problem leading ultimately to anemia and irreversible nerve damage. Prudent vegans will include sources of vitamin B12 in their diets. Vitamin B12 is especially important in pregnancy, lactation and for infants and children. Red Star Nutritional Yeast T-6635+ has been tested and shown to contain active vitamin B12." It has a delicious tasting cheese-like flavor. I sometimes use it as a base for a lemon sauce served over sautéed tofu or tempeh, or lightly steamed green vegetables.

> "What happens when a breatharian goes on a fast?"
> —Swami Vegananda

TRANSITION SLIPSZZZZZZZZZ

EXPERIENCE IS THE BEST TEACHER

Sometimes the transition can be like taking one step forward and two steps back. This might actually be a positive approach because experience is the best teacher. Dr. Paavo Airola, one of my nutrition mentors, used to teach that we should eat healthy 29 days of the month (except February). Then one day a month, *"Break all the rules and see how you feel; that would be your greatest teacher!"*

QUESTION: What about people wanting to start the transition with full commitment to change, yet they are drawn back to eating animal products?

ANSWER: Do the best you can from where you are and bite by bite you will reach your goal as long as you keep on keeping on. Keep in mind that the transition takes as long as it takes.

UNCONSCIOUS EATING

For some people, old eating patterns and conditionings may slip in and out of the picture so quickly we don't even know what happened. We may lose conscious awareness and trip over old habits. For example, a client of mine had enthusiastically made her commitment to the transition. One week later, when I met with her for a consultation, she claimed she had "failed." She had eaten a pizza (with cheese) and, at another time, sushi (with fish). I asked her, "At what point did the thought enter to choose this?" She replied that she never gave it a thought; it never entered her mind. The old eating pattern, especially surrounded by friends with whom she had shared these meals many times, was so firmly established, so well integrated in her lifestyle, that there was no warning or feeling that food was *now* a new arena requiring conscious and different choices. This discussion in itself gave her the boost she needed to continue toward her goal with full acceptance on my part and renewed zeal on her part.

FOOD HAS A VOICE

How many of us, just before we eat, will hear a small, quiet voice within saying "this food is good for us," or "this food is bad for us?" Could that voice be called our conscience, intuition, or just the noise in our minds? Or could it be our bodies trying desperately to guide us toward good health?

I have heard it said that intuitively and instinctually our body's intelligence knows exactly what is good for us, and the opposite is also true. The challenge is in staying *conscious* of what our bodies do say. Do we hear our bodies more clearly when we feel stuffed up with congestion, or bloated with gas? Or maybe we just feel lousy and our mood is like "Crabby Appleton — rotten to the core" because we haven't had proper elimination. If we listen carefully to our bodies, we stay in the exact harmony of the vibration of our food choices.

> "A mistake is something you make so that you recognize it as a mistake the next time you make it."
> —Swami Vegananda

RELAPSE IS NATURAL

Many people can make the transition with the first step; it could be an ethical issue or something else that impressed them deeply and urged them to walk this path. For others, the taste buds will start dancing with desire at the thought of missed favorite flavors and they will be tempted to revisit their former food habits. So what is important for them to know is that, although I don't ever recommend animal or dairy products in good conscience, I do understand that they are doing the best they can. They can give themselves credit, as I do, for their openness to a healthier lifestyle and the willingness to continue moving forward. This is all a natural part of the transition process.

Slip-sliding away... In my own attempt to *experience* the transition from vegan to raw vegan, I experienced similar slips. I would eat a 98% raw food diet and then be tempted to go for a pancake breakfast with my husband. I would try to say that my body had no reaction but I knew that I was kidding myself because, no kidding, I did not like the way I was feeling compared to how the raw foods made me feel. What I noticed was that each time I (so to speak) "fell off the wagon" and then got back on again, staying with the raw foods diet was easier. I learned that the transition was really working; it just takes as long as it takes. The main thing is not to judge or make ourselves wrong as we struggle to make dietary change.

The buddy system: If you find you need extra help with the transition, buddy up with a friend who wants to make the same transition or someone who already has some knowledge about transitioning to veganism.

PURIFICATION

Special Cleansing: There is no need for a special cleansing diet. It is cleansing in itself to eliminate all animal products. The transition to a vegan diet begins a natural detoxification of the body. Because toxic animal/dairy foods and refined/ processed[8] foods are no longer coming in, the body is automatically less contaminated. When pure foods are introduced on a regular basis, the body will start to wash out the old debris. As whole, plant-based foods start to give the body what it needs to build up immunity; this will automatically start the elimination of existing toxins. ALWAYS DRINK LOTS OF WATER.

Caution: Sometimes, not always, toxins will start circulating in the bloodstream before they exit. There could be a mild headache, some feelings of nausea or temporary lack of energy. It is important to know this ahead of time so that you understand this is a process of *elimination* rather than a cause for alarm. This phase passes quickly. If you feel a little off one day, the next day you will almost always feel a heightened sense of accomplishment, more energy and vitality. ALWAYS DRINK LOTS OF WATER.

Signals: If you do feel these indicators of cleansing, this is a signal to employ additional support such as drinking extra, EXTRA water and doing things to flush out the system. I recommend that you see a holistic medical doctor for support. Check online or at a natural foods store for products and ideas that will give you additional support.

Carry on: As you continue with the transition, as you go deeper, there will be more cleansing and the diet itself will be refined with time. Be looking for books on the subject of detox and fasting.[9] Periodically a deeper cleansing can be beneficial.

ALWAYS DRINK LOTS OF WATER. ALWAYS DRINK LOTS OF WATER. ALWAYS DRINK LOTS OF WATER. Oh, ...Did I say ALWAYS DRINK LOTS OF WATER?

---

[8]   It is hoped that refined foods will go in the first pantry sort but this is not a prerequisite in the beginning.
[9]   Please see recommended reading list and website links at the end of this book.

DINING AWAY FROM HOME

BEING A GUEST

If you are invited to someone's home for a meal, forewarn your host or hostess. Do not apologize. Say something like, "I have found this wonderful new way of eating. I'm grateful to have it and am clear this is right for me. I would like to have your support." Then explain what you can and cannot eat or just ask if there is anything on the menu that will be suitable.

A FEW RESTAURANT TIPS

There are some steps/tips you can take in advance to make the experience a smooth one:

- ✧ Call ahead before you go, if you know the name of the restaurant and ask your questions. Then your decisions are premeditated and safe. Ask if there are eggs in the pasta or bread. Do they have vegan choices?

- ✧ Inform your companions that you have adopted a vegan diet and may have to ask the waiter some questions about the food.

- ✧ It never hurts to ask: A part of the dietary transition lifestyle is about understanding what we can eat away from home, and in which restaurants. The word "vegan" is becoming more and more widely known and understood. An individual can experiment with this and see if it is something common or rare in their environment.

If this doesn't seem suitable, there are other options such as telling the waiter:

"I am a strict vegetarian, no animal products including eggs or dairy. What do you suggest from your menu?"

"I am allergic to all animal and dairy products including eggs." The possibility of a customer having an allergic reaction to their food is often a strong motivation to deliver the desired (vegan) food.

If you have questions about a certain ingredient, ask further.

For example: Ask if the soup is made with vegetable broth; often chicken or beef broth is used.

BE SPECIFIC

When ordering a sandwich, tell them no mayonnaise. (Mayonnaise contains eggs.) Ask for mustard or (salad) dressing as a replacement for mayo. It's embarrassing to forget that and have to decide between: sending it back to be redone, paying for something that you cannot eat or eating something that is against your principles.

Note: There may not be eggs in bread, however, sometimes the breads have an egg-white glaze baked on the crust and you may need to ask this specifically. When in doubt, ask!

TRUST IS GOOD BUT TRUST YOURSELF

Often the waitress/waiter doesn't know the ingredients in a recipe, and they will sometimes *try* the shortcut and say what you would like to hear. More than a few times I have had to reiterate, asking them to please double-check, reminding them I am allergic to certain foods, and they will often come back with a completely different answer, an apology and often a thank you for heightening their awareness.

EVERYTHING BUT THE KITCHEN SINK

Here is a list of subjects I have found to be additionally important in maintaining good health. Although they are all directly related to good health and are tremendously supportive of the transition, it is nearly impossible to take in so much information at one time. To keep the transition simple and focused, I have put these subjects on a back burner but mention them here because they are important once you have established your basic vegan lifestyle and wish to expand on health-aware subjects. Each topic is listed here with a few words about it so that when you feel ready you can research whatever appeals to you or comes up in your explorations as the next thing to check out further.

- ✧ Digestive Wellness — For good digestion it is important to understand enzymes and metabolism, as this knowledge has great value.
- ✧ Organic — Familiarize yourself with Farmer's Markets, organic markets and resources.
- ✧ Weight Loss — (Waste loss) Occurs naturally when you are eating a vegan style.
- ✧ GMOs — For the dangers of genetically modified foods, see Chapter Four.
- ✧ Elimination and Bowel Cleansing — Extremely useful, helpful and *important* for good health.
- ✧ Herbs — This is a vast field to explore. Start with the flavorful culinary herbs. Most culinary herbs were first used medicinally and/or as digestive aids.
- ✧ Food Dehydration — There's a whole world of practicality and new raw tastes here. This is also a healthy way to preserve seasonal produce, especially when it's on sale!
- ✧ Exercise — Yoga, walking, all forms of exercise are an obvious must!
- ✧ Sprouting — Living foods have the highest vitamin, mineral and protein content.
- ✧ Proper Food Combining — Very helpful for better digestion and elimination.

- ✧ Water Quality and Quantity — Your body needs high-quality, pure, alkaline water and lots of it. Raw fruits and vegetables contain natural water, valuable for the body.
- ✧ Fasting and Juicing — Highly beneficial to your health and healing. A great way to detoxify the body.
- ✧ Vitamin/Mineral content in foods — There are some great charts/books that can help you select the foods you need for your particular health condition.
- ✧ Raw Foods — This is high up there on my list of food preferences. Raw foods are becoming more and more prevalent.
- ✧ Sea Vegetables — High nutritional and mineral content.
- ✧ Fermented Foods — Such as Sauerkraut, Kim Chee, Miso, Umeboshi plum paste. They are rich in enzymes and excellent for digestion.

"The transition in a nutshell: Eat a variety of plant foods until it crowds the 'nasty stuff' off your plate."
—Swami Vegananda

Chapter Two
Karma Kitchen:
The True Meaning of "Soul Food"

The essence of my work with the transition is to ease suffering, to do my best to help readers understand the connection between becoming vegan and the law of karma. My purpose for writing about karma is to shine a light, to encourage a relaxed and warm expansion. Allow me to illustrate this with a very old (560 BCE) story:

THE NORTH WIND AND THE SUN

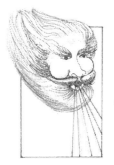

"A dispute arose between the North Wind and the Sun; each claiming that he was stronger than the other. At last they agreed to try their powers upon a traveler to see which could soonest strip him of his cloak. The North Wind had the first try.

Gathering up all his force for the attack, he came whirling furiously down upon the man, and caught up his cloak as though he would wrest it from him by one single effort: but the harder he blew, the more closely the man wrapped it round himself. Then came the Sun's turn. At first he beamed gently upon the traveler, who soon unclasped his cloak and walked on with it hanging loosely about his shoulders. Then the Sun shone forth in his full strength, and the man, before he had gone many steps, was glad to throw his cloak right off and complete his journey more lightly clad.

The gentle persuasion of a warm light is more convincing than a forceful fight."

— AESOP'S FABLES

A DEFINITION OF KARMA

Karma is the sum of all that an individual has done, is currently doing and will do. The effects of all deeds create past, present and future experiences, thus making one responsible for one's own life, and the pain and joy it brings to others. The word karma itself means "action," but implies both action and reaction. All actions have consequences; some immediate, some delayed. Every action has to be balanced in some way, in this or another life. It is not punishment or reward; karma simply deals with what is. By doing certain actions, certain energies are set in motion, which bring certain effects. There is a tendency toward balance in the universe, and karma is the law that continually restores this balance.

SPIRITUAL HEALTH

I believe that understanding spiritual health calls for an awareness of karma. My own meditative path embraces the concept of harmlessness to all living beings. This yogic practice encompasses teachings about the law of karma; whenever we cause suffering, that suffering comes back to us. Because this is such a central point in my life, and the reason behind my adherence to a vegetarian/vegan lifestyle for such a long span of years, I feel compelled to share this with you.

Health is not only on one level; we are spiritual, emotional, mental and physical. Whenever we are out of balance on any one of these levels we experience dis-ease. The key to health is being in harmony on all of these levels simultaneously. We study and discuss physical and even mental health at great length but what is spiritual health and how does it apply to this transition?

> ## "PLANT CORN, HARVEST CORN.
> ## PLANT THORNS, HARVEST THORNS."
> —*Swami Vegananda*

THE LAW OF COMPENSATION

According to Ralph Waldo Emerson, in his essay on the Law of Compensation,[1] we live in a universe that is not only well ordered but that demands compensation. The Law of Compensation is: "The absolute balance of Give and Take, the doctrine that everything has its price…"

THE LAW OF CAUSE AND EFFECT

Will Tuttle, in his book titled *The World Peace Diet*, states: "The most universal teaching, found cross-culturally in virtually all the world's religious traditions, is based on the truth of our connectedness. It is presented both positively, in what we

---

[1] Ralph Waldo Emerson, Essays, First Series (1841).

call the 'Golden Rule' (to do unto others as we would have them do unto us) and more neutrally as the law of cause and effect (that whatever we do unto others will rebound to us)."

THE INTERCONNECTEDNESS OF ALL

This law of cause and effect is based on the interconnectedness of all. Since there is a price for everything and a result for every cause, what is the price for causing the suffering of animals that we kill for our food? Every action, positive or negative, sets in motion a return effect. It is the automatic, unbiased cosmic boomerang. Our past actions determine the present and whatever we think and do now influences the future. The karmic accounting office sends out the bill or the paycheck accordingly.

SPIRITUAL SCIENCE

Earth science can explain many of the mysteries of the human body through biochemistry. There is a mass of scientific data that describes the physical results of humans eating animals. This is one way to calculate the cost. Spiritual science, however, is a more powerful means of understanding why eating meat is harmful.

In his book, *Life is Fair,* Brian Hines writes, "Spiritual scientists, who have attained clarity of perception, speak with one voice: the law of justice is reality; every effect has a cause, every cause has an effect. Every action is a seed that will one day be harvested.

"The law of karma guides every particle of our universe, including our own body and mind. Cause and effect are the order of the day — yesterday, today and every day until a soul is able to experience the purely spiritual realm where love and positive energy reign. In this physical world, what we do and what we think makes us what we are.

"When we look at the effect of the food we eat from a spiritual perspective, we see a specific application of the overarching rule of karma. The suffering that animals endure to fill the stomachs of meat eaters can be seen reflected in the diseases and disabilities that make humans suffer in turn."

"Recognize meat for what it really is: the antibiotic and pesticide-laden corpse of a tortured animal."
—Ingrid Newkirk, President of People for the Ethical Treatment of Animals

"A man of my spiritual intensity does not eat corpses."
—George Bernard Shaw

SPIRITUAL HEALTH IS A CHOICE

There may not be choices about some essentials of life such as air and water, but when it comes to food, there are choices. Meat, it has been proven,[2] is not the only source for protein nor is it necessarily the best source of protein for human beings. If large, powerful animals such as elephants, gorillas, and horses get adequate protein from plants, humans can do the same. Statistics show that the amount of energy and resources that go into producing animal protein foods can feed many more people with much less harm to the environment.[3]

LIFE LIVES ON LIFE

Everything here has to subsist by killing. In the taking of life there is a karmic price to pay. Here the argument arises that we also kill vegetables when we eat them. True, but the load of karma is weighed not by the act of killing itself, but by the *level of consciousness* of that which is killed. Take a look at the man-made laws regarding killing. What have we determined is fair punishment?

Example:

If you pluck a flower from a lady's garden you may get a scolding.

If you kill her chicken, you will be fined.

If you kill her cow, you will be put in jail.

If you kill her, you may be sentenced to death.

At each stage there is a killing, but the degree of punishment is different due to the *level of consciousness* of that which is being killed.

---

[2] "We now know that through enormously complex metabolic systems, the human body can derive all the essential amino acids from the natural variety of plant proteins that we encounter every day." –T. Colin Campbell, PhD, from *The China Study*.

[3] Source: *The Food Revolution* by John Robbins.

THE GOLDEN RULE

Golden Nuggets

Please answer "true" or "false"—
If I were a chicken, I would gladly
suffer and die to become a "nugget".

BIZARRO.COM
8-15-07

Cartoon above by permission of Dan Piraro

"Morality is Reality," says Brian Hines.[4] This principle is simple and needs no elaboration. Examples of the Golden Rule quoted from various paths and cultures repeat this theme: "What you do not want others to do to you, do not do to others." —*Confucius, c. 500 BCE*

"The question was once put to Aristotle how we ought to behave to our friends; and his answer was, 'As we should wish them to behave to us.'" —*Diogenes Laertius, c. 150 BCE*

"This is the sum of all true righteousness; deal with others as thou wouldst thyself be dealt by." —*The Mahabharata, c. 150 BCE*

"All things whatsoever ye would that men should do to you, do ye even so to them; for this is the law of the prophets." —*Matthew c. 75*

DOES EVERY CREATURE HAVE A SOUL?

*"A tool
in your hand I am, dear God,
the sweetest instrument you have shaped my being into.*

*What makes me now complete —
feeling the soul of every creature against
my heart.*

*Does every creature have a
soul?*

*Surely they do; for anything God has touched
will have life
forever,*

*and all creatures He
has held."*

Saint Francis of Assisi — from the book *Love Poems From God*[5] by Daniel Ladinsky

---

[4] From Brian Hines' *Life is Fair* p. 99 and 100.
[5] From the Penguin anthology *Love Poems from God,* copyright 2002 Daniel Ladinsky and used with his permission.

GANDHI AND AHIMSA

"Ahimsa," or "Dynamic Compassion," is a principle of non-harming and non-violence. Possibly the most famous (Ahimsa) exponent of this century was Mahatma Gandhi who was profoundly influenced by and propagated the Jain[6] doctrine of Ahimsa. The first Jain spiritual father lived between 599 and 527 BCE. He exhorted his followers to: "Regard every living being as thyself and hurt no one." It was this statement that Gandhi acknowledged as pivotal to human ethics and it led him to adopt the principle of the harmless life. Gandhi wrote that, "Ahimsa is the highest duty. Even if we cannot practice it in full, we must try to understand its spirit and refrain as far as humanly possible from violence." Ahimsa says that we have no right to inflict suffering and death onto another living creature and, that if harmlessness were the keynote of our lives, then this would do more to produce harmonious conditions than any other discipline.[7]

> "To my mind, the life of a lamb is no less precious than
> that of a human being. I should be unwilling to take
> the life of a lamb for the sake of the human body."
> —Mahatma Gandhi

SAGES AND HOLY MEN/WOMEN

The philosopher, E. F. Schumacher, observed: "There have been no sages or holy men/women in our or anybody's history who were cruel to animals or who looked upon them as nothing but utilities and innumerable are the legends and stories which link sanctity as well as happiness with a loving kindness toward these creatures."

BUDDHISM, KARMA AND ANIMALS

QUESTION: "Dr. Page,[8] what's your understanding of karma and eating animals?"
ANSWER: (Dr. Tony Page) "Karma is the spiritual law of justice that makes us experience the good and the bad effects of what we do to others. So, if we harm animals by killing them, eating them, or experimenting on them, we

ANIMALIA

"Breath, life, and soul were known as "anima" in Latin. Our word "animal" comes from this. There are always people who live in harmony with Animalia, kingdom of the animals. Many have been saints and sages who live in legend still."

*Barbara Berger
from her book
Animalia*

---

[6] Jain religion: A small but influential religious minority with at least 4.2 million practitioners in modern India and more in growing immigrant communities around the world. Jainism stresses spiritual independence and equality of all life with particular emphasis on non-violence.

[7] From an article titled *"Ahimsa, Animal Rights and Spirituality"* by Claudette Vaughan, Source: New Vegetarian and Natural Health, May 1999.

[8] Dr. Tony Page, author of *Buddhism and Animals* interviewed on Australian animal rights website: *http://www.animal-lib.org.au/* Animal Liberation NSW.

will have to suffer analogous experiences ourselves in the future — or at least have to undergo some form of suffering. Only when we ourselves go through what the animals have been through will we definitely know that hurting animals is wrong. So eventually we will develop empathy, a belief in our kinship with all sentient beings, including animals. It is interesting to note, also, that if we are kind to animals, kindness and happiness flow back to us. The Buddha says that if you perform one act of kindness to an animal, you will be recompensed a hundredfold."

> "Dr. Martin Luther King Jr.'s wife, Coretta, and son Dexter became vegans, rejecting all products of animal suffering, including meat, dairy, eggs, leather and fur. Their opposition to violence extended to the violence perpetrated against billions of innocent, sentient animals in America's factory farms and slaughterhouses. Their passion for justice extended to the most oppressed living beings on the planet — animals bred, abused and killed for food."
> —Letter to Editor, from Pedro Diego, 1-29-08, Providence Journal

RESPECT

Life on Earth is a non-stop relationship:

- ✧ Human to Spirit
- ✧ Human to Human
- ✧ Human to Animals
- ✧ Human to Environment
- ✧ And all possible combinations of the above

One of the keys to success in all relationships is mutual respect. Problems arise wherever that is missing. The transition to a plant-based diet is anchored in respect and fosters natural harmony in the human relationship to Spirit, Animals, and Environment. Conversely, a meat-based diet severely weakens these connections and causes damage to all concerned. Respect for the creation (and the Creator) is not only ethical; it is *essential* for the survival of all.

"YOU KNOW YOU HAVE FOUND GOD when you observe that you will not murder (that is, willfully kill, without cause). For while you will understand that you cannot end another's life in any event (all life is eternal), you will not choose to terminate any particular incarnation, nor change any life energy from one form to another, without the most sacred justification. Your new reverence for life will cause you to honor all life forms — including plants, trees and animals — and to impact them only when it is for the highest good."

— From *Conversations with God* by Neale Donald Walsch

Expanding our view of Life:

Question: "Master, the most helpful thing I have received from your lips is when you said, "You get only what you deserve."

Answer: "What I mean by 'we get only what we deserve' is that whatever we have done in the past, we have sown certain seeds to deserve what we are getting now. We reap what we have sown in the past, and now we deserve it. Therefore, we should always do those actions of which we want to reap the desired results."[9]

—*Maharaj Charan Singh,* The Master Answers

"They are not brethren; they are not underlings.
They are other nations, caught with ourselves
in the net of life and time, fellow prisoners of
the splendor and travail of the earth."

—*Henry Beston*

---

[9] Excerpted (and edited) from a taped question and answer session with Master Charan Singh, Beas, India.

Chapter Three
Truth or Consequences:
Meat Ain't Neat and Dairy is Scary

SIMPLE STATEMENTS

My personal health library is teeming with writings on the adverse effects of meat and dairy and the advantages of vegan cuisine. Beyond that library are magazines, websites, videos and a myriad of events promoting plant-based diets and warning people about the dangers associated with the consumption of animal products. If you are reading this book, you already have a clue. I could spend a lot of time just repeating what other authors and experts have said, but I want to make some simple statements here, statements that may not have been emphasized or highlighted before, although they are available from many sources.

If we are concerned with protein at all (and who isn't?), what are the central questions we should be asking about it? If dairy is scary, why? Most people have a fondness for milk, cheese, ice cream, and yogurt and consider them comforting, harmless and even health-promoting. What do we need to know about the casein[1] case?

UNBIASED RESEARCH

I am going to be writing about the subjects of meat and dairy with a quantity of quotes from medical and scientific research sources. It's one thing for me to tell you that meat and dairy are health destroying foods and quite another to back that up with some of the latest, most impressive and unbiased research that validates and supports the foundation of a vegan diet.

THE PROTEIN MYTH

PROTEIN

The word protein comes from the Greek word *proteios*, which means 'of prime importance.'

---

[1] Casein is the milk protein found in dairy products.

31

"The story of protein is part science, part culture and a good dose of mythology."[i]

The following paragraph has been paraphrased from *The China Study* by T. Colin Campbell: Ever since the discovery of protein in 1839, it has been regarded as sacred. Early scientists recommended twice the amount needed because of the cultural bias of the time. It became a status symbol; the rich ate meat and the poor ate potatoes. These early scientists had great influence on government agencies such as the US Department of Agriculture. Original USDA recommended daily allowances for protein intake were 118 to 125 grams per day.[ii] Presently "...the US Recommended Dietary Allowance (RDA) for protein intake is 0.8g per kilogram body weight per day."[iii] So the protein myth grew out of personal and cultural bias rather than solid scientific research.

"We have been indoctrinated since early childhood to believe that animal protein is a nutrient to be held in high esteem. We have been brought up with the idea that foods are good for us if they help us *grow bigger and faster*. Nothing could be further from the truth.

"...The slower a child grows, the slower he or she is aging."[iv]

"...Scientists have discovered reducing one's consumption of animal protein slows the aging process."[v]

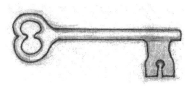

A KEY QUESTION: The word protein is almost always associated with meat. Protein is at the top of the list when questions pop up about being vegan or vegetarian. There is one question, however, that may have been missed. Until now there has not been enough valid research to even prompt this question.

WHAT IS THE RIGHT KIND OF PROTEIN?

High on my list of research scientists is T. Colin Campbell, PhD, author of *The China Study*. Much of his research is focused on protein and it allows him to shed light on this core issue. The following statements, that I have quoted or paraphrased from *The China Study*, form a daisy-chain connection that is easy to follow:

- ❀ "Protein, often regarded with unsurpassed awe, is the common thread tying together past and present knowledge about nutrition."
- ❀ Protein and meat have become synonymous. "Protein is the core element of animal-based foods."
- ❀ Protein from animal foods is considered high-quality.
- ❀ "The concept of quality really means the efficiency with which food proteins are used to promote growth."

- ..."high-quality" would be well and good if the greatest efficiency equaled the greatest health, but it doesn't, and that's why the terms *efficiency* and *quality* are misleading.
- The key question: Is "high-quality" protein and efficient rapid growth the best thing for humans?
- Answer: "There is a mountain of compelling research showing that "low-quality" plant protein, which allows for slow but steady synthesis of new proteins, is the *healthiest* type of protein for humans. Slow and steady wins the race."
- "We now know that through enormously complex metabolic systems, the human body can derive all the essential amino acids from the natural variety of plant proteins that we encounter every day."

Yes, meat is a "high-quality" protein, but is it the *RIGHT* protein for the human body? NO! The human body works best on slowly assimilated "low-quality" protein. This is from research found in the China Study. All of that medical/scientific research and it points to this simple, crucial fact. How powerful is that? So, basically, Dr. Campbell's research states that the amount and quality of protein we get from eating a plant-based diet is not only sufficient but the healthiest. The best sources of protein *for the human body* are found in plants. I cannot imagine a stronger, more compelling statement concerning protein.

❀❀❀❀❀❀❀❀❀❀❀❀❀❀❀❀❀❀❀❀❀❀❀❀❀❀❀❀❀❀❀❀❀❀❀❀❀

COMMONLY ASKED QUESTIONS REGARDING PROTEIN

"What we don't know — what we don't understand — about nutrition can hurt us."
—*T. Colin Campbell, PhD*, The China Study

WHERE DO VEGETARIANS GET THEIR PROTEIN?
This question can be answered with another question: Where do elephants get their protein? Elephants, gorillas and horses, some of the strongest, largest animals on the planet get their protein from plants.

To give you a basic idea, here is a partial list[2] of plant foods with grams of protein per serving:

NUTS/SEEDS (¼ cup)	PROTEIN (GRAMS)	BEANS (1 cup cooked)	PROTEIN (GRAMS)
Almonds	7.59	Adzuki Beans	17.30
Brazil Nuts	4.76	Black Beans	15.24
Cashews	5.24	Black-eyed Peas	13.30
Coconuts	0.67	Fava Beans	12.92
Flaxseeds	7.68	Garbanzos	14.53
Hazelnuts	4.30	Great Northern	17.74
Macadamia nuts	2.65	Kidney Beans	15.35
Peanuts	9.42	Lentils	17.86
Pecans	2.27	Navy Beans	14.98
Pumpkin seeds	8.47	Pinto Beans	15.41
Sesame seeds	6.38	Soy Beans	22.23
Sunflower seeds	2.39	Split Peas	16.35
Walnuts	3.81	White Beans	16.06

GRAINS (1 cup cooked)	PROTEIN (GRAMS)	VEGETABLES (cooked)	SERVING	PROTEIN (GRAMS)
Amaranth	9.35	Artichoke	Medium	3.47
Barley (pearled)	3.55	Asparagus	4 spears	1.44
Buckwheat groats	5.68	Beets	½ cup, slices	1.43
Corn Tortilla (one)	1.37	Broccoli	½ cup, chopped	1.86
Millet, hulled	6.11	Cabbage	½ cup, shredded	0.95
Oat, bran	7.03	Carrot	½ cup, sliced	0.59
Quinoa	8.14	Cauliflower	½ cup	1.14
Rice, brown	4.52	Chard, Swiss	1 cup	3.29
Soba Noodles	5.77	Corn, Sweet	1 large cob, yellow	3.92
Spelt, berries	10.67	Kale	1 cup	2.47
Teff	9.75	Onion	½ cup	1.43
Whole-Wheat Bread (2 slices)	7.25	Peas	½ cup	4.29
		Potato	Medium	4.33
		Sweet Potato	Medium, baked	2.29

---

2   *The USDA National Nutrient Database for Standard Reference.*

Most fruits have little protein. Here are a few examples with 1 gram or higher per cup or per fruit.

FRUIT	SERVING	PROTEIN (GRAMS)
Avocado	1 Medium	4.02
Blackberries	1 cup	2.00
Casaba Melon	1 cup, cubes	1.89
Cherimoya	1 cup, diced	2.57
Currant	½ cup	0.78
Date	2 dates	0.86
Orange	1 fruit	1.26
Peach	1 Medium	1.36
Pineapple	1 cup, chunks	0.89
Raspberries	1 cup	1.48
Sapote	1 Medium	4.77
Watermelon	1 cup	0.93

"The argument that flesh must be eaten in order to supply the body with sufficient protein is unreasonable; it is found in abundance in beans, peas, lentils, and all kinds of nuts. Nut butters prepared without roasting (raw) are superior in nutritive and hygienic value to the best cuts of meat and to dairy, butter and cheese. The protein of (raw) nuts is of greater value for the renewal of the body cells than the protein derived from the muscular tissues of a dead animal with all its waste poisons."

—Jethro Kloss, Back to Eden

WHAT IS THE PROTEIN RDA?

Physician's Committee for Responsible Medicine uses this formula: Body weight (in pounds) x 0.36 = recommended protein intake (in grams).[vi] "…about 44 grams for a 120-pound woman and 55 grams for a 150-pound male. This is a recommended amount, not a minimum requirement."[vii] According to PCRM our actual requirements are far less. I find it remarkable that "…the average American consumes an unhealthy amount, over 100 grams per day."[viii]

FROM MY MENTOR, Dr. Paavo Airola's book *Are You Confused?*

"Research from one of the leading institutions for nutritional research in the world, The Max Plank Institute, showed that many vegetables, fruits, seeds, nuts and grains are excellent sources of proteins. This is corroborated by research from many other research centers. Soybeans, sunflower seeds, sesame seeds, almonds, potatoes and most fruits and green vegetables contain complete proteins.

"Vegetable proteins are higher in biological value than animal proteins. For example: proteins in potatoes are biologically superior to proteins in meat, eggs or milk.

"Raw proteins have higher biological value than cooked proteins. You need only one half the amount of proteins if you eat raw vegetable proteins instead of cooked animal proteins."[ix]

PROTEIN OVERLOAD

John McDougall, MD: Too much protein, animal protein in particular, is seen as a major cause of the most common diseases in America. This is graphically illustrated in Dr. John McDougall's book, *McDougall's Medicine: A Challenging Second Opinion.* Each chapter is an actual case history exemplifying one of the most common and destructive diseases in America. The chapter titles are: Heart Disease, Diabetes, Atherosclerosis, Hypertension, Arthritis, Urinary Disease, and Cancer.

"Muscle, vitality, strength, power, energy, vigor, aggressiveness, and liveliness are words that come to mind when people think of the benefits of protein in their diet. The truth is quite the opposite. Bone loss, osteoporosis, kidney damage, kidney stones, immune dysfunction, arthritis, cancer promotion, low-energy, and overall poor health are the real consequences from overemphasizing protein. Protein serves as raw material to build tissues. Without sufficient protein from your diet, your body would be in trouble — but, aside from starvation, this never happens. Yes, a little protein is good, but more is not better. Protein consumed beyond our needs is a health hazard as devastating as excess dietary fat and cholesterol. Unfortunately, almost everyone on the typical western diet is overburdened with protein to the point of physical collapse. The public has almost no awareness of problems of protein overload, but scientists have known about the damaging effects of excess protein for more than a century.

"In his book, *Physiological Economy in Nutrition*, Russell Henry Chittenden, former President of the American Physiological Society (APS) and Professor of Physiological Chemistry at Yale, wrote in 1904, "Proteid (protein) decomposition products are a constant menace to the well-being of the body; any quantity of proteid or albuminous food beyond the real requirements of the body may prove distinctly injurious... Further, it requires no imagination to understand the constant strain upon the liver and kidneys, to say nothing of the possible influence upon the central and peripheral parts of the nervous system, by these nitrogenous waste products which the body ordinarily gets rid of as speedily as possible."[x]

Everyday Cooking with Dr. Dean Ornish "Americans tend to be overly concerned about getting enough protein. In fact, meat eaters tend to get too much. Eating too much protein, especially animal protein, can increase your risk of cancer, diabetes and heart disease. And because there is a connection between protein intake and calcium loss, excess protein may lead to osteoporosis."

In an interview, *The Diet War: Low-Fat verses High-Protein* — Dean Ornish, MD states: "Most people get too much protein in their diet, which may put a strain on their liver and kidneys and hasten illnesses such as osteoporosis. If you eat a good assortment of fruits, veggies, greens, beans, and soy products, you will be getting plenty of protein but you won't be getting many of the toxic substances such as cholesterol, saturated fat, and oxidants, which often lead to heart disease, cancer, and other illnesses."

From the book, *Senior Fitness: The Diet and Exercise Program for Maximum Health and Longevity* by Ruth Heidrich: A SIDE EFFECT OF HIGH PROTEIN INTAKE: "One of the major causes of the epidemic of osteoporosis in this country is excess protein. As is generally recognized, protein is made up of amino acids. These acids are, logically, acidic — that is, they have a pH[3] of less than 7, which is neutral. The human body cannot operate in an acidic environment — it must be alkaline, that is, above 7 or about 7.2. So when you take in protein powders, pills, or animal protein such as egg white, fish, dairy, poultry or beef, this acid load has to be neutralized. Our bodies have the perfect buffering system. We use the same mechanism you see advertised on TV ads for antacids, for "acid stomach," which is calcium. And where do we store our calcium? In our bones. Our bones are very active living tissue, and calcium is constantly moving in and out of them, so if we consume a high acid meal, especially animal protein, our bones are called upon to give up some calcium to neutralize or buffer this acid so that we can keep the heart beating,

---

[3]   pH — Acid levels measured in bodily fluids: blood, urine and saliva.

muscles contracting, and nerves firing. These processes all stop if we go into acidosis, a state of too much acid."[4]

BACK AT THE CLASSROOM

When I was studying with Dr. Airola, I learned that a leading cause of degenerative disease is caused by over consumption of protein, especially from animal sources. Too much protein in the diet creates a variety of unhealthy conditions, such as over-acidity from biochemical imbalances. The body, in order to heal must have an alkaline environment, which is fostered by a plant-based diet.

> "I don't think the vegan diet is extreme.
> Heart diseases and cancers, they are extreme."
> —Swami Vegananda

BASED ON MY EXPERIENCE

In the early 80s, I was working for a doctor as a colon therapist in Las Vegas (where people are willing to gamble). It seems that my work has centered around the topic of "what goes in and what comes out" of the body. I observed two things consistently; 1) those clients that were most open-minded, and 2) those clients that abstained from eating animal products and dairy were the ones that got the best elimination results. The bottom line is that meat and dairy are hard to digest and just plain constipating.

I was so impressed, that it was one of the major influences that turned my head in the direction of becoming vegan. (I had been vegetarian for about 13 years before I became vegan.) Before becoming vegetarian I experienced "drowsiness" and "sluggishness" after eating a meat/dairy meal. This led me to believe that I was having difficulty in digesting this type of food, so I began eliminating these foods. Simultaneously, I had an emotional experience, which you can read about in "Life Is Just A Bowl Of Cherish," under the caption of "REFRIGERATOR EPIPHANY."

> "There is strong medical evidence that complete
> freedom from eating animal flesh or cow's milk products
> is a gateway to optimal nutritional health."
> —Michael Klaper, MD from the book, May All Be Fed by John Robbins

---

[4] Ruth Heidrich, PhD, is a triathlete, vegan, cancer survivor, health book author, and more. Check her website for more information. *www.ruthheidrich.com.*

Research in China[xi] has shown that consumption of meat and dairy can lead to and promote the following health problems:[5]

- ✦ Cancer
- ✦ Obesity
- ✦ Cataracts
- ✦ Osteoporosis[6]
- ✦ Heart Disease
- ✦ Kidney Stones
- ✦ Dementia and Alzheimer's Disease
- ✦ Autoimmune Diseases: (Examples) Arthritis, MS, Diabetes, Crohn's Disease

"Today's pallbearers need to be weightlifters. Obesity has 'widened' the demand for making super-size caskets."
—Swami Vegananda

Regarding protein in a vegetarian diet, in *Eat to Live* Dr. Joel Fuhrman writes: "It is only when a vegetarian diet revolves around white bread and other processed foods that the protein content falls to low levels. However, the minute you include unprocessed foods such as vegetables, whole grains, beans, or nuts, the diet becomes protein-rich."

TRUE OR FALSE?
1. Plant proteins are incomplete.
2. Animal protein is superior to plant protein.
3. Only certain (limited) plant foods contain protein.
4. Children need meat and dairy for healthy growth.
5. Ham has more protein than oatmeal or tomatoes.
6. Only animal products contain all the essential amino acids.
7. Plant proteins must be mixed/matched in a complex way to provide complete protein.

All of the above statements are false.[xii]

---

[5] There are actually more but I simplified the list.
[6] In osteoporosis research, "It was found that 70% of the fracture rate was attributable to the consumption of animal protein." — 1992 Yale University School of Medicine researchers, *The China Study*, p. 205.

QUESTION: Is it necessary to combine plant foods to get complete protein?

ANSWER: Plant foods provide all the necessary protein for even the largest of animals. Dr. Joel Fuhrman writes: "Plant foods have plenty of protein, and you do not have to be a nutritional scientist or dietician to figure out what to eat; you don't need to mix and match foods to achieve protein completeness. Any combination of natural foods will supply you with adequate protein, including all eight essential amino acids as well as unessential amino acids. It is unnecessary to combine foods to achieve protein completeness at each meal."[xiii]

QUESTION: Are protein supplements/powders advisable for more active people?

ANSWER: I don't believe protein powders are necessary. Powders are processed and hard to digest. I recommend using raw nuts or raw nut butters. This same recommendation comes from many other nutritional scientists and cookbook authors.[xiv]

QUESTION: Do athletes, weightlifters and pregnant women need more protein?

ANSWER: In the personal experience of Dr. Joel Fuhrman, yes, more protein is needed, (for athletes) but lots more of everything, especially calories, is needed. "When you take in more food, you get the extra protein, extra fat, extra carbohydrates, and the extra nutrients that you need. …Your protein needs increase in direct proportion to the *increased* caloric demands and your increased appetite. Guess what? You automatically get enough. The same is true during pregnancy."[xv]

"When you meet your caloric needs with an assortment
of natural plant foods, you will receive the right
amount of protein — not too much, not too little."
—Joel Fuhrman, MD Eat to Live

You will find there is a great deal of controversy between governmental agencies and health experts regarding protein requirements.

I KNOW AN OLD LADY WHO SWALLOWED A FLY

By Rose Bonne and Alan Mills
(c) 1952 by Peer International (Canada) Ltd.
Copyright Renewed   Used by Permission

"I know an old lady who swallowed a fly.
I don't know why she swallowed the fly.
Perhaps she'll die.

"I know an old lady who swallowed a spider
That wiggled and jiggled and tickled inside her.
She swallowed the spider to catch the fly
And I don't know why she swallowed the fly.
Perhaps she'll die.

"I know an old lady who swallowed a bird.
How absurd to swallow a bird.
She swallowed the bird to catch the spider
That wiggled and jiggled and tickled inside her.
She swallowed the spider to catch the fly
But I don't know why she swallowed the fly.
Perhaps she'll die.

"I know an old lady who swallowed a cat.
Think of that, she swallowed a cat.
She swallowed the cat to catch the bird.
She swallowed the bird to catch the spider
That wiggled and jiggled and tickled inside her.
Swallowed the spider to catch the fly
But I don't know why she swallowed the fly.
Perhaps she'll die.

—What a hog to swallow a dog! Swallowed the dog to catch the cat... (Repeat)
—Opened her throat and swallowed a goat! Swallowed the goat to catch the dog... (Repeat)
—I wonder how she swallowed a cow! Swallowed the cow to catch the goat... (Repeat)

"I know an old lady who swallowed a horse.
She died of course."

At each step, what the old lady swallows becomes bigger and more absurd until it kills her.

In our meat/dairy industry there are similar progressions, similar absurdities that consumers swallow. Cows[7] swallow chemicals, drugs, and other animals.

Humans swallow cows and other animals/poultry and everything that's in them.

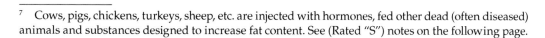

[7]   Cows, pigs, chickens, turkeys, sheep, etc. are injected with hormones, fed other dead (often diseased) animals and substances designed to increase fat content. See (Rated "S") notes on the following page.

Humans swallow medicines to treat the diseases caused by swallowing animals.

Humans swallow diet pills to lose the weight resulting from (the fat in) meat and dairy products.

RATED "S"

(May contain facts that will make you "*Squeamish*")

In my studies with Dr. Paavo Airola, my mentor in the early 70s, I learned that meat, poultry and dairy products contain chemicals such as DDT and other insecticides, residues of hormones, antibiotics and drugs used to speed animal growth. It should be noted — and it stands to reason — that the faster the growth, the faster the aging.

From Howard Lyman, in his lectures and from his book, *Mad Cowboy*, I learned that the rendering process where animals are ground and steam-cooked is made up of entire bodies of cows, and other farm animals known to be diseased. This witches' brew also contains euthanized pets and road kill. The rendering process is partly described by the following quote from his book: "The heavier protein material is dried and pulverized into a brown powder — about a quarter of which consists of fecal material. The powder is used as an additive to almost all pet food as well as to livestock feed. Farmers call it 'protein concentrate.'" Howard goes on to say: "Cows still munch on ground-up dead horses, dogs, cats, pigs, chickens and turkeys, as well as blood and fecal material of their own species and that of chickens. About 75% of the ninety million beef cattle in America are routinely given feed that has been 'enriched' with rendered animal parts."

Reading Howard Lyman's books *Mad Cowboy* and *No More Bull!* are an absolute must for anyone who wants to know the truth about animal-based foods. I won't elaborate more on this subject, because *Vegan Bite by Bite*, which includes recipes, is designed to *give* you an appetite, not take it away!

The above information is sometimes difficult to digest, perhaps because taste buds are extremely fond of the foods that are getting a bad rap. My only interest in revealing these unpleasant facts is to assist readers in understanding why animal foods are potentially hazardous and why the bite-by-bite transition to a plant-based diet is so nourishing and life sustaining.

"When you give up meat and dairy, the only thing
you will be deprived of is your misery."
—Swami Vegananda

DAIRY IS SCARY

CASEIN

The word casein comes from the Latin word *caseus,* which means "cheese." Casein is a form of protein found in milk and cheese.

When I think of dairy today, my mind drifts toward Halloween. I don't think of tricks or *treats,* I think of tricks and *threats.* The *trick* is that our conditioning has led us to believe that dairy is a *healthy* food, that it is valued as a good source of calcium. Although the *treat* of ice cream, whipped cream, butter, cheese and milk is so appealing, there is a *threat* within those treats that robs us of their pleasures. These *comfort* foods soon lead to *discomfort!*

The dairy/calcium trick has been exposed by scientific documentation, proving that dairy is not our best source of calcium. It is actually our worst source because it is so high in animal protein that it leeches calcium *out* of the bones.[8][xvi] It is also now documented that casein, a milk protein, promotes cancer growth.[xvii]

Dairy is known to cause mucous in the body and to clog facial pores. A good facialist can tell by your skin whether you consume dairy or whether you are vegan because the skin makes its own statement. In my experience I have found that dairy products cause facial blemishes such as pimples. When dairy is taken out of the diet, the skin clears up and becomes radiant. I have experienced this by observing my clients.

I wanted to include the subject of dairy in this book about transition because it is so relevant to becoming vegan. Most people, when they start eliminating meats from the diet, "beef" up on dairy. I did it that way myself. It is easy to understand because dairy is represented as a *healthy* food. Wrong! It is important to re-educate ourselves, to put some facts where they can do the most good.

BUDS vs. BRAINS

When our taste buds are in love, but the object of our affection could cause serious health conditions, which one rules? Is this a no-brainer? I am the first to agree that it may mean giving up some desirable tastes but there are ways around this dilemma. We speak of substitutes but I'm willing to assert that many of the substitutes for dairy products are better than the original, once your taste buds have transitioned.

Our taste buds have certainly been programmed to enjoy ice cream. Baskin Robbins ice cream is famous for how many flavors? But John Robbins, son of the founding (Baskin) Robbins, and heir to that fortune, abandoned the ice cream icon and wrote a revolutionary book titled *Diet for a New America,* exposing the harmful effects of dairy and meat.

---

[8] Quote from *McDougall's Medicine: A Challenging Second Opinion* — osteoporosis chapter.

CREAM OF THE CROP

In the recipe section of this book you will find my version of cream cheese, and sour cream, which I have been told, is tastier than the dairy source. Some manufacturers have come close to duplicating some cheese flavors including the "melt." Others will often use casein (dairy source) to make it melt.[9] Nut and seed milks: almond, sunflower seed, sesame seed and hempseed milks make up easily in the blender, taste delicious, and take only a few minutes to prepare. You can make seed and nut milks fresh *as needed* and not worry about it going sour.

"Dairy has surpassed beef in terms of
America's top source for saturated fat."
—Dr. Michael Greger, MD

Optimal calcium[10] sources are abundant in whole foods:

- ✧ Dark leafy greens such as Kale and Collards
- ✧ Broccoli
- ✧ Sesame seeds
- ✧ Carrot juice
- ✧ Oranges
- ✧ Beans

CHILDREN AND DAIRY

Michael Klaper, MD, in his book, *Pregnancy, Children, and the Vegan Diet,* has a chapter titled "Be Wary of Dairy." Dr. Klaper writes: "To many mothers it seems natural to give children cow's milk to drink, and dairy products like cheese and ice cream. However, clinical experience suggests that cow's milk is not a natural food for human children (or adults) and is actually linked to many of the health problems (runny noses, allergies, ear infections, recurrent bronchitis, etc.) that bring people to the doctor's office. Human children have no nutritional requirements for cow's milk and grow up healthy and strong without it. Ample calcium and protein for growing children can be obtained from plant sources exclusively."

---

[9] It is important to read labels on "veggie" cheeses. Refer to Brand Name Shopping Guide in Chapter Four.

[10] The book *Composition and Facts about Foods* by Ford Heritage lists all calcium foods as well as sources of vegetable protein, vitamins and minerals.

CASEIN AND CANCER

I find Dr. Campbell's research conclusions compelling and credible. He states very clearly that casein promotes cancer growth. "The initiation stage is far less important than the promotion stage of cancer. This is because we are very likely 'dosed' with a certain amount of carcinogens in our everyday lives, but whether they lead to full tumors depends on their *promotion* or lack thereof."[xviii]

DAIRY — THE SACRED COW

Excerpts from an article titled: "Milk Can Kill": Educate yourself and your patients that "milk does NOT do the body good!" by Elizabeth Noble, Founder: *Section on Women's Health, APTA*[11]

"When I started the SOWH in the mid-seventies, osteoporosis was not the common, deadly disease it is today (hip fractures are the twelfth leading cause of death). As a student in Australia during the decade before, osteoporosis was diagnosed only after a fracture caused by minimal trauma (e.g. falling from standing).

"...To consider the consumption of dairy products as the *culprit*, not the cure or prevention of osteoporosis is to attack a very sacred cow for families, and also for the Big Business of dairy products. And osteoporosis is only part of the problem...

"In 1992 Frank Oski, Jr. MD, who was chief of Pediatrics at Johns Hopkins wrote *Don't Drink Your Milk: New Frightening Medical Facts about the World's Most Overrated Nutrient*. Dr. Oski had already linked milk consumption with juvenile diabetes and claimed that at least 50% of all children in the United States are allergic to milk, many undiagnosed, suffering among other ailments: constipation, diarrhea, and fatigue. Cutting out dairy products, he found, eliminated many cases of asthma and sinus infections. Dr. Oski considered dairy products the leading cause of food allergy and advised against drinking milk or eating dairy products for all ages.

---

[11] American Physical Therapy Association.

"...Another, better-known pediatrician, Benjamin Spock, in the 7th edition of his *Baby and Child Care*, admitted that "Research has forced us to rethink this recommendation...dairy products contribute to a surprising number of health problems...

"...Then in 1997 Robert Cohen, published *Milk: The Deadly Poison*, an expose of Monsanto's greed in causing BGH[12] to be added to America's milk supply beginning in 1994. Cohen created the Dairy Education Board; its website is worth exploring: *www.notmilk.com*."

"...Milk producers treat their dairy cattle with recombinant bovine growth hormone (rBGH or rBST, as it is also known) to boost milk production. But rBGH also increases udder infections and even pus in the milk. It also leads to higher levels of a hormone called insulin-like growth factor (IGF-1) in milk. In people, high levels of IGF-1 may contribute to breast, prostate, and colon cancers.[13]

"...In 2001, Robert Cohen published *Milk: A-Z*, which is a book of cartoon illustrations on the right-hand page, and medical citations for the particular malady (e.g., asthma–zits) on the left-hand page.

"...The *Townsend Medical Letter*,[xix] Harvard School of Public Health,[xx] and Julian Whitaker, MD[xxi] admitted that milk causes many health problems. Of course, if milk is a problem, then cheese (12 pints are needed to make one pound) and ice cream (10 pints to make one pound) are worse for being more concentrated.

> "More than 50 diseases have been linked to
> the consumption of dairy products."
> —Elizabeth Noble

"...In *The Calcium Bomb, www.calciumbomb.com*, the authors present research linking cancer and heart disease, and review the role of excess calcium in many diseases including osteoporosis.[xxii]

"The 12-year Harvard study of 78,000 adult women found that those who drank milk three times a day actually broke more bones than women who rarely drank milk. In countries like the US, Australia, Scandinavia and Europe, where dairy product consumption is among the highest in the world, osteoporosis and fracture rates are also among the highest. By the same token the incidence is low among the Chinese and Japanese whose traditional diets contain no dairy products at all."[xxiii]

T. Colin Campbell revealed the benefits of the Chinese diet during the China-Cornell-Oxford project. He grew up on a dairy farm, studied veterinary science and thus had every reason to believe that milk was "Nature's perfect food" until his research proved that wrong.

---

[12] Bovine Growth Hormone.
[13] Rick North, project director of the Campaign for Safe Food at the Oregon Physicians for Social Responsibility.

The following paragraphs are excerpts from:

"THE MILK LETTER: A MESSAGE TO MY PATIENTS"
By Robert M. Kradjian, MD[xxiv]

WHAT IS MILK?
"Milk is a maternal lactating secretion, a short-term nutrient for newborns, nothing more, and nothing less. Invariably, the mother of any mammal will provide her milk for a short period of time immediately after birth. When the time comes for 'weaning,' the young offspring is introduced to the proper food for that species of mammal.

SCIENTIFIC LITERATURE
"Out of over 2,700 articles dealing with milk, recorded in the 'Medicine' archives, 1,500 had milk as the main focus. There is no lack of scientific information on this subject. How would I summarize the 500 articles I reviewed? They were only slightly less than horrifying. The main focus of the published reports seems to be on:

- Intestinal colic
- Intestinal irritation
- Intestinal bleeding
- Anemia
- Allergic reactions in infants and children, as well as, infections such as salmonella

"More ominous is the fear of viral infection with bovine leukemia virus or an AIDS-like virus as well as concern for childhood diabetes.

Contamination of milk by blood and white (pus) cells as well as a variety of chemicals and insecticides was also discussed.

"Among children the problems were allergy, ear and tonsillar infections, bed-wetting, asthma, intestinal bleeding, colic and childhood diabetes.

"In adults the problems seemed centered more around heart disease and arthritis, allergy, sinusitis, and the more serious questions of leukemia, lymphoma and cancer.

MILK IS NOT JUST MILK
"The milk of every species of mammal is unique and specifically tailored to the requirements of *that* animal. For example, cows' milk is very much richer in protein than human milk, three to four times as much. It has five to seven times the mineral content. However, it is markedly deficient in essential fatty acids when compared to human mothers' milk. Mothers' milk has six to ten times as much of the essential fatty acids, especially linoleic acid. (Incidentally, skimmed cow's milk has no linoleic acid.) It simply is not designed for humans.

"The milk each animal provides contains the crucial elements that allow a particular species to develop its unique specializations. Clearly, our (human) specialization is for advanced neurological development and delicate neuromuscular control. We do not have much need of massive skeletal growth or huge muscle groups, as does a calf. Think of the difference between the demands made on the human hand and the demands on a cow's hoof. Human newborns specifically need critical material for their brains, spinal cord and nerves.

WELL, AT LEAST COW'S MILK IS PURE, or is it?

"Fifty years ago an average cow produced 2,000 pounds of milk per year.
Today the top producers give 50,000 pounds!
How was this accomplished?

- ✧ Drugs
- ✧ Antibiotics
- ✧ Hormones
- ✧ Forced feeding plans
- ✧ Specialized breeding

"A related problem is that it causes a marked increase (50 to 70 per cent [*sic*]) in mastitis (infected udders). This, then, requires antibiotic therapy, and the residues of the antibiotics appear in the milk. Any lactating mammal excretes toxins through her milk. This includes antibiotics, pesticides, chemicals and hormones. Also, all cows' milk contains blood!

"The latest high-tech onslaught on the poor cow is bovine growth hormone or BGH. This genetically engineered drug is supposed to stimulate milk production but, according to Monsanto, the hormone's manufacturer, does not affect the milk or meat… Obviously, there have been no long-term studies on the hormone's effect on the humans drinking the milk. Other countries have banned BGH because of safety concerns. One of the problems with adding molecules to a milk cows' body is that the molecules usually come out in the milk. I don't know how you feel, but I don't want to experiment with the ingestion of a growth hormone.

WELL, AT LEAST MOTHER'S MILK IS PURE!

"A huge study showed that human breast milk in over 14,000 women had contamination by pesticides! Further, it seems that the sources of the pesticides are meat and — you guessed it — dairy products. Well, why not? These pesticides are concentrated in fat and that's what's in these products. (Of interest, a subgroup of lactating vegetarian mothers had only half the levels of contamination.)

OTHER PROBLEMS

"Let's just mention the problems of bacterial contamination.
Salmonella, E. coli, and staphylococcal infections can be traced to milk. In Finland there is "…the world's highest rate of dairy product consumption and the world's highest rate of insulin dependent diabetes. Milk is also the leading cause of childhood allergy.

THE (MILK) PROTEIN MYTH

"You should know that the protein content of human milk is the lowest amount (0.9%) in mammals." Given the earlier points made in this chapter about amounts and "quality" of protein humans need, it is Nature's common sense that a mammal whose milk has a low protein content is out of balance when consuming milk from a mammal with high protein content in the milk.

"A common cautionary word is: "Make sure you get plenty of good protein." Protein was the nutritional "good guy" when I was young. As regards protein, milk is indeed a rich source; "liquid meat" it was called. In actual fact it is a source of difficulty. Nearly all Americans eat too much protein.

"The protein RDA[14] is only 45 grams per day for the 60-kilogram adult.[15] You can "get by" on 28 to 30 grams a day! Now 45 grams a day is a tiny amount of protein. That's an ounce and a half! Consider too, that the protein does not have to be animal protein. Vegetable protein is identical for all practical purposes and has no cholesterol and vastly less saturated fat. Do not be misled by the antiquated belief that plant proteins must be carefully balanced to avoid deficiencies. This is not a realistic concern.

Authorities test for only 4 of the 82 drugs in dairy cows.

"Therefore virtually all Americans, Canadians, British and European people are in a protein-overloaded state. This has serious consequences when maintained over decades. The problems are osteoporosis, atherosclerosis and kidney damage. There is good evidence that certain malignancies, chiefly colon and rectal, are related to excessive meat intake. Barry Brenner, an eminent renal physiologist was the first to fully point out the dangers of excess protein for the kidney tubule. The dangers of animal fat and cholesterol are well known to all.

IS THAT ALL OF THE TROUBLE?

"Lactose problems: Nature provides newborns with the enzymatic equipment to metabolize lactose, but this ability often extinguishes by age four or five years. Let's think about this for a moment. Nature gives us the ability to metabolize lactose for a few years and then shuts off the mechanism. Is Mother Nature trying to tell us something? Clearly all infants must drink milk. The fact that so many adults *cannot* seems to be related to the tendency for Nature to abandon mechanisms that are not needed. At least half of the adult humans on this earth are lactose intolerant.

---

[14] All RDAs are calculated with large safety allowances in case you're the type that wants to add more just to "be sure."
[15] January, 1992 edition of the Recommended Dietary Allowances produced by the National Research Council, edited by Dr. Richard Havel of the University of California in San Francisco.

LOW FAT

"Low fat milk isn't low fat. The term "low fat" is a marketing term used to gull the public.

Low fat milk contains from 24 to 33% fat as calories! The 2% figure is also misleading. This refers to weight. They don't tell you that, by weight, the milk is 87% water!

"So don't drink milk for health. I am convinced on the weight of the scientific evidence that it does *not* "do a body good." Inclusion of milk will only reduce your diet's nutritional value and safety. Most of the people on this planet live very healthfully without cows' milk. You can too."

> "Cow's milk is also linked to chronic infections, constipation, multiple sclerosis, and prostate cancer. The protein in milk is the causative link. Consuming low-fat and fat-free cow's milk is even more risky for health since the protein is then more concentrated. The science is quite clear that all cow's milk products are best avoided, but low-fat or no-fat products are worse than full-fat milk products."
> —Dr. Pam Popper

I rest my CASEIN CASE.

CHAPTER SUMMARY AND KEY POINTS

1. The right kind of protein for the human body is the low-quality, slowly digesting protein found in plant-based foods.
2. Protein is easily found in plant-based foods.
3. If you are eating enough calories, you are automatically getting enough protein, provided the sources are from a variety of whole, unprocessed plant foods.
4. Protein overload, especially animal protein, causes disease.
5. Animal food production is hazardous to your health.
6. Dairy is scary.
7. Plants are a much better source of calcium than dairy.
8. Animal milk is not meant for human beings.

RECOMMENDED CASEIN READING AND RESOURCES

Appleton, Nancy, *Healthy Bones.* Garden City Park, NY: Avery, 1991

Brown, Susan, PhD *Better Bones, Better Body.* New Canaan, CT: Keats, 1996

Campbell, T. Colin and Thomas M. Campbell, II *The China Study: The Most Comprehensive Study of Nutrition Ever Conducted and the Startling Implications for Diet, Weight Loss and Long-Term Health.* Dallas, TX: Benballa, 2006

Cohen, Robert, *Milk A–Z.* Argus Publishing, PO Box 229, Oradell, NJ 07649, (201-967-7001). 2001

_____ *Milk: The Deadly Poison.* Englewood Cliffs, NJ: Argus, 1997

Colbin, Annemarie *Food and our Bones.* New York: Plume, 1998 *Food and Healing* Ballantine Books, NY 1986

Cummings, Russell SR, MC Nevitt, WS Browner, et al. Risk factors for hip fracture in white women. *N Engl J Med* 1995; 332: 767–773

Kradjian, Robert M., MD "The Milk Letter: A Message To My Patients." *www.rense.com/general29/milkt.htm*

Mulhall, Douglas, and Katja Hansen *The Calcium Bomb*, The Writers Collective, Cranston, RI.

Noble, Elizabeth *Having Twins — and More,* 3rd edition, Boston: Houghton Mifflin, 2003

Oski, Frank, MD *Don't Drink Your Milk: New Frightening Medical Facts About the World's Most Overrated Nutrient.* TEACH Services, Inc., Route 1, Box 182, Brushton, NY 12916. 1996

CASEIN RESOURCES

- *www.calciumbomb.com*
- *www.birthworks.com*
- *www.milksucks.com*
- *www.nancyappleton.com*
- *www.notmilk.com*
- *http://www.nutrition.cornell.edu/ChinaProject/*
- *www.pcrm.org/* Physicians Committee for Responsible Medicine, 5100 Wisconsin Ave. N.W. Suite 404, Washington, D.C. 20016. (202) 686-2210. Much good information about diseases caused by dairy products can be found in their publication *Good Medicine* and the books of Neal Barnard, MD, one of the founders.

Endnotes

i.   Campbell, PhD, T. Colin; *The China Study*, p. 27

ii.   ibid, pp. 28–29

iii.   Davis, B. and M. Vesanto; *Becoming Vegan*, p. 40

iv.   Fuhrman, MD, Joel; *Eat to Live*, p. 80

v.   ibid, p. 81

vi.   Source: Dietary Reference Intakes for Energy, Carbohydrate, Fiber, Fat, Fatty Acids, Cholesterol, Protein, and Amino Acids (2002/2005). This report may be accessed via *http://www.nap.edu/books/0309085373/html/*

vii.   Fuhrman, MD, Joel; *Eat to Live*, p. 139

viii.   ibid

ix.   Airola, Paavo, PhD, *Are You Confused?* p. 32

x.   McDougall, MD, John, Used with his permission

xi.   Campbell, PhD, T. Colin, *The China Study*, all pages

xii.   Fuhrman, MD, Joel; *Eat to Live*, p.137, + random sources

xiii.   Fuhrman, MD, Joel; *Eat to Live*, p.137

xiv.   Jethro Kloss recommends raw nuts in *Back to Eden*. See: Zel Allen's interview, Chapter Eight of this book, and her website *www.vegparadise.com* featuring *The Nut Gourmet Cookbook*

xv.   Fuhrman, MD, Joel; *Eat to Live*, p. 140

xvi.   McDougall, MD, John, *McDougall's Medicine: A Challenging Second Opinion*, Osteoporosis chapter, Campbell, PhD, T. Colin, *The China Study*, p. 205

xvii.   Campbell, PhD, T. Colin, *The China Study*, p. 62

xviii.   ibid, p. 65

xix.   Cohen, Robert, *www.notmilk.com/deb/townsend.html*, Townsend Medical Letter May 1995

xx.   Harvard School of Public Health, Calcium and Milk — What Should You Eat? — The Nutrition Source — Harvard School of Public Health, *http://www.hsph.harvard.edu/nutritionsource/what-should-you-eat/calcium-full-story/index.html*, Calcium and Milk

xxi.   Latson, Deanna, *http://www.gotohealth.com/articles/read.cfm?article_id=30*, "Tomorrow's Medicine Today" by Julian Whitaker MD, October 1998 Vol. 8, No. 10

xxii.   Mulhall, Douglas and Katja Hansen — *The Calcium Bomb: The Nanobacteria Link to Heart Disease & Cancer* (Hardcover, Illustrated)

xxiii.   Feskanich D, WC Willett, MJ Stampfer, GA Colditz. Milk, dietary calcium, and bone fractures in women: a 12-year prospective study. *Am J Publ Health* 1997;87:992–7

xxiv.   Kradjian, MD, Robert M., Retired Breast Surgery-Chief Division of General Surgery, Seton Medical Centre, used with his permission

Chapter Four
What To Stash and
What To Trash

KITCHEN TRANSITION

I magine… that I am going into the kitchen with you to help sort out your current food supply. I appreciate your openness in allowing me to come into your home. Our beginning step is to sort out what does and does not support your health. As we work together, be prepared to let go of some favorite foods but relax as we sort it all out. The goal is to make a fresh start and that entails moving out the old as well as bringing in the new.

IF THE FOOD NO LONGER SERVES YOU, YOU NO LONGER SERVE THE FOOD

In this step we go through kitchen cupboards, pantry, refrigerator and freezer and take out foods that contain harmful ingredients. "LABEL READING 101" begins here and is continued later in the food markets. Be prepared to pass along non-perishable food items to your local food bank or charity by having a box or two handy. Have a trash container ready for the perishable rejects. Some foods are better off somewhere else besides in your body. This includes outdated items as well as foods containing ingredients such as hidden sugars, fats and other undesirable, riffraff ingredients. Foods will be sorted into four basic categories:

1. TOSS OUT
   - ✦ All opened packages of animal or dairy foods or anything containing them
   - ✦ Anything outdated
   - ✦ Perishable packages of animal/dairy even if unopened — frozen or refrigerated

2. GIVE AWAY
   - ✧ Non-perishable, unopened packages of food containing meat, fish (including shell fish, fowl, eggs or dairy — in other words, if it didn't have roots at one time, it belongs somewhere else besides in your kitchen)

3. USE UP, BUT DO NOT BOTHER TO REPLENISH — Note: It is best to give these away also, just to expedite a healthier beginning.
   - ✧ White flour or items made with it — white bread, pasta, grains, cookies, muffins and donuts, white sugar or items containing it — candies, baked goods, and cereals
   - ✧ Foods with ingredients such as: artificial flavor, color, and preservatives

4. KEEPERS (Examples):
   - ✧ All fruits and vegetables
   - ✧ Canned vegetable products
   - ✧ Sun-Dried Tomatoes
   - ✧ Artichoke Hearts
   - ✧ Vegan cheeses
   - ✧ Vegan salad dressings
   - ✧ Maple Syrup
   - ✧ Vinegars — apple cider or balsamic
   - ✧ Mock-meats and processed proteins

GOOD! KEEP IT AND RESTOCK WHEN IT RUNS OUT

SHELF-AWARENESS
— What's on the Label Goes on Your Table

> ### SIX COMMON INGREDIENTS TO BE ON THE ALERT FOR:
>
> *Toss out any animal or dairy ingredients such as:*
>
> 1. Chicken or beef stock
> 2. Lard
> 3. Butter
> 4. Eggs, egg whites, albumin
> 5. Gelatin (made from animal hooves)
> 6. Milk, powdered milk, whey, skimmed milk powder, casein

VEGAN BUT NOT RECOMMENDED:

❖ GMO:[1] Foods containing genetically modified crops or ingredients derived from them should be replaced with organic foods whenever possible. GMO crops: CORN, SOY, CANOLA OIL, COTTONSEED OIL, DAIRY PRODUCTS (rBGH injected dairy cows), HAWAIIAN (non-organic) PAPAYA, SUGAR BEETS (the sugar derived from beets) + derivatives of these; like high fructose corn syrup

❖ Hidden sugars: There are many names for sugar. If there is more than one sweetener, put this product on your suspect list.
   ○ Maltodextrin
   ○ (High Fructose) Corn Syrup
   ○ Fructose (Fructose accounts for about half the sugar molecules in table sugar and in high-fructose corn syrup, the sweetener used in many packaged foods.)

❖ Fats:
   ○ Hydrogenated Oils
   ○ Fried Foods, chips, roasted (in oil) nuts

❖ Additives

❖ Preservatives — A preservative is to a plant what embalming fluid is to a human

❖ Food Dyes

❖ Artificial anything

❖ Sodium Chloride Salt (I recommend using sea salt instead of over-processed, bleached and iodized table salt) Get iodine sources from Kelp, Dulce, and many green vegetables. (Google iodine foods)

❖ Bad Guys Wearing White Hats: Refined white sugar, Refined white flour

LABEL FABLES — "TRICKSTER" INGREDIENTS

As you shop always read the labels searching for chemicals, hidden sugars, poor quality ingredients, and of course — animal/dairy. Also, sometimes a company changes ingredients in a product you have always used. Recheck labels every so often just to be reassured.

TRICK FOOD EXAMPLES	INGREDIENT
Worcestershire Sauce	Anchovies
Refried Beans	Lard
Marshmallows	Gelatin
Assorted Chocolates	Egg whites, gelatin, dairy
Soy or Rice Cheeses	Many have casein to make it melt
Corn or Soy ingredients	Can be GMO unless organic
Marinara Sauce	Parmesan cheese in some brands

---

[1] GMO stands for Genetically Modified Organism. In some (not all) GMOs, scientists can combine animal DNA with plant DNA and come up with something that looks like a plant but includes animal or fish molecules.

WHAT'S IN A NAME? PEANUT BUTTER BY ANY OTHER NAME: I was giving a lecture on label reading and its importance in health at the world famous Cal-a-Vie Spa. I had shopped ahead of time at two distinctly different stores; one was a traditional supermarket, and the other was a natural foods store. By buying the same basic items in each store, but not the same brands, I was able to demonstrate to the guests that a similar food does not necessarily contain similar ingredients. For instance: peanut butter from the natural foods store contained only peanuts and sea salt. The same product from the supermarket had a much longer ingredient list including sugars, hydrogenated fats and preservatives.

> "I have no doubt that it is a part of the destiny of the human race, in its gradual improvement, to leave off eating animals, as surely as the savage tribes have left off eating each other..."
> —*Henry David Thoreau,* Walden, 1854

RESEARCH DEVELOPMENTS
Biggest Study Yet Proves Superiority of Organic Foods

In the biggest study of its kind ever conducted, scientists have discovered that foods "contain up to 40 percent more nutrients if they are grown without chemical fertilizers and pesticides." The study, which was conducted at Newcastle University and funded by the European Union and food companies, found that the "health benefits were so striking that moving to organic food was the equivalent of eating an extra portion of fruit and vegetables every day."[2]

A TIP FROM AN ORGANIC GROWER — The Shoppers Detective System

There is a PLU (stands for Produce Labeling Unit), which is a sticker on fruits and vegetables intended for the check-stand scanner for purposes of identifying retail produce pricing. This is done nationwide (including Canada).

- ✧ The sticker reads #9 followed by 4 numbers if it is organic.
- ✧ The sticker reads #4 followed by 4 numbers if it is conventional.

---

[2] From Vegetarian Organic Life Website: *www.vegetarianorganiclife.com/50.htm.*

GOING COLD TURKEY (minus the turkey of course)

In this first stage we are concerned mainly with the transition from meat/dairy to vegan foods. However, if you care to go further by eliminating plant-based foods that do not support health, it can give you an extra advantage. I would like to make a point here, based on my experience of transition coaching; if you transition gradually, then you will feel only a gradual difference. When a person pulls out all the stops, clearing out all the foods that don't support health, giving up refined foods, sugar, etc., they will notice in a greater way how much better they feel. They may feel, for example, a higher level of energy, improved elimination, less congestion and less depression.

WHAT STAYS AROUND PLAYS AROUND

I have noticed that clients, who ask to keep the refined and/or undesirable products in their kitchen, using the excuse that they will serve it only to their friends, usually end up with these foods on their own plate. This also seems to give permission to continue with the old eating habits. I find the person who is willing to let go of the foods that compromise health is the person who attains the greatest results from the transition. This is where it is important to find a balance between being too strict and too loose. Parents know that taking a loving but firm stand sends the right message to the child. You are in charge of your own program and you will be choosing how you want to feel.

According to research findings published in the September 2005 edition of the *American Journal of Medicine:*

The study of 64 overweight postmenopausal women looked at how well people cope with switching to a vegan diet. Half of the study's subjects were placed on a low-fat vegan diet that excluded all animal products. The other half was put on a low-fat diet that included animal products.

Among the vegan diet group, 89 percent reported that they were mostly or completely used to the diet by the end of the 13-week study. Perhaps most surprising was that 93 percent of the women said they enjoyed the entirely plant-based diet. In fact, 86 percent said they planned to continue with the diet at least most of the time.

According to the researcher, Dr. Neal Barnard, it's often easier for people to give up animal products *altogether* than it is to limit intake and many people are willing to make the change in their diet because of the numerous health benefits, including weight loss and lower cholesterol levels.

GMO OR GENETICALLY ENGINEERED FOOD

Following are selected contents from the book *Genetic Roulette* by Jeffrey Smith (Institute for Responsible Technology).

SCIENTIFICALLY DOCUMENTED HEALTH RISKS OF GMO FOODS

 ✧ Multiple health problems in animals fed GM products
 ✧ Pigs and cows become sterile from GM corn
 ✧ GM crops create allergies and illness
 ✧ GM crops may cause kidney damage and retard growth
 ✧ GM food supplement caused death of 100 humans
 ✧ Gene insertion disrupts the DNA and can create unpredictable health problems
 ✧ May accidentally switch on harmful genes and dormant viruses in plants
 ✧ May accidentally create genetic instability and mutations
 ✧ May alter natural chemicals in plants, increasing toxins and reducing nutrients
 ✧ May create antibiotic-resistant diseases (in humans)
 ✧ Transfers to human gut bacteria
 ✧ May turn our gut into living pesticide factories
 ✧ May act as endocrine disruptors
 ✧ May increase risk of cancer (milk rBGH)
 ✧ Pregnant mothers eating GM foods may endanger offspring
 ✧ GM foods are more dangerous for children than adults

Other notable GMO-related issues are:
1. There are no mandatory labeling requirements for GMO; therefore, the choice to discriminate against their consumption is made very difficult. Obviously, eating almost any processed food (except organic, natural food) will put us at risk of consuming GMOs if they contain the common GMO crops of soy, corn, canola or cottonseed oil, sugar beets or rBGH dairy products. More than 70 to 90% of such crops are now GMO.
2. The health risks of consuming GMO are poorly researched.
3. There are fundamental flaws in the regulatory processes governing GMOs. Giant companies in the GMO industry have a revolving door policy with the FDA. Whistle blowers in independent research have even been fired.

The foregoing is a wake-up call for those who are not already fully aware of the impact of GMO food. Therefore, increase your knowledge and awareness of GMOs and then you can choose whether or not to consume them. In the absence of regulations, I urge you to do your own research and make your own informed choices.

A Few Recommended Resources:

❖ *Seeds of Deception*, Jeffrey Smith *www.seedsofdeception.com*

❖ *What's in Your Milk?* Samuel S. Epstein, MD — An Exposé of Industry and Government Cover-Up on the DANGERS of the Genetically Engineered (rBGH) Milk You're Drinking

❖ *DVDs* available through *www.seedsofdeception.com*: *The World According to Monsanto, GMO Trilogy: The Future of Food, A Silent Forest* (For an eye opening look at the genetic engineering now overtaking the forestry industry, I highly recommend watching the documentary film "A Silent Forest," available in full on MeFeedia.com *[http://www.mefeedia.com/watch/25978940])*, *Sweet Misery, The Corporation, Seeds of Deception, Genetic Roulette,* and *Your Right to Know* (Note: Hidden Dangers in Kids' Meals and the two audio CDs are in these disc collections.)

❖ There is a very useful website that lists the major foods that are GMO and non-GMO: *http://www.truefoodnow.org/shoppersguide/guide_printable*

❖ Organic Consumers Association: *http://www.organicconsumers.org/gelink.cfm*

❖ *Seeds of Doubt*, written by staffers at the Sacramento Bee

THE SUBSTITUTE TEACHER — Replace with Plant-Based Foods

HAPPY HABITS

Rather than thinking about "giving up" favorite foods and feeling deprived, we look for ways to replace those food habits with healthy alternatives.

MILK SUBSTITUTES

❖ Soy milk
❖ Almond milk
❖ Rice milk
❖ Oat milk
❖ Hemp milk
❖ Hazelnut milk
❖ Any nut or seed milks

MEAT SUBSTITUTES

❖ Tofu
❖ Tempeh
❖ Seitan

- ✧ Nuts
- ✧ Seeds
- ✧ Beans/legumes
- ✧ Sprouts[3]

EGG SUBSTITUTES
- ✧ Ener-G egg replacer
- ✧ Flaxseeds
- ✧ Silken tofu
- ✧ Tapioca

SWEETENER OPTIONS
- ✧ Maple syrup
- ✧ Brown rice syrup
- ✧ Fruit juices
- ✧ Dried fruits
- ✧ Evaporated cane sugar
- ✧ Agave nectar
- ✧ Stevia
- ✧ Molasses (black strap)

DAIRY ALTERNATIVES — Say "Cheese" but Substitute Please

CHEESE — Always check the label for casein (see product shopping guide in this chapter)
- ✧ Soy cheese
- ✧ Rice cheese
- ✧ Almond cheese
- ✧ Vegan cheese (says Vegan on the front label)

Those who drop dairy notice a great difference in their health; it shows in their complexion. A complexion that once looked clogged with mucous, now looks clear and soft. However, it doesn't mean that the dairy cheese varieties are not missed; they can be. The solution is to prepare the nut cheeses.[4] Also there are a few of the store-bought non-dairy cheeses that will substitute for the "real thing." It's good to be reminded here that the "real thing" is being able to feel good, with increased energy, this is the trade-off.

At the store: Some dairy alternatives are becoming as advanced as meat imitations in their technology for duplicating flavor and texture without using casein

---

[3] Sprouting seeds, nuts, beans and legumes raises the protein, vitamin/mineral content and makes them more digestible.

[4] See Chapter Six.

(milk protein) — the ingredient that makes cheese melt. Recently, manufacturers have produced cheeses that melt like dairy cheeses. Vegetarian alternative cheeses that contain casein are also delicious replicas, however they are not vegan, therefore, not on the recommended list.

Medical research has documented that casein is a carcinogen.[5] For the cheese lover there are some limitations; vegan cheese varieties are limited to the most commonly used cheeses such as Cheddar, Jack and Mozzarella and do not appear in varieties such as Gouda, Brie, and Camembert. However, I personally would rather go for the trade-off of a healthier body. I'd rather have fewer choices at the supermarket than more choices at the doctor's office.

Homemade cheeses[6] can be made from nuts and seeds. For example, nut cheeses and pâtés are similar in texture and surpass the flavors of cream cheese so that one can achieve health without having to compromise.

MORPHING THE "MOO JUICE"

MOOOVE OVER, COWS!

You will find complete instructions for making your own seed and nut milks in Chapter Six. This is a NON-FATTENING, fresh source of protein and an excellent substitute for dairy products.

Many supermarkets now carry soy and rice milks, while natural foods stores expand that to include items such as oat, hempseed, almond, and hazelnut milks. At home, seeds and nuts are easily made into milks with just a blender and some water.[7] You can make sesame, almond or sunflower seed milk, which are very high in calcium and protein, and taste delicious. Try combining seeds/nuts and adding cinnamon, vanilla, maple syrup, and other flavors. As an added bonus, these milks are non-fattening and do not cause allergies, lactose intolerance or mucous build-up as in the case of animal milk.

---

[5] "It is a powerful, convincing and consistent effect. ...Casein affects the way cells interact with carcinogens, the way DNA reacts with carcinogens and the way cancerous cells grow." —T. Colin Campbell, from *The China Study*.

[6] See Chapter Six.

[7] See Chapter Six, under Nut Milks and Fruit Smoothies (Nut/Seed Milk Basics recipe).

WHEAT SUBSTITUTES FOR THOSE WITH WHEAT ALLERGIES

Labeling clarification: There is a distinction between "wheat" and "whole wheat"; wheat is processed while whole wheat still contains the healthy wheat germ.

Non-gluten products:

Rice	Millet
Quinoa	Kamut
Buckwheat	Amaranth
Spelt	

COFFEE SUBSTITUTES,[8] COFFEE, TEA, OR SOMETHING BETTER?

My clients are always happy when I introduce a coffee alternative to them, as many of them are used to a hot beverage in the morning. An example might be *Teeccino*, a coffee alternative that can be made in a French Press, similar to the way many are used to preparing their coffee. It comes in exotic flavors as well as Java. There are many other coffee substitutes on the shelf today, such as Roma. Try combining them for a richer flavor.

. . . .

"The main problem with coffee is that it causes detox symptoms
that drive overeating behavior and enhanced eating frequency.
In larger amounts it can cause Cardiac arrhythmias and
enhance risk of autoimmune disease, such as arthritis."

—Dr. Joel Fuhrman

. . . .

Coffee Caution: When making this transition, one is likely to experience a headache, possibly for several days, which is the result of the body releasing poison accumulated from the "real coffee" habit.

SHELF LIFE — KEEPING THE *"LIFE"* ON THE SHELF

FOOD STORAGE TIPS

Oils and foods containing oil tend to go rancid if not refrigerated or kept in a cool place, especially after opening. Rancid oils are carcinogenic.

✧ Avoid highly refined oils and oils with preservatives

✧ Flaxseed oil or any Omega 3 oils always require refrigeration

✧ Purchase and/or store oils in dark bottles

---

[8] I wholeheartedly recommend transitioning from coffee as a healthy step in supporting your health.

Some people like to store oils in the refrigerator but have a small bottle of it out for everyday use. Note: Olive oil solidifies if refrigerated and is easier to use at room temperature.

Fresh produce should be washed in a citrus-based produce wash product to help kill parasites and reduce contamination. ✓

A lettuce spinner is handy. Dry lettuce (and other greens like parsley) keeps longer than wet lettuce. Inserting a paper towel in the produce bag before refrigerating, and squeezing the air out of the bag before sealing also helps preserve freshness. The paper towel will absorb excess moisture. Buying organic also gives fruits and vegetables a longer refrigeration life.

Scrub produce such as root vegetables with a natural bristle veggie brush.

Uncut keeps better. Once the skin, tops or bottoms are cut off, the plant deteriorates more rapidly. Root vegetables, however, should have their leaves cut off because the plant's life energy will continue to go into the leaves until cut. You want it in the root after harvesting.

Keep potatoes out of direct light. Their skins turn green and become toxic when exposed to light. Remember that potato eyes see best in the dark. (Just kidding!) Store potatoes in a paper bag or porous container rather than a sealed or plastic one; they tend to break down faster in a non-porous, sealed container.

Always use glass containers instead of plastic whenever possible. The power and pungency of spices, for example, will leach out of plastic but will stay fresh and strong much longer in glass. Do a "sniff" comparison if you have the same herb in plastic and glass. The one in plastic will be flat and the one in glass will smell alive and lend richer flavor to a recipe.

Never store tomatoes or acidic foods in aluminum or other metals. The acid in the tomatoes eats into the metal and the metal becomes part of the food.

Whole grains store very well in Ziplock bags in the freezer. The advantage to this type of storage is that "bugs" do not infiltrate the grains while allowing the grains to remain fresh and cold, without actually freezing.

INVESTMENT

The basic transition is an investment in good health. In Stage One it is simply a matter of substituting one product for another. Financial considerations may prevent some people from getting on board with the organic foods completely; they are more expensive. In the long run, however, it is cheaper to have good health than to take time off from work plus the cost of seeing a doctor. One budget booster would be to shop at a Farmer's Market to find more economical organic foods. Many supermarkets now have an organic section. In some areas organic may not be available. Do the best you can with your newfound awareness.

> "Health is valuable because it's something money can't buy."
> —Swami Vegananda

The Organic Trade Association states: "Organic production is based on a system of farming that maintains and replenishes soil fertility without the use of toxic and persistent pesticides and fertilizers. Organically produced foods also must be produced without the use of antibiotics, synthetic hormones, genetic engineering and other excluded practices, sewage sludge, or irradiation. Cloning animals or using their products would be considered inconsistent with organic practices. Organic foods are minimally processed without artificial ingredients, preservatives, or irradiation to maintain the integrity of the food."

SHOPPING OPTIONS

With this transition in mind, and the idea of eating happily ever after, do you know where you want to shop? If you live in a big city, do you know all the places to choose from? If there are no natural foods store options nearby, it is possible to find many things you need in a supermarket.[9] Most modern markets and some super stores, for example, now carry soy milk and many carry vegan and even "organic" vegan frozen foods. Is there a Farmer's Market or a food co-op in your neighborhood? Request "free" tops of greens from beets or other edible produce. Some items that might be hard to get in your immediate area can be purchased online or though a mail order catalogue.[10] Knowledgeable clerks in the stores where you shop, especially at a natural foods store, can answer many questions. Suggestion: ask a clerk if someone in the store is vegan; they may be able to offer assistance.

MAKING A LIST

OPTION ONE: MAKE NEW FRIENDS AND KEEP THE OLD — Make a list of all your favorite foods. Shop as usual but substitute vegan foods for the meat and dairy ingredients. Example: If you are used to cereal and milk for breakfast, have cereal and soy or rice milk.

OPTION TWO: Check in the menu and recipe sections of this book and make a list.
Refer to Chapter Five (menus) and Chapter Six (recipes) and make a shopping list for stages one and two for ingredients to purchase from the recipes you choose to prepare.

OPTION THREE: Combine the two options above.

BASICS: A list of vegan basic items to stock is provided. Check the "Repantry" list below and/or take a copy of it with you to the store just to get familiar with it. There is no pressure to have everything on the list before you start. Your first week or two should be simplified as much as possible, without a lot of detail.

---

[9] See Supermarket Tour at the end of this chapter.
[10] See web links and suggested resources at the end of this book.

REPANTRY
— A LIST OF BASIC STOCK ITEMS TO ALWAYS HAVE ON HAND

OILS (purchase in dark glass bottles, organic whenever possible)

- Olive oil — extra virgin, cold pressed
- Coconut oil
- Flaxseed oil: (Keep refrigerated) It can be used as butter on potatoes, popcorn, etc.
- Almond oil, Sesame oil and Safflower oil

SWEETENERS — Select one or two

- Maple syrup
- Brown rice syrup
- Agave nectar
- Dehydrated cane juice
- Black strap molasses
- Barley malt syrup

SPICES, CONDIMENTS and FLAVORINGS

- Vanilla, peppermint, orange, lemon, butterscotch (Vanilla is most commonly used)

HERBS:

- Basil, cilantro, dill, chives, parsley and tarragon — Dried for stock, fresh is best

SEASONINGS/SALT[11]

- Celtic sea salt and Sea salt
- Kelp
- Gomasio (macrobiotic blend of sea salt and sesame seeds)
- Pepper — black pepper, white pepper and cayenne pepper

---

[11] For those on a lower sodium diet, try Liquid Aminos or kelp. If less sodium is desired, dilute Liquid Aminos with water to taste.

- ✧ Liquid Aminos (has a salty flavor without the salt; the amino acids have a naturally salty taste)
- ✧ Vinegars (apple cider, rice, balsamic, fruit)
- ✧ Vegenaise[12]
- ✧ Earth Balance margarine[13]

NUTS AND SEEDS — Whole, raw and organic, whenever possible

BASICS TO STOCK FOR EVERYDAY USE:

- ✧ Almonds
- ✧ Sunflower seeds
- ✧ Cashews
- ✧ Sesame tahini
- ✧ Almond butter[14]

OPTIONAL:

- ✧ Pine nuts
- ✧ Walnuts
- ✧ Pumpkin seeds
- ✧ Pistachio nuts
- ✧ Hazelnuts

MILK — Soy, rice, oat, hempseed or nut milks[15]

MOVIN' RIGHT ALONG

Now that the kitchen has been properly raided, you are all set to start on your NEW-tritional kitchen! We are ready to go shopping at a natural foods store, or the closest you can get to natural, where you will learn to select vegan foods.

---

[12] Brand name Vegenaise, purple lid has the highest quality oils. Yellow lid has reduced fat, high quality oils.

[13] Brand name.

[14] I have avoided listing peanut butter here because it is not as easy to digest. Peanuts are legumes, not nuts.

[15] Made fresh at home just before use is best. The water and solids tend to separate when held over, unless you blend in some guar gum or xanthan gum. These milks are also available already made up in box-type packages that are not refrigerated.

VEGAN ALTERNATIVES

FAMILIAR FOODS	REPLACE WITH
Bacon	Tempeh bacon strips, vegan bacon, bacon-bits
Hamburger	Veggie burgers — many varieties made from tofu, tempeh (soy) Caution: some brands have eggs, buy organic to avoid GMO
Hot Dogs, Sausage	Soy and/or gluten-based products
Chicken, Turkey	Soy and/or gluten-based products
Cold Cuts	Soy and/or gluten-based products
Pork	Soy and/or gluten-based products
Beef	Seitan (wheat gluten)
Mayonnaise	Vegenaise,[16] Most other eggless soy mayonnaise is usually found on shelves with regular mayonnaise if the market carries it
Honey[17]	Maple or brown rice syrup, agave nectar, dehydrated cane juice, black strap molasses, barley malt syrup, stevia (avoid refined white sugar)
Scrambled Eggs	Scrambled tofu (select texture preference — firm, soft or silken tofu)
Cows' milk	Soy milk, rice milk, hemp milk, seed milk or nut milk
Butter	Earth Balance butter, margarine, flaxseed oil
Cheese	Vegan cheeses (check label for casein)
Yogurt	Soy yogurt and other non-dairy yogurts

MOCK MEATS — The masquerade: This is the stage where *vegan* processed foods are introduced, such as mock cold cuts, sausages, hot dogs and hamburgers, tofu and tempeh burgers and seitan. These are plants dressed up to look like meat. Most people enjoy this part of the transition and include mock meats from time to time during other stages of the transition.

TIPS ON PRODUCE SELECTION — THE IDEAL AND THE REAL:

ORGANIC is the byword here. We try to avoid produce sprayed with pesticides, fertilized with chemicals and/or genetically modified (GMO).[18] Although organic produce tends to cost more than non-organic, in my estimation the quality, taste and nourishment in organic produce far outweighs the difference in price. Insecticides, pesticides, chemicals and GMO used in non-organic fertilizers are processed by the liver and can cause great harm to this vital organ.

---

[16] Follow Your Heart brand has the best taste. It is stored in the refrigerator section.
[17] Vegans avoid honey because it is not plant-based.
[18] A genetically modified organism (GMO) is an *organism* whose *genetic* material has been *modified* using DNA technology. In lay terms, this means that scientists have learned how to introduce, among other things, animal genes into plants. In vegan terms, organic produce is the safest and "GMO" produce *could* include animal genes.

IN SEASON is another favorite guideline. For example, it is always better to buy strawberries in the spring and apples in the fall. Spring and summer apples are the last of last year's crop.

YOUR NEW-TRITIONAL KITCHEN — READY, SET, SHOP!

BUY LOCAL AND ORGANIC
Buying seasonal, locally-produced food helps in a number of ways. Most food travels 1,500 miles from "farm to fork." But buying local food drastically reduces the energy spent on food shipping. Local goods also tend to use minimal packaging, are fresher and come in more varieties. The best way to track down local food is at your local Farmer's Markets or through the Community Supported Agriculture (CSA) department. Farmers who grow produce organically use less fossil fuel and release fewer greenhouse gasses into the atmosphere. Organic farming is better for the land, for the farmers, and for the consumers.

PICKY, PICKY
We don't want to get too picky when picking produce. Picking your own produce is as fresh and perfect as you can get. The ultimate produce, of course, is straight from your own organic garden.

GMOs — (Genetically Modified Organisms)
What bio-engineering scientists consider *progress* may in fact be a travesty of Nature. By altering the DNA of plants through various chemical and biological processes, the health and safety of humans and the planet itself may be in imminent danger. Large corporations[19] have gained a monopoly on the production of seeds, the alteration of plant genes and a complete chemical system of farming. This system is now multi-national. Pollution and corruption of plant genes has spread around the world. Plants with altered genes cannot be contained and succeed in contaminating non-altered crops. These GMOs are patented. The patents have created

Cartoon by permission of Dan Piraro

a worldwide network of financial destruction among farmers who don't wish to grow GMO foods but are legally forced to comply with patent infringement laws.

---

[19] Monsanto is predominant in this field.

From an article by John Robbins, "Is Your Favorite Ice Cream Made With Monsanto's "Cancer Causing" Artificial Hormones?"

> "...*Injecting the **genetically engineered hormone** (emphasis added) into cows increases the levels of a substance called IGF-1 in their milk. Monsanto's own studies found that the amount of IGF-1 in milk more than doubled when cows were injected with rBGH. Studies by independent researchers show gains as much as six-fold...*
>
> *The excessive levels of IGF-1 found in the milk of cows injected with rBGH may pose serious risks of breast, colon and prostate cancer.*"

Please take the time to understand what GMOs can do to our food supplies, our health, and the safety of the planet by viewing documentaries, visiting related websites and reading the following books.

DVDs:

✦ *The Future of Food*, Deborah Koons Garcia

Websites:

✦ Google 'GMO websites'

Books:

✦ *Seeds of Deception*, Jeffrey M. Smith
✦ *The Food Revolution, Diet for a New America*, John Robbins
✦ *Seeds of Doubt*, by staffers at the Sacramento Bee
✦ The True Food Shopping Guide is a great tool for helping you determine which brands and products contain GMO ingredients. It lists 20 different food categories that include everything from baby food to chocolate. *www.greenpeace.org/usa/news/true-food-shopping-list*

> "If beef is your idea of 'real food for real people' you'd better live real close to a real good hospital."
> —Neal Barnard, MD

VEGAN PRODUCTS BRAND NAME SHOPPING GUIDE

Author's note: Products and companies come and go. There are many new products on the market all the time. This list is just to give you an idea of where to start and how much vegan food is actually available.

PRODUCT NAME	MANUFACTURER	WEB ADDRESS	STORE LOCATION	ALTERNATIVE
Agave Nectar	Natures First Law	www.sunfood.com	Online store	Maple Syrup
Agave Nectar	Madhava	www.madhavahoney.com	Shelf	Brown Rice Syrup
Bragg Liquid Aminos	Bragg™	www.bragg.com	Shelf	Tamari Nama Shoyu Liquid Aminos
Cacao NIBS – raw chocolate	Sunfood Nutrition™	www.sunfood.com	Online store	Non-dairy carob chips
Carob Chips	SunSpire®	www.vegangoods.com	Online store	Any non-dairy chocolate
Cheeses (see soy & vegan cheeses in chart)	Daiya	www.daiyafoods.com	Refrigerated	Tofutti
Chicken-free Chicken	Follow Your Heart®	www.followyourheart.com	Refrigerated	Un-chicken
Chocolate Chips – Tropical Source	SunSpire®	www.worldpantry.com	Online	Carob chips
Coconut Butter	Artisana®	www.premierorganics.com	Shelf	Any organic coconut butter
Dairy-free Cakes and Ice Cream	Mudslingers Freestyle™	www.maggiemudd.com	Online, shelf	Any vegan ice cream
Earth Balance® Whipped Buttery Spread	GFA Brands, Inc.	www.earthbalance.net	Refrigerated	Vegetable margarine
Egg Replacer	Jolly Joan	www.ener-g.com	Refrigerated	Tofu, Tapioca
Ezekiel Breads, Rice Breads, Cereals	Food For Life®	www.foodforlife.com	Shelf	Any egg-dairy-free breads; rice bread
Grillers® Vegan	Morningstar Farms®	www.seeveggiesdifferently.com	Refrigerated	Any vegan product
Ground Rounds	Yves® Veggie Cuisine	www.yvesveggie.com	Refrigerated	Any vegan meat products
Ketchup	Muir Glen® Organic	www.muirglen.com	Shelf	Organic Valley
Meatless Breakfast Patties	Yves® Veggie Cuisine	www.yvesveggie.com	Refrigerated	Gimme Lean patties; see others by manufacturers
Miso	Cold Mountain	www.coldmountainmiso.com	Refrigerated	All variety of flavors

VEGAN PRODUCTS BRAND NAME SHOPPING GUIDE

PRODUCT NAME	MANUFACTURER	WEB ADDRESS	STORE LOCATION	ALTERNATIVE
Miso Cup®	Edward & Sons	www.edwardandsons.com	Shelf/Ref.	Miso Masters Org.
Miso	Eden® Organic	www.edenfoods.com	Refrigerated	Ohsawa® Miso
Muffins Fibercakes Scones	Zen Bakery®	www.zenbakery.com	Shelf	Read ingredients on other brand products
Nama Shoyu	Ohsawa®	www.goldminenaturalfoods.com	Online, shelf	Liquid Aminos
Organic Broths & Soups	Imagine Foods	www.imaginefoods.com	Shelf	Any non-dairy broth soups
Pancake mixes, soups, cookies, breads	Orgran	www.orgran.com	Online store	Read ingredients on other brand products
Pasta noodles	De Boles	www.deboles.com	Shelf	Any without egg
Pasta noodles (rice)	Tinkyada	www.ricepasta.com	Shelf	Any without egg
Pizza + a variety of vegan products	Amy's Kitchen	www.amys.com	Freezer	Any vegan pizza
Rice & Corn Pasta	Orgran®	www.orgran.com	Online, shelf	Any vegan product
Rice Dream Beverage	Rice Dream®	www.tastethedream.com	Shelf	Non-dairy beverage
Rice Dream Ice Cream Ice cream	Rice Dream® Soy Delicious	www.tastethedream.com www.purelydecadent.com www.turtlemountain.com	Freezer Freezer	Non-dairy ice cream Non-dairy ice cream
Sauces, herbs, mixes	Harvest Direct	Telephone: 217-422-3324	Mail order	Any vegan options
Sauces: Mr. Spice (Brand) Ginger Stir Fry Hot Wing Sauce Thai Peanut Sauce Garlic Steak Sauce Tangy Bang Sauce	Lang Naturals	Available at www.mrspice.com and also some stores	www. mrspice.com	Note: These sauces are vegan and have good ingredients
Seitan	White Wave®	www.whitewave.com	Refrigerated	Boxed shelf Seitan
Silk® Soymilk	Silk®	www.silksoymilk.com	Refrigerated	Boxed shelf soy milks

VEGAN PRODUCTS BRAND NAME SHOPPING GUIDE

PRODUCT NAME	MANUFACTURER	WEB ADDRESS	STORE LOCATION	ALTERNATIVE
Soy Cheese / Soy Bleu	Sunergia™ Soyfoods	www.sunergiasoyfoods.com	Refrigerated	Tofutti
Soy Cheese/ Soy Feta	Sunergia™ Soyfoods	www.sunergiasoyfoods.com	Refrigerated	Tofutti
Soy Garden™ Natural Buttery Spread	Earth Balance®	www.earthbalance.net	Refrigerated	Vegetable margarine
Soy Yogurt	Silk®	www.silksoymilk.com	Refrigerated	White Wave
Tahini	MaraNatha	www.worldpantry.com	Shelf	Arrowhead Mills
Tempeh – Organic	Lightlife®	www.lightlife.com	Refrigerated	Use extra firm tofu
Tempeh, Sausages, Deli, Grounds, Strips	Lightlife®	www.lightlife.com	Refrigerated	Any vegan product
Tofu, baked Teriyaki and various flavors	Wildwood	http://www.pulmuone wildwood.com	Refrigerated	Any tofu flavor
Turkey, Bologna, Ham, Pepperoni, etc.	Yves® Veggie Cuisine	www.yvesveggie.com	Refrigerated	Any vegan cold cuts
Vegan Chocolates	Sjaaks	http://sjaaks.com	Online store	Any vegan chocolate
Vegan cookies	Boston Cookies	www.bostoncookies.com	Shelf	Uncle Eddie's
Vegan cookies	Uncle Eddie's™	www.uncleeddies vegancookies.com	Shelf	Any vegan cookies
Vegan Gourmet® Cheese Alternatives	Follow Your Heart®	www.followyourheart.com	Refrigerated	Non-casein vegetarian cheese
Vegan Grain meats, sausages, etc.	Field Roast	www.fieldroast.com	Refrigerated	Yves, Lightlife, or any vegan products
Vegan Mozzarella, American, Parmesan	Galaxy Nutritional Foods	www.galaxynutritional foods.com	Refrigerated	Non-casein American and mozzarella cheese

TOURS OF TYPICAL STORES

A NATURAL FOODS STORE TOUR (Summer, 2007)[20]

When I take people on a tour of a natural foods store, it is to teach them how the market is set up. I lead them through the various departments and explain some of the products that may be unfamiliar to them, show them what foods to be careful about (label reading) and how to choose quality vegan products. The following is a written sketch of such a tour.

DEPARTMENTS, DISPLAYS AND COMMENTS AS WE GO:

COFFEE ALTERNATIVES

These are made from herbs and grains, have a taste similar to coffee and are not only caffeine-free but are actually good for you. Two brand names would be Teeccino, (which is ground like coffee and can be used in the same way you normally use coffee), and Roma. These are good individually and excellent when combined. These products can be very helpful for someone trying to quit drinking coffee. Often people complain of tiredness or they may be having stomach problems caused by caffeine exhaustion and irritability.

REFRIGERATED DELI SECTION

In the refrigerated deli section there are prepared, packaged foods. Especially during the first week (as you adapt to this diet), stock up on vegan deli foods. They may have items such as vegan potato salad, packaged salads, vegan soups, grain and pasta dishes and much more. This is a great way to eat right, get satisfying flavor and not have to spend a lot of time exploring new recipes in the kitchen.

REFRIGERATED SECTIONS OTHER THAN DELI

Vegan (mock) meats and vegan cheeses are usually found in this same deli area. This is where you will find tofu, tempeh, and mock meats such as cold cuts, sausage, burgers and hot dogs. Caution: some cheeses say vegetarian but are not vegan because they include casein. Read all labels carefully before you purchase products. It may save you a trip to the store for a return.

Yogurt — There are several brands of yogurts. Check for no casein or whey. Yogurt is famous for its acidophilus culture, which produces the beneficial intestinal flora, aka friendly bacteria.

In this section you will also find fresh soy milks, soy creamers, baby-size soy yogurts and puddings.

If seeking alternatives to wheat, there are choices of corn or brown rice tortillas and many wheat-free types of bread (spelt tortillas may contain honey). Small stores

---

[20] Hot off the Press: Since the supermarket tour, more non-dairy cheeses have been added to some major supermarket chains.

will have these in the freezer section but the larger chain markets may also have them fresh and/or refrigerated instead of frozen.

Fresh miso is found in the refrigerator section, as is Vegenaise. Fresh miso is better than the powdered miso. There are many different flavors and colors (red, white, yellow) of miso. Try them as you go and decide which ones you like best. Miso is a fermented food that replenishes the intestinal flora or friendly bacteria.

Take your time and explore fresh Omega 3-6-9 oils — Flax, Borage, Primrose and/or blends of these: good for the cardiovascular system, hair, skin and nails.[21]

Probiotics — intestinal flora in vegetarian capsules and liquid forms, many varieties and combinations.

- ✧ Fresh salsa
- ✧ Hummus and Baba Ghanouj
- ✧ Organic juices — They are best if made fresh at a juice bar
- ✧ In some stores there are fresh refrigerated dill pickles

OILS: The best oils are in dark (glass) bottles, organic, and with as little processing as possible. With olive oil you want cold pressed, virgin and unrefined. If you can't find all of this, take the next best.

SOUPS: Check soup labels carefully. Some soups include yeast. This is okay unless you are dealing with Candida.

CRACKERS: The European rye crackers and brown rice crackers are excellent. Skim milk powder or whey is sometimes an ingredient in many crackers. Don't assume, read your labels.

SWEETENERS (Avoid refined white sugar)

- ✧ Maple syrup — Grade B is more nutritious
- ✧ Molasses — black strap is a higher quality
- ✧ Date sugar
- ✧ Barley malt syrup
- ✧ Brown rice syrup
- ✧ Fruit juice syrups (concentrated) (refrigerate after opening)
- ✧ Whole cane — unrefined, unbleached
- ✧ Evaporated cane juice
- ✧ Sucanat — dehydrated cane juice (organic)

---

[21] For extra research on oils, read *Fats That Heal, Fats That Kill* by Udo Erasmus.

LEGUMES/GRAINS, SEEDS/NUTS, DRIED FRUIT — PACKAGED AND BULK (Bulk is cheaper)

SEEDS AND NUTS

✧ Bulk or packaged — Buy raw, not roasted. Whole nuts retain the quality of the oils (within them). Avoid "pieces" so that oils do not become rancid.

LEGUMES AND GRAINS

✧ Red or black colored beans/legumes are high in iron
✧ Lentils are high in protein — can be very easily sprouted
✧ Steel Cut Oats strengthen the reproductive system. Soak and rinse before cooking. They require a longer cooking time than regular oatmeal
✧ Mung Beans can be sprouted[22]

DRIED FRUIT: No sulfur dioxide or preservatives

SEA VEGETABLES

✧ Kombu
✧ Nori
✧ Dulse
✧ Arame
✧ Hizike

THICKENERS

✧ Kudzu
✧ Arrowroot powder
✧ Agar Agar
✧ Guar gum
✧ Potato starch

MILK SUBSTITUTES

(Usually in dry packaging, these boxes are located on the shelf rather than in the refrigerator)

✧ Soy milk
✧ Rice milk
✧ Almond milk
✧ Hemp milk
✧ Hazelnut milk
✧ Oat milk

---

[22] Soak Mung Beans 12 hours in a jar, in low light, rinse and drain. Rinse 2 to 3 times daily for 3 days, until they sprout.

CEREALS
- ✦ Whole grain, organic is best
- ✦ Avoid cereals containing refined white sugar

Peanut butter and jelly — Buy organic whenever possible, some jams and jellies are sweetened with fruit juice instead of sugar. This is a plus!

CONDIMENTS AND SALAD DRESSINGS, ETC.:
Watch for non-vegan ingredients, sugars, wheat and yeast if you are allergic to them. Liquid Aminos has a salt flavor without the salt. BBQ sauce has sugars or some form of sweetener.

PRODUCE
Look for produce labels near each fruit or vegetable that indicate whether it is organically or conventionally grown. Buy local produce wherever possible. If it says organic but is from Mexico or South America or some distant place like that, their organic farming methods may be questionable due to the fact that American organic certification standards cannot be regulated there. A variety of fruits and vegetables are important because of their uniqueness in vitamin and mineral content.

- ✦ Portabello Mushrooms have a meat-like texture. They can be prepared many different ways, such as stuffed with tofu or tempeh and herbs
- ✦ Lettuce — so many varieties — Make sure the butter lettuce is non-dairy (just kidding)
- ✦ Beets — liver food[23]
- ✦ Celery — sodium food
- ✦ Cilantro — pulls heavy metals from the body
- ✦ Spinach — high in iron
- ✦ Carrots — Vitamin A and calcium
- ✦ Kale, Collards, Broccoli and greens in general are rich in calcium

FROZEN
- ✦ Organic no-cheese pizza[24]
- ✦ Cornmeal or brown rice pizza crust (buy organic to avoid GMO)
- ✦ Wheat-free, eggless waffles
- ✦ Veggie-burgers
- ✦ Frozen vegetables — handy to have on hand for soup ingredients
- ✦ Ice Creams (non-dairy) and Sorbets
- ✦ Various entrées

---

[23] Notes here about the health value of these foods are taken from Dr. Bernard Jensen's book, *Foods that Heal.*

[24] Some pizzas have soy cheese but check the label for casein as a cheese ingredient. Z Pizza has a delicious non-dairy melted cheese. They are located in 16 states, with 100 stores.

BREADS AND BUNS

- ✧ Whole-wheat pita, Whole-grain breads, Spelt, Kamut, Rye, Millet
- ✧ Avoid yeast by purchasing sourdough breads (if you buy sourdough bread, you must know if the baker has added commercial yeast or if the bread is truly the non-yeast based traditional recipe or "formula" in baking)

SUPERMARKET TOUR (Summer, 2007)

AN ESCORT IN UNFAMILIAR TERRITORY

Today I went to a major national chain supermarket. I don't frequent these types of stores often because I usually shop at natural foods stores. I spoke with the store manager who was considerate enough to take a tour of the store with me. I put on my Sherlock Holmes garb, grabbed my magnifying glass and off we went, searching for the comparisons; natural foods vs. chain supermarket. This manager was not only kind enough to escort me around the store; he even carried my shopping basket.

ROLE REVERSAL

When I speak with people who are not vegan, I slip into an unsolicited health educational role. SURPRISE! This time I was the one who got the unexpected education. When I consult with clients and students, I usually take them shopping on familiar turf — the natural foods store. I was short of shock and close to ecstatic when I saw that organic food is IN! According to the manager, my shopping partner, who regularly reads the trade publication, *Supermarket News*, "Organics are growing faster than any other food category."

UNDER THE MAGNIFYING GLASS

So here's the scoop from under the magnifying glass: I found out that in this store, and I assume the same is true in most large chains, "Corporate" decides what to order. Within that framework, there is a specialty foods company that stocks the kind of foods that a reader interested in vegan products may be shopping for. This adds up to approximately 5% of what the store orders. Since this is a huge chain store, 5% amounts to a decent variety of friendly foods to choose from. You can decide for yourself; this is the evidence I found.

ORGANIC VARIETY

Foods in this store are not necessarily categorized under "Organic" except in areas in the fruit and vegetable produce section. I was pleased to see how well stocked that was: potatoes, varieties of greens and herbs, boxed salads, carrots, beets, cauliflower, tomatoes, and varieties of bananas, shitake mushrooms, fruits in season and much more. It was just like a mini Farmer's Market,[25] from local packaged growers. There were some items that were not organic that we often use, such as fresh baby coconuts, avocados (some were also organic). They even had a raw fruit energy bar and a candy bar that was gluten-, wheat- and dairy-free. Organic items are not all in one place but mixed in with other choices.

There was no vegan section, yet I was pleasantly surprised to see that some store items had a certified vegan icon on the label. How easy does that make it?

AN ATTRACTIVE ARRAY OF INVENTORY

- ❖ In the frozen section there were some Amy's organic food products
- ❖ In their dairy refrigerated section I found soy yogurts, soy milk and creamer
- ❖ On the (non-refrigerated) shelf they carry packaged soy and rice milks
- ❖ To go with your non-dairy milks, they have a section of organic whole-wheat cereals
- ❖ On the subject of breakfast, I did find organic maple syrup
- ❖ I found tofu mixed in with mock meat products like "Tofurky," sausage, cold cuts, organic baked marinated tofu varieties and ground round
- ❖ Also in this (refrigerated) section I found vegan cream cheese, organic Earth Balance (tastes like butter), Vegenaise and more!
- ❖ In the Asian section I found organic tofu
- ❖ There were varieties of organic frozen vegetables, even Edamame (soy bean)
- ❖ Frozen juices were plentiful (only not organic)
- ❖ The store carried alternatives to coffee and a variety of organic teas
- ❖ Organic sesame oil and olive oil in glass jars and cooking spray
- ❖ Organic sea salt
- ❖ Whole-wheat breads
- ❖ Taco shells
- ❖ Pickles
- ❖ Apple cider vinegar
- ❖ Liquid Aminos
- ❖ Some vegan packaged products such as couscous (all of the grains were refined)

---

[25] Keep in mind that this store is in southern California. Things might be different in other parts of the country.

- ✧ Hummus
- ✧ Bean and rice burritos
- ✧ Tofu mayonnaise (non-refrigerated section)
- ✧ Dressings
- ✧ Barbeque sauces
- ✧ Canned coconut milk
- ✧ Roasted sesame seeds
- ✧ Olives
- ✧ Dry herbs
- ✧ An organic natural line of chips
- ✧ Organic pasta sauces
- ✧ Whole-wheat pasta
- ✧ Organic Lasagna pasta[26]
- ✧ There were no bulk grains, legumes, or beans bins (packages of beans were not organic)

MORE DETECTIVE WORK

I found out it was wise to shine my flashlight and magnifying glass on the ingredient list of a packaged Miso soup. There was one product listing MSG (a harmful flavoring additive) and an aisle away I found a similar Miso soup cup that was healthy and actually marked with a "CERTIFIED VEGAN" label. See how labels can protect your health? On the subject of soups, the manager told me he had found various packaged soups such as "No-Chicken" broth and a variety of other vegetable broths. (When he told me he found them, I asked him if Corporate knew they were lost.)

THE BEST FOR LAST

I saved the best for last; the dessert case stocks Rice Dream and Purely Decadent (soy) Ice Cream. I did some comparative price shopping. A couple of natural foods stores, although they carried many more flavors, had a price between $3.85 and $3.99 and the supermarket price was 2 for $5.00.[27] How sweet is that for a dessert topping?

---

[26] Organic doesn't necessarily mean that the flour is not processed — read your labels.
[27] Tour done in 2007.

Chapter Five
Food Is A Meal In Itself —
Menus and Miscellaneous

STAGE ONE: LOVE AT FIRST BITE

Bite by bite we go, with the first bite being the transition from animal and dairy products to a plant-based diet. Just about anything else goes. Although I strongly advise you to eliminate other health-hazardous foods in this first sweep, such as sugar, fried foods, refined products (white rice, white flour, etc.), the only for-sure requisite here is eliminating meat and dairy. The love comes in when we start loving our bodies by treating them to vegan, healthier foods.

STAGE TWO: GET THEE BEHIND ME, SEITAN![1]

Plants are packaged by Nature; they come with skins, shells, husks, or hulls and contain their own unique combinations of oils, vitamins, minerals, proteins, fiber, chlorophyll and water. This is Nature's perfect balance. Processed foods are not as Nature made them; they often give a quick energy rush because their packages have already been *opened* or broken down and certain elements isolated so that the contents cook or digest faster. There is an immediate supply of food-fuel but not a lasting one; the body's cells feel temporarily satisfied but begin sending out hunger signals a short while later because they are not whole foods. This stimulates a *snack attack*, a constant craving for more food with less satisfaction. This is one explanation for obesity problems; consumers have to eat more because the body is not satisfied with denatured foods. Whole foods, on the other hand, release their sugars and nutrients into the bloodstream bit by bit, keeping your blood sugar steady and holding hunger at bay for longer periods of time. Although vegetarian food is superior karmically and nutritionally compared to animal foods, whole, unprocessed, *vegan* foods are out in front of them all. In Stage Two, we progress from everything vegan to less processed, more whole foods.

---

[1]   Seitan is a processed food containing gluten and is not easily digestible. Therefore we leave it behind when progressing to foods that are more whole.

MENUS AS MODELS

The transition stages and menus are designed as a model or example of meals. You can either choose to follow it, or adapt to it based on your personal likes and dislikes (and the folks you are cooking for). You can also substitute products if they are not available, or in your budget.

SURFING THE MENUS

Please feel free to choose any recipe at any time, making substitutions in the menu plans as you go. Stage Two recipes are welcome in Stage One and many readers may choose Stage One recipes and ingredients while following Stage Two. Desserts are located in the recipe section, Chapter Six. Dessert choices are up to you, if and when you want to include them.

RAW FOOD

Raw food recipes are abundant in the recipe section. Health-supportive raw food recipes are included in both menu stages.

> "When you are in the kitchen there are no rules;
> who says it has to be just one way?
> Flavor it with your own creativity!"
>
> —Marilyn Peterson

"I DON'T DO RECIPES!"

Making it up as I go is one of my favorite ways to play. A chef is an artist using food flavors instead of paint colors. Although I generally try to pay attention to the food combining rules as I go, sometimes it's a no-holds-barred romp in the kitchen. It's more pleasing and fun for the family and yourself if you understand how to give food preparation a personal touch. This can increase the pleasure of eating at home, and make it even tastier than restaurant cooking.

For me, because I love what I do, working with food is therapy. For example, when I'm on a bummer, the best way for me to get out of it is to come into the kitchen and channel that energy in a positive way. I feel the healing power in food and know that the effect of food is an extremely potent force. So, I step into the kitchen and mix it up with the fruits and vegetables and dissipate the downward energy by taking positive action and creating a tasty dish.

TIPS ON RECIPE READING

COMPATIBLE RECIPES

If one or more companion recipes are mentioned within a recipe, it is done in bold and it means that recipe is also in this book and is compatible with that particular recipe. For example: **Caesar Salad Dressing** will be noted within the **Caesar Salad** recipe or **Cashew Vanilla Cream** is noted as a topping for **Wendel's 'Other Love' Chocolate Mousse**.

BEING EXACT

Recipes can either be followed to the letter or they can be used as a guide. Sometimes ingredients that are listed in a recipe cannot be found. If a recipe calls for a tiny amount of an ingredient and you don't have it maybe because you don't think you will use it often, leave it out of the recipe. One exception is cayenne pepper, although used in tiny amounts, it's a spice that gives a lift to a recipe. You must learn to improvise. Learning in this way can take a bit of experience, but I'm going to give you as many helpful hints as possible to make recipe preparation easy for you.

THICKENERS

Sometimes a recipe may indicate an ingredient that is used specifically for the purpose of thickening. Here is a list of thickener options.

- ✧ Lucuma Powder (found in natural foods stores)
- ✧ Coconut oil
- ✧ Nuts/Seeds
- ✧ Agar Agar
- ✧ Tofu (firm or silken, depending on texture desired)
- ✧ Dried fruits

SALT

All salts are not the same salty strength. I personally prefer Celtic salt. Other salts may vary. Add salt slowly and taste as you go. Liquid Aminos or soy sauces have a salty taste.

SAME RECIPE, DIFFERENT TASTE

The same recipe can be prepared several times and still taste somewhat different. These variations can be due to a wide range of factors such as:

- ✧ Quality of product — different manufacturer brand names vary in taste
- ✧ The difference between organic and non-organic produce varies in quality and flavor

- ◇ When using a fruit like strawberries, some are sweeter than others
- ◇ Lemon flavors vary in tartness. Meyer lemons are sweeter

LEARN TO REVAMP YOUR RECIPES

For example: If you think a recipe needs more garlic, (all garlic is not created equally pungent) then add more garlic. The same thing goes with herbs. Always season salt and pepper to taste. My taste buds may differ from yours. With an ingredient like tomatoes, you'll find that some tomatoes could be juicier than others. Some lemons can be sweeter or tarter so you may need to adjust the amount of lemon. Apples may vary in sweetness, thus causing a need to adjust sweetener in the recipe.

COOKING IS FUN AND EASY

However if there is any recipe that challenges you, please visit my website at *www.veganbitebybite.com* for contact information.

AMOUNTS

Don't sweat over the exact amounts in a recipe. Maybe the size of an ingredient varies from the size available to you. This can all be compensated for somewhere in the recipe. It may not have a huge impact after all.

LOVE

The main ingredient in every recipe is love. If you add that quality to all of your recipes, they will be enjoyed because of that flavor!

MISCELLANEOUS NOTES

KITCHEN EQUIPMENT

Good kitchen equipment is needed when an abundance of fruits and vegetables and a different dietary lifestyle is being recommended.

BLENDERS: I realized fairly early on that the issue of Vita-Mix vs. a regular blender would come up, so I tried testing in a regular blender where I could. Many people don't even own a blender. The bottom line is that an investment in a good blender is important for this type of food preparation. The high-powered Vita-Mix is highly recommended here but if that is out of budget range, get the most powerful blender possible.*

Vita-Mix

*See page 283 for a special discounted price on shipping.

FOOD PROCESSOR: I use a food processor often in my kitchen and recommend owning one just to save time.

JUICER: For health's sake this is a wise investment. Vegetable pulp from the juicing process can also be saved, frozen and added to recipes later on.

CITRUS JUICER: An electric one makes citrus juicing so much faster and easier but a hand juicer will still do the job.

ICE CREAM MAKER: Many versions of ice cream can be tried in the Vita-Mix Blender and frozen directly. However, if an ice cream maker is in your budget it will do the job more professionally. For making ice creams and sorbets I started out with a less expensive ice cream maker, which works perfectly fine if that is within your budget. Because I was trying to focus on the transition to raw foods I invested in a commercial machine. They can also be bought used and can be found online, at resale sites.

EASY DOES IT

Especially for Stage One, as an introduction to the transition, the menu is designed for simplicity so that a minimum amount of time is spent in the kitchen. My aim is to eliminate as much *newness* as possible so that you will not feel overwhelmed with the change. Menu items are repeated so that the prepared foods will be used within a reasonable time. At any time during the transition, feel free to select menus and recipes from outside the menu plan, according to your personal tastes. Keep in mind that the menu stages are there as a guide only. During the first few weeks you may choose to purchase ready-made products or deli items at a natural foods store for your transition ease. Please do whatever it takes to make everything easy.

FROZEN FOODS MENU

I am recommending that you take a few hours each week and prepare some freezable entrées and soups. I have created a list of recipes that can be prepared in advance and frozen so that you can conveniently pull them out for a quick meal. This group of entrées and soups have been conveniently noted as *Pull from freezer* in the menu. Although fresh recipes are the tastiest and have the highest nutrition, the menu is designed purposely so that when you start the transition it will be easier for you. There is a good deal to learn as you begin using new foods while understanding the change itself and spending less time in the kitchen *before* each meal is a big help.

FOR STAGE ONE

You may also want to stock your freezer with pizza (Amy's vegan style) or any vegan entrée from the frozen natural foods section. A well-stocked freezer takes the panic out of *"What shall I fix for dinner?"* and provides that *fast-food* option while still maintaining quality ingredients. Preparing dishes like soups, casseroles, marinara sauce, stuffed baked potatoes, and stews will give you a variety to select from. Before you freeze your recipes, be sure that you portion out the size you will be serving into the appropriately sized containers. Make certain that everything you put into the freezer has a waterproof[2] label noting the dish and date.

After you've been cooking up a storm once a week, your freezer will be built up with a nice variety of entrées and soups. I recommend that you don't keep them stored too long so you have *freezer fresh* meals that retain their flavors. Pull your meals from the freezer about 24 hours in advance, and thaw slowly in the refrigerator. Warm it on low heat in a covered pot.

NUMBERS AND AMOUNTS

Although the menus are designed for seven days, they are not designed for specific numbers of people. The recipes will give you approximate yields. You may choose to go out for a meal now and then. Because of this, you will probably have leftovers.

Use your own judgment as to whether or not the recipe volume needs to be cut in order to meet your shelf-life requirements. If, for instance, you don't know how to cut down a salad dressing recipe because you don't feel you will use the recipe within five days or so, then purchase a prepared salad dressing and refrigerate it to make things easier for yourself, especially in the beginning of the transition.

INGREDIENTS

If you don't have everything a recipe calls for on hand, substitute similar ingredients that you do have. It doesn't have to be exact. For example; Nama Shoyu, (a popular soy sauce for macrobiotic and raw fooders) is called for in a recipe, instead use Liquid Aminos or whatever soy sauce you have on hand.

GRAINS

You can make an extra quantity of grains for breakfast, keeping in mind that the same grain can be put into a loaf recipe. For instance, if you make quinoa for breakfast, and you have another recipe that calls for millet, in millet burgers, you can substitute quinoa for millet. Don't be afraid to let your creative juices flow! Mistakes are often our best teachers.

Cereal grains can be flavored with vegan butter, margarine, or olive oil and seasoned with Liquid Aminos or Nama Shoyu for a savory dish. If you want to sweeten grains, you could add (soaked) raisins, prunes, dried fruits or fresh chopped apple or banana at the very end of the cooking time. You may also use agave nectar or maple syrup as a sweetener.

---

[2]   Use permanent markers that won't run or fade.

HOW TO PRESS THE WATER OUT OF TOFU

Directions:
1. Take tofu out of package, drain excess water, place on board or flat plate. You may want a kitchen or paper towel underneath to absorb water.
2. Place additional board or flat plate on top.
3. Place any heavy weight on top for 15 minutes.

HOW TO OPEN A COCONUT

Coconuts are so flavorful and healthy. Once you get the hang of opening a coconut you will have mastered the art! Blended coconut meat and coconut milk freeze great. Thaw and re-blend before using.

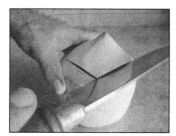  

Directions:
With a large and fairly heavy cleaver, strike the coconut at an angle. Continue making these cuts around the top until all sides have been cut open. Remove the top and proceed to empty out the water and spoon out the coconut meat. Trim off all dark spots until you have only the pure white coconut meat. Try the **Avocado Ambrosia** recipe in Chapter Six.

NUT CREAMS are made from any soaked, rinsed and drained nut of your choice. Add water, agave nectar, vanilla, (or various other flavorings of your choice) and blend in your blender.

SEED MILKS are made from sunflower seeds or sesame seeds. Sesame seeds do not need to be soaked. Soak sunflower seeds overnight, rinse and drain. Add pure water, agave nectar and vanilla flavor and blend until smooth. The amount of water in nut/seed milks determines the consistency. If seed milks are strained, the pulp can be frozen for use in raw dehydrated crackers.

SOAKING OR TOASTING

It is healthier to soak raw nuts and seeds before using them in recipes for easiest digestibility. They keep several days in the refrigerator. Once seeds and nuts are soaked, rinsed, drained and patted dry, they can be refrigerated for several days before use. Patting them dry prevents them from molding.

Nuts do not break down like fresh produce does because they contain natural preservatives. But this preservative also keeps the nuts/seeds from breaking down in the digestive tract.[3] Soaking and then draining off the soak water and rinsing them will make them easier to digest. A nut or seed that is toasted will have a more flavorful, nutty taste. For the cook who is transitioning to the vegan style of cooking, perhaps their taste buds prefer the raw nut being toasted on top of the stove to bring out that type of nutty flavor. However, for more health benefits, one may choose to soak nuts and seeds. The recipes basically turn out the same way with a slightly different flavor.

"The healthiest blood type is Be Positive."
—Swami Vegananda

---

[3] Soak only raw nuts. This is not intended for nuts that have been roasted or toasted.

	BREAKFAST	LUNCH	DINNER
MONDAY	Granola *Soy or Rice Milk Muffin *Almond Milk is also an option	Mixed Greens Salad Thousand Island Dressing Curried Tofu Egg(less) Sandwich	Coleslaw *Potato Salad Tofu Hot Dogs (bun optional) Condiments *Purchase or see recipe
TUESDAY	Whole grain dry cereal Soy or Rice Milk Banana	Spinach Salad Tahini Dessing Grilled Cheese Sandwich	Arugula Salad Italian Dressing *Mushroom Marinara Sauce Pasta Garlic Toast *Pull from freezer
WEDNESDAY	Oatmeal Raisins Cinnamon Soy or Rice Milk Toast	Coleslaw *Cold Cuts Club Sandwich *Any brand Vegan cold cuts	Mixed Greens Salad Thousand Island Dressing *Seitan Stew Dinner Roll (purchased) *Pull from freezer
THURSDAY	Granola Soy or Rice Milk Muffin	Dandelion Greens Salad Mock Bleu Cheese Dressing *Sweet & Sour Cabbage Soup *Pull from freezer	Spinach Salad Tahini Dressing *Burger (bun) Lettuce, tomatoes, sliced onions, condiments *Amy's Vegan, pull from freezer
FRIDAY	Whole grain dry cereal Soy or Rice Milk Banana	Sprout Salad Tarragon Vinaigrette Curried Tofu Egg(less) Wrap	Coleslaw Baked Yam Steamed Broccoli Mushroom Cashew Gravy
SATURDAY	*Strawberry Banana *(see Fruit Smoothies recipe) Sesame Tahini	Greek Peasant Salad *Cold Cut Club Sandwich *Any brand Vegan cold cuts	Arugula Salad Mock Bleu Cheese Dressing *Pizza *Amy's Vegan, pull from freezer
SUNDAY	Scrambled Tofu Canadian Mock Bacon Crispy Potatoes Toast Coffee alternative or Herbal Tea	Mixed Greens Salad Tarragon Vinaigrette *Creamy Cauliflower Soup *Pull from freezer	Caesar Salad Pine Nut Dressing Macaroni and Cheese

MENU PLAN: STAGE ONE, WEEK TWO

	BREAKFAST	LUNCH	DINNER
MONDAY	*Waffles/Maple Syrup Sausage Links Coffee alternative or Herbal Tea *Can purchase frozen waffles	Coleslaw Mock Chicken Salad Sandwich	Sprout Salad Pimento Dressing *Seitan Stew Dinner Roll (purchased) *Pull from freezer
TUESDAY	Oatmeal Raisins Cinnamon Soy or Rice Milk Toast (optional)	Cream of Spinach Soup *Hummus Crackers *Hummus can be purchased	Arugula Salad Tarragon Vinaigrette *Hearty Hot Chili Brown Rice *Pull from freezer
WEDNESDAY	Granola Soy or Rice Milk Soy Yogurt Fruit	Kale Cranberry Salad Sesame Lemon Dressing Curried Tofu Egg(less) Sandwich	Mixed Greens Salad Italian Dressing *Eggplant Minestrone Stew Quinoa (optional) *Pull from freezer
THURSDAY	*Strawberry Plum *(see Fruit Smoothies recipe) Almond Butter	*Sweet & Sour Cabbage Soup Mock Chicken Wrap *Pull from freezer	Caesar Salad Caesar Dressing Portabello Mushrooms Peas
FRIDAY	Whole Grain Dry Cereal Soy or Rice Milk Banana	Dandelion Greens Salad Asian Dressing Pimento Cheese Dark Whole-Rye Flatbread	Mixed Greens Salad Italian Dressing *Mushroom Marinara Sauce Garlic Toast *Pull from freezer
SATURDAY	*Pancakes/Maple Syrup Coffee alternative or Herbal Tea *Pancake mix can be purchased	*Miso Soup Smoky Tempeh Wrap *Miso soup packages can be purchased	Hot and Cold Slaw Baked Yam Steamed Broccoli Mushroom Cashew Gravy
SUNDAY	Scrambled Tofu with peppers and onions Sausage Links Toast Coffee alternative or Herbal Tea	Spicy Beet Borscht Cashew Sour Cream Curried Tofu Egg(less) Wrap	Watercress Salad Tarragon Vinaigrette Tacos Guacamole Sour Cream 'n' Chives *Salsa can be purchased

MENU PLAN: STAGE ONE, WEEK THREE

	BREAKFAST	LUNCH	DINNER
MONDAY	Oatmeal Raisins Cinnamon Soy or Rice Milk Toast	Mixed Greens Salad Thousand Island Dressing Cold Cuts Club Sandwich	Spinach Salad Pimento Dressing *Hearty Hot Chili Dinner Roll (purchased) *Pull from freezer
TUESDAY	Granola Soy or Rice Milk Muffin Soy Yogurt	*Lentil Soup Mock Chicken Salad Dark Whole-Rye Flatbread *Pull from freezer	Caesar Salad Caesar Dressing *Pizza *Amy's Vegan, pull from freezer
WEDNESDAY	Whole Grain Dry Cereal Soy or Rice Milk Banana	Greek Peasant Salad Smoky Tempeh Wrap	*Split Pea Soup Macaroni and Cheese String Beans *Pull from freezer
THURSDAY	*Waffles/Maple Syrup Herbal Tea *Waffles can be purchased	Coleslaw Cold Cuts Club Sandwich	Dandelion Greens Salad Mock Bleu Cheese Dressing *Burger Lettuce, tomato, onion, bun, condiments *Amy's Vegan, pull from freezer
FRIDAY	Fruit Smoothie *Make your own smoothie. See Fruit Smoothies recipe under note suggestions. Sesame Tahini	Sprout Salad Sesame Lemon Dressing Curried Tofu Egg(less) Stuffed Tomato	Mixed Greens Salad Italian Dressing *Polenta Croquettes Bruschetta *Pull from freezer
SATURDAY	Oatmeal Raisins Cinnamon Soy or Rice Milk Toast	Watercress Salad Thousand Island Dressing Mock Chicken Wrap	*Creamy Cauliflower Soup *Seitan Stew Dinner Roll (purchased) *Pull from freezer
SUNDAY	Scrambled Tofu Sausage Links Tortilla Wrap Coffee alternative or Herbal Tea	*Miso Soup Curried Tofu Egg(less) Sandwich *Miso Soup packages can be purchased	Coleslaw *Hearty Hot Chili Tofu Hot Dogs (bun optional) Condiments *Pull from freezer

MENU PLAN: STAGE TWO, WEEK ONE

	BREAKFAST	LUNCH	DINNER
MONDAY	Quinoa Toasted Sunflower Seeds Almond Milk	Sprout Salad Creamy Cilantro Dressing Sun-Dried Tomato Pâté Crackers	Mixed Greens Salad Italian Dressing Spaghetti Squash *Mushroom Marinara Sauce Bruschetta *Pull from freezer
TUESDAY	Mixed Fruit Bowl Cashew Lemon Cream	Coleslaw *Millet Burger Bun, lettuce, tomato and condiments (optional) *Pull from freezer	*Split Pea Soup Roasted Root Vegetables *Pull from freezer
WEDNESDAY	Steel Cut Oats Cereal Raisins Nuts Almond Milk	*Tabouli *Red Pepper Hummus *Pita Bread *Stuffed Grape Leaves *This whole meal can be purchased	Mixed Greens Salad Italian Dressing Tempeh Tacos Guacamole Sour Cream 'n' Chives *Salsa (optional) *can be purchased
THURSDAY	Banana Berries Cashew Vanilla Cream	*Sweet and Sour Cabbage Soup Mock Liver Pâté Sandwich *Pull from freezer	Watercress Salad Creamy Cilantro Dressing *Neat Loaf Mashed Potatoes Peas *Pull from freezer
FRIDAY	Toasted Buckwheat 'n' Greens Toasted Pumpkin Seeds Green Tea	Mixed Greens Salad Thousand Island Dressing Tempeh Tuna Wrap	Arugula Salad with Pea Shoots and Edamame Sesame Lemon Dressing Vegetable Stir Fry Brown Rice
SATURDAY	Scrambled Tofu with broccoli, onions, peppers Smoky Tempeh Strips Toast Coffee alternative or Herbal Tea	Spicy Beet Borscht Cashew Sour Cream Avocado Tofu Cheese Pita Bread	Mixed Greens Salad Creamy Cilantro Dressing Golden Flower Squash Soup Mock Liver Pâté Crackers
SUNDAY	*Fruit Smoothie (*see recipe for suggestions and variety) Sesame Tahini Hempseeds	Sea Slaw Sun-Dried Tomato Pâté Dark Whole-Rye Flatbread	*Creamy Cauliflower Soup Tempeh Stroganoff *Pull from freezer

MENU PLAN: STAGE TWO, WEEK TWO

	BREAKFAST	LUNCH	DINNER
MONDAY	Millet Cereal Toasted Sunflower Seeds Blended Greens Green Tea	Jazzy Jerusalem Artichokes *Lentil Soup Dill Chives Cream Cheese Celery Sticks *Pull from freezer	Watercress Salad Miso Ginger Dressing *Marinara Sauce Zucchetti *See recipe
TUESDAY	*Avocado Ambrosia *(see Fruit Smoothies recipe)	Spinach Salad Creamy Cilantro Dressing Pimento Cream Cheese Dark Whole-Rye Flatbread	Hot and Cold Slaw *Polenta Croquettes Steamed Beets *Pull from freezer
WEDNESDAY	Steel Cut Oats Raisins Nuts Almond Milk	Sea Slaw *Miso Soup Rice Crackers *Miso Soup packages can be purchased	Kale Cranberry Salad Tarragon Vinaigrette *Neat Loaf Mashed Potatoes String Beans *Pull from freezer
THURSDAY	Quinoa Cereal Toasted Pumpkin Seeds Blended Greens Green Tea	Hot and Cold Slaw BLT Sandwich	Mixed Greens Salad Italian Dressing Tempeh Tacos *Taco recipe Guacamole Sour Cream 'n' Chives Salsa (optional)
FRIDAY	Mixed Fruit Bowl Cashew Vanilla Cream (Make your own nut or seed milk using Nut and Seed Milk Basics recipe)	Watercress Salad Thousand Island Dressing Pimento Cream Cheese Dark Whole-Rye Flatbread	Arugula Salad Tarragon Vinaigrette Dressing Neatballs Peas
SATURDAY	Cornmeal Mash Toasted Sunflower Seeds Toast	*Creamy Cauliflower Soup Tempeh Tuna Stuffed Tomato/Lettuce Greens *Pull from freezer	Greek Peasant Salad Shish Kebab Confetti Couscous
SUNDAY	Scrambled Tofu with broccoli, onion, peppers Smoky Tempeh Strips Toast Coffee alternative or Herbal Tea	Spicy Beet Borscht Cashew Sour Cream Falafel Pita Pockets	Mixed Greens Salad *Millet Burger Cashew Mushroom Gravy Peas *Pull from freezer

MENU PLAN: STAGE TWO, WEEK THREE

	BREAKFAST	LUNCH	DINNER
MONDAY	Manna Bread Almond Butter Fruit Jam Coffee alternative or Herbal Tea	Spinach Salad Thousand Island Dressing Curried Tofu Egg(less) Stuffed Tomato	*Split Pea Soup Stuffed Baked Potato Steamed Broccoli and Zucchini Squash *Pull from freezer
TUESDAY	Mixed Fruits Cashew Lemon Cream Muffin (purchased)	Kale Cranberry Salad Tarragon Vinaigrette Dressing Avocado and Sprout Sandwich	Watercress Salad Sesame Lemon Dressing Spaghetti Squash *Mushroom Marinara Sauce Bruschetta *Pull from freezer
WEDNESDAY	Cornmeal Mash Raisins Cinnamon (Make your own nut or seed milk. See Nut and Seed Milk Basics recipe)	Sprout Salad Pimento Dressing *Miso Soup Rice Crackers *Miso Soup packages can be purchased	Greek Peasant Salad Squash Enchiladas *Spanish Rice *(see Brown Rice recipe) Bean Dip (Optional)
THURSDAY	Blueberry Muffin *(purchased) Almond Butter Coffee alternative or Herbal Tea	Mixed Greens Salad Tarragon Vinaigrette Dressing Grated Carrots, and Beets Mock Liver Pâté Crackers	Arugula Salad Italian Dressing Fiesta Tostada
FRIDAY	Berries and Bananas Cashew Vanilla Cream Muffin (Purchased)	Marinated Kale/Spicy Ginger Peanut Sauce Curried Tofu Egg(less) Wrap	Sprout Salad Creamy Cilantro Dressing *Neat Loaf Mashed Potatoes Peas *Pull from freezer
SATURDAY	*Waffles/Maple Syrup Coffee alternative or Herbal Tea *Frozen, can be purchased	Sea Slaw Dill Chives Cream Cheese Carrot and Celery sticks	Greek Peasant Salad Eggplant Roll-ups *Mushroom Marinara Sauce (optional) String Beans *Pull from freezer
SUNDAY	Scrambled Tofu with mushrooms & onions Toast Coffee Alternative or Herbal Tea	Watercress Salad Pimento Dressing *Sweet and Sour Cabbage Soup Rice Crackers *Pull from freezer	*Creamy Cauliflower Soup Udon Noodles with Broccoli and Tempeh Spicy Ginger Peanut Sauce *Pull from freezer

PRE-PREP FREEZER RECIPES

Eleven recipes are suggested to prepare for the freezer before the transition is started. These recipes can be prepared in several cooking sessions for the whole six weeks or they can be prepared before each week. This will allow meals to be easily pulled from the freezer at times when you just want to relax. When cooking freezer recipes, use freezer containers suitable for the serving sizes and number of people. You will need airtight containers for the freezer, labels and a marking pen to identify your dishes.

During any day of the week you can easily substitute any menu meal with foods that you have in your freezer. This *fast food* convenience is the primary benefit of preparing a larger quantity for storage in the freezer than you might for a regular meal. In this way you can better adjust your meals to your family's size and preferences.

Stage One, Week 1
1. Creamy Cauliflower Soup
2. Mushroom Marinara Sauce
3. Seitan Stew
4. Sweet and Sour Cabbage Soup

Stage One, Week 2
5. Eggplant Minestrone Stew
6. Hearty Hot Chili

Stage One, Week 3
7. Split Pea Soup
8. Lentil Soup
9. Polenta Croquettes

Stage Two, Week 1
10. Millet Burgers
11. Neat Loaf

Stage Two, Weeks 2 and 3
New recipes are introduced. Keep in mind that if you have any frozen leftover dishes in the freezer, they will come in handy for preparing future quick meals.

COMPLETE LIST OF FREEZER RECIPES FOR STAGES ONE & TWO

Creamy Cauliflower Soup
Eggplant Minestrone Stew
Hearty Hot Chili
Lentil Soup
Millet Burgers
Mushroom Marinara Sauce
Neat Loaf
Polenta Croquettes
Seitan Stew
Split Pea Soup
Sweet and Sour Cabbage Soup

RECIPE LIST

SALADS

Antipasto
Arugula Salad with Pea Sprouts and Edamame
Caesar Salad
Coleslaw and Dressing
Dandelion Greens Salad
Greek Peasant Salad
Hot and Cold Slaw
Kale Cranberry Salad
Mixed Greens Salad
Potato Salad
Sea Slaw
Spinach Salad
Sprout Salad
Watercress Salad

SOUPS

Cream of Spinach
Creamy Cauliflower
Golden Flower Squash
Lentil
Spicy Beet Borscht
Split Pea
Sweet and Sour Cabbage

SANDWICHES & WRAPS

Avocado Tofu Cream Cheese
BLT Sandwich
Cold Cut Club Sandwich
Curried Tofu Egg(less)
Falafel Pita Pockets
Grilled Cheese Sandwich
Millet Burgers
Mock Chicken Salad
Smoky Tempeh Wrap
Tempeh Tuna

ENTRÉES

Eggplant Minestrone Stew
Eggplant Roll-ups
Fiesta Tostada
Hearty Hot Chili
Macaroni and Cheese
Marinara Sauce Zucchetti
Mushroom Marinara Sauce
Neatballs (see Falafel Pita Pockets)
Neat Loaf
Polenta Croquettes
Portabello Mushrooms
Roasted Root Vegetables
Scrambled Tofu
Seitan Stew
Shish Kebab
Squash Enchiladas
Stuffed Baked Potato
Tacos and Tempeh Tacos (see Tacos recipe)
Tempeh Stroganoff
Udon Noodles/Broccoli/Spicy Ginger Peanut Sauce (Tofu or Tempeh)
Vegetable Stir Fry

GRAINS

Brown Rice
Buckwheat 'n' Beet Greens
Confetti Couscous
Cornmeal Mash
Millet
Quinoa

SIDE DISHES
Crispy Potatoes
Jazzy Jerusalem Artichokes
Marinated Kale
Mashed Potatoes

NUT MILKS AND FRUIT SMOOTHIES
Almond Milk
Avocado Ambrosia (see fruit smoothies)
Nut/Seed Milk Basics
Strawberry Banana (see fruit smoothies)
Strawberry Plum (see fruit smoothies and check out suggestions)

SAUCES, SPREADS, DIPS, DRESSINGS
Asian Dressing
Bean Dip
Bruschetta
Caesar Dressing
Cashew Sour Cream (see Spicy Beet Borscht recipe)
Coleslaw Dressing (see Coleslaw recipe)
Cream Cheese (Basic)
Creamy Cilantro Dressing
Dill Chives Cream Cheese
Garlic Olive Oil (used for garlic toast, etc.)
Greek Dressing (see Greek Peasant Salad)
Guacamole
Italian Dressing
Miso Ginger Dressing
Mock Bleu Cheese Dressing 1 and 2
Mock Liver Pâté
Mushroom Cashew Gravy
Pimento Cream Cheese
Pimento Dressing/Dip
Pine Nut Dressing
Salsa
Sea Slaw Dressing (see Sea Slaw recipe)
Sesame Lemon Dressing
Sour Cream 'n' Chives
Spicy Ginger Peanut Sauce (see Udon Noodles/Broccoli and Tofu or Tempeh)
Sun-dried Tomato Pâté
Tahini Dressing
Tarragon Vinaigrette

Thousand Island Dressing
Tofu Feta Cheese
Twisted Sour Cream 'n' Chives (see Sour Cream 'n' Chives)

DESSERTS
Cashew Lemon Icing
Cashew Vanilla Cream
Chocolate Mint Mousse
Chocolate Orange Cranberry Cheesecake
Kids Kandy Yums
Lemon Blueberry Cheesecake
Rainbow Parfait
Sesame Candy
Tangerine Ice Cream
Tangy Lemon Tango Sorbet
Tutti-Frutti Ice Cream
Wendel's 'Other Love' Chocolate Pudding
Yummy Yam Pie

Chapter Six

Recipes

SALADS

Antipasto

This is a fun platter to bring out your individual creativity. Garnishes for this platter are ingredients used for color and presentation. Complement the Antipasto by serving the **Pimento Cheese** recipe in a small bowl.

1 box cherry tomatoes
4 to 6 celery stalks, cut into sticks
1 bag baby carrots
15 radishes, trimmed
1 can garbanzo beans, drained
1 small jar Pepperoncini, drained
2 red and 2 yellow peppers, roasted and de-seeded
1 package each, vegan mozzarella/cheddar cheese slices
1 package each, vegan cold cuts: pepperoni, turkey, bologna slices

[1]Garnish: 1 medium green head lettuce, leaves
[2]Garnish: 1 small whole red cabbage, cut across ¼ from bottom of cabbage for 9 leaves to be used as holders for vegetables. Pull them apart gently, patiently
[3]Garnish: flower tops, any flowers or herbs of your color choice (optional)

Directions
1. [1]Arrange lettuce leaves around the platter.
2. [2]Garnish: Use red cabbage leaves as vegetable holders for the vegetables, preparing all of the vegetables as noted above either in sticks, florets, or left whole, according to the directions.
3. Design and arrange the cold cuts, cheeses, beans, and the rest of the ingredients.
4. [3]Garnish with flower tops for additional color and flair.

Yield 1 party platter

Note: Amounts for ingredients and size of platter are figured depending on the number of guests. Prepare either 1 or 2 cabbage leaves for your garnish to hold each vegetable.

Some markets have roasted red peppers in the jar or deli-olive cases.

Arugula Salad with Pea Sprouts and Edamame

Wakame seaweed is a great addition to this salad. If desired, you may make the dressing the day before and store it in the refrigerator. **Asian Dressing** also complements this salad.

2 cups arugula leaves
1 cup pea sprouts, cut bite size
¼ head large red butter lettuce, torn
½ cup edamame soy beans (out of the pod)

2 tablespoons black or white sesame seeds
3 wakame seaweed strips, soaked, rinsed, drained and sliced fine (optional)
1 **Tarragon Vinaigrette** recipe

Directions
1. In a large bowl, combine the first four ingredients. Set aside.
2. Prepare the vinaigrette dressing according to the recipe.
3. When ready to serve the salad, toss together the salad mixture with **Tarragon Vinaigrette**.
4. Serve in individual bowls and garnish with sprinkles of sesame seeds.

Yield serves 4

Caesar Salad

Caesar Dressing or **Pine Nut Dressing** complements this salad.

4 cups romaine lettuce, torn, compressed
2 tablespoons capers, drained

1 cup smoky tempeh bacon strips, cut in squares
½ cup croutons

Directions
1. Place the above ingredients in a medium size bowl.
2. Prepare dressing.
3. Chill and serve.

Yield serves 4

"Leaf lettuce is much richer in iron than head lettuce. I do not advocate using head lettuce in the diet, for it contains little nourishment. It contains significantly lower amounts of vitamins A and C than green Romaine lettuce. Also, Romaine lettuce is excellent for those who would like to lose weight."
Foods That Heal *by Dr. Bernard Jensen*

Coleslaw and Dressing

I like making up this salad and putting it in a Ziploc bag and storing it in the refrigerator. Hold off on dressing the coleslaw until serving. This dressing also complements green steamed vegetables.

3 cups cabbage, green (1 small head) shredded

½ cup green pepper, diced small

¾ cup green scallions (2 to 3), sliced thin

1½ cups carrots, peeled and shredded

½ cup curly parsley, minced

Directions

1. Place the above ingredients into a bowl and toss together.
2. Whisk together the ingredients for the dressing.
3. If serving 4, toss the cabbage with all of the dressing or save until serving time.

Yield serves 4

Coleslaw Dressing

½ cup Vegenaise

2 tablespoons lemon juice

½ teaspoon sea salt

¼ teaspoon black pepper

Yield about ¾ cup

Note: Add lemon juice according to your taste because lemon tartness varies. The Meyer lemon flavor is sweeter than regular lemons.

"Cabbage, both red and green, is one of the least expensive of the vitamin protective foods and is one of the most healthful vegetables. It is an excellent source of vitamin C. Cabbage contains many minerals. It is rich in calcium and potassium, and contains chlorine, iodine, phosphorous, sodium and sulfur. Red cabbage has more calcium, but less of the other minerals than white or green cabbage."

Foods That Heal by Dr. Bernard Jensen

Dandelion Greens Salad

Thinly sliced or shavings of fresh fennel bulb would be a great addition to this salad. Green butter lettuce or Boston Bib may be easier to find than the red, so use whatever is readily available. Usually the more exotic greens like the red butter lettuce can be found in local Farmer's Markets.

1 bunch *dandelion greens, cut
    leaves and stems thin
¼ large head red butter lettuce,
    torn

1 medium carrot, shredded
¼ cup cilantro leaves
2 tablespoons golden raisins
1 recipe Tarragon Vinaigrette

Directions
1. In a large bowl, combine together the first five ingredients. Set aside.
2. Prepare the vinaigrette dressing according to the recipe.
3. When ready to serve the salad, toss together the salad mixture with the **Tarragon Vinaigrette** dressing. Serve immediately.

Yield serves 4

Note: *There is a slightly bitter taste to the dandelion greens but it is well balanced by the rest of the salad ingredients. The bitterness is what makes it effective as a liver cleanser. **Asian Dressing** also complements this salad.

> "Dandelion greens are a wonderful liver cleanser and are valuable in helping bile flow. The greens stimulate the glands. Besides cleansing the liver, the body will be relieved of many toxic conditions that are indicated by eczema, skin rashes, etc.
> Foods That Heal by Dr. Bernard Jensen

Greek Peasant Salad

The American restaurant version is often adjusted for cost-factors by adding thin confetti sliced romaine lettuce, thin scallions and adding dill instead of oregano.

Elina Katsioula, born and raised in Greece, gave me these authentic ingredients of the Greek Peasant Salad. Try either of these non-dairy versions of Feta Cheese.

4 small tomatoes, quartered
1 large cucumber (2 cups) peeled, cut in ¼–⅛ inches (*save peelings)
1 medium green bell pepper, cut in thin strips lengthwise, then cut in half

1 small red onion, cut in quarters, then sliced thin
20 kalamata olives, pitted
1 recipe **Tofu Feta Cheese** or 1 package of Sunergia Foods Feta Cheese

Directions

1. Assemble the above ingredients in individual bowls. Add salt and pepper, sprinkle the vinegar first, then the olive oil. Allow your guests to mix the salad so the fixings remain crisp and fresh.

Yield serves 4

Note: *Cucumber peelings are applied to the face for beauty. Apply for 5 minutes over the eyes to refresh them.

Oregano is the national Greek spice that grows wildly and abundantly in the mountains of Greece. Spice Hunter brand is a high-mountain Greek oregano.

Greek Dressing

2 tablespoons olive oil
2 tablespoons apple cider vinegar
½ teaspoon dried oregano

¼ teaspoon sea salt
¼ teaspoon black pepper, ground

Directions

1. Mix the **Greek Peasant Salad** in individual bowls. Whisk the **Greek Dressing** ingredients together and serve over individual salads. See salad directions #1.

Yield ¼ cup dressing

Hot and Cold Slaw

I made this dish for a potluck and it was a major hit! Two years later I got a call from the hostess, inviting me back to another party requesting this same dish!

1 small head green cabbage (4 cups) shredded
2 red onions, small (2 cups) pressed tight, sliced thin
1 yellow pepper, small (¾ cup) cut bite size
1 red pepper, small (¾ cup) cut bite size

½ green pepper, small (½ cup) cut bite size
3 tablespoons olive oil
5 tablespoons balsamic vinegar
5 tablespoons seasoned rice vinegar
1 tablespoon + 1 teaspoon garlic, minced
½ teaspoon red pepper flakes

Directions

1. Place the shredded cabbage in a medium size bowl and set aside.
2. In a medium pan sauté the onions and peppers in 1 tablespoon of olive oil and cover them with a lid. Cook them on low heat until caramelized.

> "Rice vinegar detoxifies, invigorates blood circulation, inhibits bacteria, acts as an astringent, and closes pores."
> The Tao of Nutrition by Maoshing Ni

3. Place the remaining 2 tablespoons olive oil, vinegars and garlic in a blender and blend until a smooth consistency is reached.
4. Place the sautéed mixture and the blended dressing into the bowl with the cabbage. Sprinkle in the red pepper flakes and toss the mixture together lightly.
5. Allow slaw to marinate. Serve warm or cold.

Yield serves 4

Note: Like the title, **Hot and Cold Slaw,** this dish can be served by adding the pepper and onion sauté hot off the stovetop, with the cabbage and dressing. Or it can be served marinated and chilled.

Kale Cranberry Salad

Kale should be as tender as possible and torn fine due to its hearty texture. Kale is known to be a good source of calcium. This recipe becomes "fast food" when stored in a gallon size Ziploc bag for future use.

1 bunch tender kale (3 cups) de-spined, torn fine, compressed
4 small carrots (2 cups) shredded
½ medium orange pepper, sliced thin

½ medium yellow pepper, sliced thin
½ cup pine nuts
½ cup pomegranate seeds, fresh
1 cup cranberries (dried)

Directions
1. De-spine kale with your fingers, tearing very finely and place in a medium bowl.
2. Add above ingredients and mix together.
3. Serve, or bag in the refrigerator for healthy "fast food".

Yield serves 4 (9 cups)

This salad can be served either as an entrée or a side dish, accompanied by a salad dressing of your choice. A clear dressing will highlight the colors of the cranberries, pomegranate, carrots and peppers, giving it a more colorful presentation. Suggested clear dressings: **Asian Dressing, Creamy Cilantro** or **Italian Dressing**

> "Kale is very high in calcium, vitamin A and iron. It is good for building up the calcium content of the body, and builds strong teeth. Kale is beneficial to the digestive and nervous systems.
> Foods That Heal *by Dr. Bernard Jensen*

Mixed Greens Salad

Beets should be added on top of the salad, after the dressing, otherwise it will bleed, turning the salad red.

Entrée size

2 cups mixed greens, compressed
1 cucumber, small, sliced
¼ cup (1 small beet), shredded

2 tablespoons green scallions, sliced thin
1 medium sized carrot

Side salad

Same as above, half the amount of ingredients

Directions

1. Lay out greens and arrange accompanying vegetables to your liking.
2. Dress and serve with your choice of dressing.

Yield serves 1 entrée or 4 side salads

Note: Use potato peeler on outside carrot skin, and then continue using the peeler for shavings over greens. This is a different texture than the shredded carrot.

Potato Salad

This potato salad is a wonderful addition to any picnic or salad plate. I like adding a hearty amount of mustard to give it a tangy flavor but you can adjust the amount of mustard to suit your taste. Adjust the Vegenaise to your liking.

4 cups russet potatoes (2 large) cut in cubes
1 cup celery sliced fine
½ cup scallions sliced fine
¾ cup Vegenaise

1 can chopped olives (4.25 ounces)
¼ cup ketchup
¼ cup Dijon mustard
⅛ teaspoon sea salt

Directions
1. Scrub potatoes with skins on, cut in bite-size cubes and steam them on top of the stove until tender. (This can take up to 12 to 15 minutes.)
2. Remove steamer basket from the pot and place potatoes in a large bowl.
3. Add the rest of the ingredients and fold together lightly.
4. Chill in refrigerator and serve.

Yield 4½ cups

Note: Marr Nealon gave me the tip of putting a generous amount of mustard in potato salad, calling it German style, an old family recipe.

Sea Slaw and Dressing

Slaw

4 cups green cabbage, shredded fine

1 cup arame seaweed, soaked 20 minutes, rinsed and drained

½ large red bell pepper, sliced fine

1 medium carrot (1 cup) shredded

15 large mint leaves, sliced fine

Garnish: black sesame seeds

Dressing

4 tablespoons seasoned rice vinegar

4 tablespoons lemon juice

2 tablespoons olive oil

2 tablespoons sesame oil

5 medium dates, pitted

5 leaves mint

2 tablespoons ginger, peeled, minced

1 teaspoon garlic, rough chop

1 tablespoon Nama Shoyu soy sauce

2 pinches sea salt

Yield about ¾ cup dressing

Directions

1. In a large bowl, combine cabbage, arame seaweed, red bell pepper, carrots and mint leaves together. Set aside.
2. In a blender, mix together all of the ingredients for the dressing, except sesame seeds.
3. If serving for 4, toss all of the dressing together with the mix. Otherwise, dress only the amount of salad to be served immediately and save the remainder for future servings.
4. For the garnish, sprinkle the top with some black sesame seeds.

Yield serves 4

Spinach Salad

The way to wash mushrooms is to take a soft, damp, paper towel and wipe the mushrooms clean. Spinach always takes several washings to get it clean. Try the **Thousand Island Dressing** recipe with this salad.

1 bunch fresh spinach, no stems
1 cup radicchio, sliced ribbon thin
4 medium (1 cup) button
   mushrooms, sliced thin

½ cup fennel, fresh, sliced thin at
   an angle
⅓ cup red onion, sliced thin

Directions
1. Wash spinach carefully, drain and pat dry. Tear and place in medium size bowl.
2. Slice radicchio, mushrooms, onions and fennel, then add them to the bowl.
3. Mix together and store in a plastic Ziploc bag in the refrigerator or serve.

Yield serves 4

'Spinach is an excellent source of vitamins C and A, and iron, and contains about 40 percent potassium. It leaves an alkaline ash in the body. Spinach is good for the lymphatic, urinary and digestive systems. Spinach has a laxative effect and is wonderful in weight-loss diets."
Food That Heal *by Dr. Bernard Jensen*

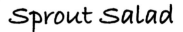

Sprout Salad

Types of sprouts: clover, alfalfa, pea, buckwheat, legumes, and broccoli sprouts are sold at Farmer's Markets and natural foods stores. Buckwheat is a more seasonal sprout. If sprouts are not easily available in your area, I suggest researching some books on sprouting. The nutritional content of all seeds, beans and legumes is greatly increased by sprouting. They are also easier to digest.

1 cup clover sprouts
½ cup sunflower sprouts
½ cup pea sprouts, cut bite size
1 medium head romaine lettuce, torn

½ cup red cabbage, sliced thin
½ cup cherry tomatoes, halved
1 yellow pepper, sliced thin
1 bunch scallions, sliced thin

Directions
1. Toss all of the ingredients together in a large bowl.
2. Add dressing and serve, or store in a Ziplock bag for future use.

Yield serves 4, entrée size

Note: When creating Sprout Salad, you can use any variety of sprouts that you like. Separate the clover sprouts until they are finely laced throughout the salad.

Watercress Salad

This salad can be stored in a gallon Ziploc bag in the refrigerator for "fast food" when you want to eat a healthy meal without prepping on demand. **Asian Dressing** also complements this salad.

2 bunches watercress leaves (5 cups) stems can be chopped fine and added
2 cups radicchio, sliced fine
½ cup yellow bell pepper, sliced thin
½ cup red pepper, sliced thin
1 cucumber (1 cup) quartered and cubed small
4 large red lettuce leaves, torn

Directions
1. Toss all ingredients prepared as directed into a medium size bowl.
2. Dress with **Tarragon Vinaigrette** recipe.

Yield serves 4

> "Watercress is a very alkaline food, and is most effective on a reducing diet. It is one of the best foods in taking care of catarrhal conditions and purifying the blood. Watercress makes an excellent addition to vegetable juices."
> Foods That Heal *by Dr. Bernard Jensen*

Cream of Spinach Soup

When using jalapeño peppers in a recipe, keep in mind that all strengths of heat are not equal. Therefore I am giving you some flexibility on the jalapeño quantity so you can adjust according to your own taste buds. Remember, the seeds pack quite the punch! This is a very simple live recipe to prepare.

1 large garlic clove, rough chop
2 cups water, pure
3 tablespoons white miso
4 tablespoons lemon juice
½ to 1 teaspoon fresh jalapeño pepper
6 ounces spinach, fresh (3 cups, pressed in cup)

1 cup raw macadamia nuts, soaked, rinsed and drained
Garnish: 6 spinach leaves (optional)
Garnish: ½ teaspoon lemon zest (see directions below) (optional)

Directions

1. In a blender, blend water, garlic, miso, lemon juice and jalapeño together.
2. Add the spinach and nuts and re-blend until you have a smooth, creamy texture.
3. Spinach garnish: Roll spinach leaves and slice thin. Lemon zest garnish: Peel the outside of a lemon and chop fine. Put 1 to 2 pinches of each garnish on top of soup.
4. Serve at room temperature or slightly chilled.

Yield 4 cups

Note: Spinach is a vegetable that needs very thorough washing. It may take several washings. If it is purchased pre-washed, re-washing is optional.

> "Spinach strengthens all organs, lubricates intestines, promotes urination, ventilates the chest and quenches thirst."
> The Tao of Nutrition by Maoshing Ni

Creamy Cauliflower Soup

You can use a stainless submerge blender by Oster, or one by Braun to hand-mix soup in the pot. If using a regular blender for hot soup, be careful because steam pressure can build up. To avoid this, start out on a low setting, and gradually increase to high.

2 cups Yukon Gold potatoes (2 medium potatoes) cut in medium pieces
5½ cups water, pure
1 cup onions, (1 small) sliced
5½ cups cauliflower (1 medium cauliflower) cut into medium pieces
4 tablespoons vegan butter
1 cup soy creamer

½ teaspoon garlic, minced
3 tablespoons white miso
2 tablespoons Liquid Aminos
1 tablespoon + 1 teaspoon Herbes De Provence
¾ teaspoon sea salt
½ teaspoon black pepper
Pinch cayenne pepper
Garnish: black sesame seeds (optional)

Directions

1. Pour water into a 5 quart soup pot and bring to a boil, add potatoes, turn heat down to medium, cook potatoes 5 to 10 minutes.
2. Add cauliflower and onions, bring to boil, turn heat down and simmer 25 minutes.
3. Stir in the remaining ingredients, except sesame seeds. Simmer 5 minutes.
4. Blend the contents in a blender until smooth and creamy.
5. Ladle into individual bowls.
6. Garnish with black sesame seeds (optional). Serve while hot.
7. If you're freezing leftovers, name and date label with a marking pen.

Yield serves 4 (8½ cups)

Note: Optional: Raw cauliflower greens chopped fine can be added in step 3. Blended, soup will come out with a light green tint. Or add greens raw in step 6. Serve hot or cold.

> "The greatest amount of calcium in cauliflower is found in the greens that are around the head. Most people throw these away, but they are good when cooked with the cauliflower or cut up in salads. It is best to undercook this vegetable. Cauliflower is easier for diabetic people to eat than cabbage.
> Foods That Heal by Dr. Bernard Jensen

Golden Flower Squash Soup

This soup was a favorite of actress Rue McClanahan (TV's Blanche, of *Golden Girls*)

1 kabocha squash = 2 cups (about 2 pounds weight)
1 teaspoon garlic, rough chop
1 teaspoon fresh ginger, sliced thin
5 cups soy creamer, regular (1 quart + 1 cup = 5 cups)
1 tablespoon Liquid Aminos

2 to 3 tablespoons white miso (see step 8 in directions)
⅓ cup water, pure
2 bay leaves
1½ teaspoons tarragon, dried
Season sea salt to taste
Garnish: parsley sprig

Directions

1. Preheat the oven to 425° F.
2. Bake the squash on a large cookie sheet, in the oven for about 45 minutes or until it is tender.
3. Cut squash in half lengthwise, de-seed and peel the squash. Scoop out the insides of the squash and reserve until step 4.
4. Place the first 3 ingredients plus 3 cups of soy creamer into a blender and blend until a smooth consistency is reached.
5. Pour the mixture into a medium soup pot and add the remaining soy creamer, Liquid Aminos, bay leaves, and tarragon.
6. Simmer with lid on for about 15 to 20 minutes.
7. Remove bay leaves.
8. Dissolve the white miso in the soup, mixing thoroughly. Turn off the heat. Once miso has been added, never let soup boil.
9. Season to taste (possibly adding 1 more tablespoon of miso or pinches of sea salt).
10. Serve hot in individual bowls with a parsley sprig.

Yield serves 4

Note: Winter squashes contain stringy fibers, some with seeds. After baking, remove them before scooping out the insides of the squash.

Lentil Soup

Rather than partial blending for a varied texture, you can also blend this soup fully, giving it a smoother, creamier texture. Never let your miso come to a boil. Miso has friendly bacteria, which is destroyed by high heat. Blended cashews enrich flavors.

2 tablespoons olive oil
2 cups red onions (1 large) diced small
2 cups carrots (3 large) peeled, diced small
2 cups celery (5 stalks) diced small
2 tablespoons garlic, minced
2 cups lentils, rinsed and drained
2 cups potatoes (5 small) peeled and cubed bite size

1 teaspoon black pepper
2 teaspoons coriander
1 tablespoon cumin
1 teaspoon sea salt
12 cups vegetable stock
4 tablespoons white miso
⅔ cup cashews
⅔ cup water, pure
Pinch cayenne pepper
Garnish: parsley sprig (optional)

Directions

1. Heat olive oil in a large pot on low flame, add onions, carrots, celery, stirring often until mixture is melted or translucent (about 20 minutes).

> "Lentil harmonizes digestion and strengthens the stomach."
> The Tao of Nutrition by Maoshing Ni

2. Add garlic into mixture and stir. Then mix in lentils, potatoes and spices.
3. Add vegetable stock, bring to boil, simmer 45 minutes, stirring often. Skim off foam.
4. Using a high-powered blender, blend 4 heaping ladles of mixture with the miso until smooth. Add ⅔ cup of cashews and ⅔ cup water and re-blend. **Caution:** increase blender speed slowly to avoid building up steam pressure.
5. Stir and simmer on stove for 15 minutes.
6. Add this mixture back into the rest of the soup on stove. Mix thoroughly and serve. Garnish is optional.
7. Allow leftover soup to cool and pour into airtight containers for the freezer.
8. Name and date label with a marking pen.

Yield about 14 cups

Note: If you prefer water instead of vegetable stock, strengthen your seasonings with 1 more teaspoon of cumin, 2 more tablespoons of white miso and 1 tablespoon Liquid Aminos.

Spicy Beet Borscht /Cashew Sour Cream

Adjust the lemon, garlic and spice to your taste. For best results, this soup is best chilled before serving, and is easy to make up in advance. This soup is a "winner" for those who like beets. You can store the borscht in the vegetable juice bottle.

Borscht

1 quart vegetable juice, bottle, organic (R. W. Knudsen "Very Veggie")
2 teaspoons garlic, minced

4 small (2 cups) beets, peeled and cubed small
3 tablespoons lemon juice
2 pinches cayenne pepper
Garnish: dill sprig (optional)

Cashew Sour Cream

1 cup cashews, whole and raw
½ teaspoon garlic, minced
5 tablespoons lemon juice

½ teaspoon sea salt
½ cup water, pure

Directions

Borscht

1. Blend ⅓ of the vegetable juice in a blender with the garlic. Add the beets, lemon juice, remaining vegetable juice, and cayenne to the blender.
2. Blend until smooth.
3. Chill in the refrigerator.

> "Beets are wonderful for adding needed minerals. They can be used to eliminate pocket acid material in the bowel and for ailments for the gall bladder and liver. Their vitamin A content is quite high so they are not only good for the eliminative system, but also benefit the digestive and lymphatic systems."
> *Foods That Heal by Dr. Bernard Jensen*

Cashew Sour Cream

4. Add all of the ingredients into a blender and blend until a smooth and creamy consistency is reached. Chill in refrigerator.

Assembly

5. Place the borscht in a serving bowl. Add two dollops of the **Cashew Sour Cream** to the top of the soup and serve. Garnish with a dill sprig.

Yield Borscht: 1 quart + 1½ cups; Sour Cream: 1¼ cups; serves 4 to 6

Split Pea Soup

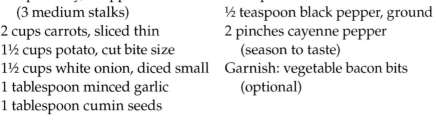

2 cups split peas, rinsed and
   drained
10 cups water, pure
2 cups celery, chopped small
   (3 medium stalks)
2 cups carrots, sliced thin
1½ cups potato, cut bite size
1½ cups white onion, diced small
1 tablespoon minced garlic
1 tablespoon cumin seeds

1 tablespoon coriander, ground
3 large bay leaves
½ cup white miso
1 teaspoon sea salt
½ teaspoon black pepper, ground
2 pinches cayenne pepper
   (season to taste)
Garnish: vegetable bacon bits
   (optional)

Directions

1. In a 5 quart soup pot, bring split peas and water to boil. During cooking time, skim off foam on top and discard.
2. Add bay leaves. Turn heat down to medium and cover with a lid. Cook until completely tender, about 45 minutes to 1 hour.
3. Toward the end of the soup cooking time, after the split peas have broken down, add vegetables with the rest of the ingredients (except salt, pepper and white miso). Cook until vegetables are al dente. Remove bay leaves.
4. Blend soup in blender, adding ½ cup water and ½ cup white miso. Pour blended mixture back into the pot. Turn off heat.
5. Season to taste.
6. Optional: Garnish with ½ teaspoon of vegetable bacon bits per bowl and serve hot. Allow leftover soup to cool before putting it in airtight containers for the freezer.
7. Name and date label with a marking pen for the freezer.

Yield about 12 cups

Sweet and Sour Cabbage Soup

Adjust the level of sweet and sour in this soup to your personal taste. See note below. A simple soup to prepare and have on hand when desired!

2 tablespoons olive oil
4 cups onions (2 medium) diced
2 tablespoons garlic, minced
1 green cabbage, medium (12 cups) sliced fine
2 – 25 ounce jars marinara sauce

8 cups vegetable stock (use 2 of the cups to rinse out marinara jars)
4 large bay leaves
7 tablespoons maple syrup
2 tablespoons lemon juice
2 teaspoons sea salt
1 teaspoon black pepper, ground

Directions

1. In a large pot, heat the olive oil on medium low. Mix and stir in the onions for about 15 minutes until golden. Add the garlic and stir again. Slowly add in the cabbage, mixing well with tongs.
2. Add the marinara sauce, bay leaves and stock, bring to a high boil, reduce heat and simmer one and a half hours, stirring often. Add remaining ingredients and season.
3. Remove bay leaves.
4. Serve hot. Allow soup to cool before ladling out extra soup into airtight containers for the freezer.
5. Name and date label with a marking pen.

Yield 16 cups (2 cups per entrée serving)

Note: Various marinara sauce brands are flavored differently; therefore I will give you some basic sweet and sour measurements according to the brand I used for testing. However, I recommend that you adjust the flavor of this soup according to your individual taste by adding either more sweetener or more lemon juice. Serve hot or cold.

SANDWICHES and WRAPS

Avocado Tofu Cream Cheese

This recipe tastes very good stuffed inside the leaves of butter lettuce. Place a couple of heaping tablespoons of the mixture inside the lettuce leaf and roll it into a log. Or serve as a sandwich or wrap filling, stuffed in a tomato, or on top of a salad.

⅓ cup Silken tofu, soft (*press water out)
1 avocado, medium, pitted and peeled
3 tablespoons Vegenaise

¼ bunch scallions (⅓ cup) sliced fine
2 tablespoons lemon juice
½ teaspoon Liquid Aminos
½ teaspoon sea salt
Pinch cayenne pepper

Directions

1. Place all of the ingredients into a bowl and mash well.
2. Chill and serve.

Yield 1 cup

Note: *For directions on how to press water out of tofu, see Chapter Five, p. 87.

> "The avocado contains fourteen minerals, all of which regulate body functions and stimulate growth. Especially noteworthy are its iron and copper contents, which aid in red blood regeneration and the prevention of nutritional anemia."
> Foods That Heal by Dr. Bernard Jensen

BLT Sandwich

For variety you can also add hummus or a pâté of your choice instead of avocado. Use the same filling rolled up inside a tortilla for a wrap instead of a sandwich.

4 slices bread

9 strips smoky tempeh bacon strips

1 tablespoon Vegenaise (each)

Bit of Dijon mustard

2 leaves romaine lettuce

1 tomato, medium, very ripe, sliced

1 medium avocado, pitted, peeled and sliced thin

Directions

1. Heat a medium skillet to medium low, spray with olive oil. Add the tempeh bacon strips and brown them on each side 3 minutes.
2. Toasting bread is optional. Spread Vegenaise inside of each slice of bread.
3. Layer the tempeh with the remaining ingredients on 2 open slices of bread, top each sandwich with the other piece of bread.

Yield 2 sandwiches or wraps

Note: Tempeh bacon strips do not need to be heated, as they are pre-cooked. They taste delicious both hot and cold.

Cold Cut Club Sandwich

The variety of vegan cold cuts, compared to meat cold cuts, is limited. Quality, flavor and tastes vary with manufacturers. The trade-off in health benefits, however, is *well* worth the small sacrifice of abstaining from animal products.

6 slices bread
4 slices veggie ham
4 slices veggie turkey
4 slices veggie bologna
4 slices vegan cheddar cheese

2 large leaves romaine lettuce, de-spined
4 slices beefsteak tomato
2+ tablespoons **Thousand Island dressing**
1 tablespoon Dijon mustard

Directions
1. Divide the ingredients in half for each sandwich.
2. Layer each ingredient between 3 slices of bread for each sandwich.
3. Use a party toothpick to hold together, cut in half and place on plate with any garnish. **Potato Salad** and/or **Coleslaw** go great with this sandwich.

Yield 2 sandwiches

Note: Martha Theus, author of *Throwin' Down, Vegetarian Style* taught me that heating the tofu cold cuts in a bit of olive oil brings out more of the flavor. Add sauerkraut to rye bread and it becomes a Reuben sandwich.

Curried Tofu Egg(less)

This recipe has all of the taste pleasure of eggs, with none of the cholesterol. Great for egg(less) salad, sandwiches, wraps, chips, or stuffed into a tomato or pepper as an appetizer. Complement this dish with leafy greens.

1 pound Silken tofu, firm,
    or regular medium/firm
    (*press out water)
⅔ cup Vegenaise
1½ cups celery, minced

½ cup green scallions, minced
1 tablespoon Liquid Aminos
1 tablespoon curry powder
Season sea salt and black pepper

> "Scallions expel external pathogens, dispel wind and cold, induce sweating, are anti-viral and anti-bacterial."
> The Tao of Nutrition by Maoshing Ni

Directions

1. Place all ingredients in a medium mixing bowl and mash together. Keep the tofu slightly lumpy for texture balance.
2. This dish gains flavor as it marinates in the refrigerator.

Yield serves 4

Note: *For directions on how to press water from tofu, see Chapter Five, p. 87.

All curry flavors are not created equal, so you may need to adjust the curry powder spice according to your taste. Textures of various brands of tofu also differ.

Falafel Pita Pockets

The *Neatballs recipe makes up 33 balls. Leftovers can be frozen and served for another meal with rice pasta and **Mushroom Marinara Sauce** or **Confetti Couscous.**

1 **Neatballs** recipe (or frozen leftovers)
3 cups lettuce, shredded, fine

2 cups tomatoes, diced, small, drained
1 **Tahini Dressing** recipe
6 Pita pocket breads (12 halves)

Directions
1. Prepare **Neatballs** recipe (if you have frozen leftovers, reheat balls by steaming them as they tend to dry out when re-baked in the oven).
2. Prepare **Tahini Dressing** recipe.
3. Put lettuce and tomatoes in separate bowls for serving.
4. Cut Pita bread pockets to half size, unless they are pre-cut.

Assembly
Fill Pita pockets with lettuce, tomatoes and 3 or 4 **Neatballs** each, spoon out 1 or 2 dollops of **Tahini Dressing** to put on top of the balls.

Yield 12 Pita pocket halves

Note: *Neatballs can be found in the recipe section under entrées. **Falafel Pita Pockets** recipe can also be assembled as a wrap. If you have any lettuce or tomato leftovers add them to your next salad.

Grilled Cheese Sandwich

This is your basic grilled cheese sandwich. The only difference is that you are using a non-dairy cheese.

2 slices whole-grain bread
2 teaspoons vegan butter
3 slices vegan cheddar cheese
1 small beefsteak tomato, sliced thin
Pinch sea salt
Pinch black pepper

Directions

1. Spread butter on (one side only) two slices of bread and grill one slice of bread, buttered side down, until toasted in a sauté pan. While this slice is toasting, place the cheese, sliced tomatoes seasoned with salt and pepper in the middle of the bread. Cover the cheese and tomato with the other (untoasted) buttered bread (buttered side up).
2. Flip the sandwich over to toast the other side. Place a lid on the pan.
3. The sandwich will be toasted/grilled when the cheese melts and the tomato is hot.
4. Remove from the heat, cut in half and serve hot.

Yield 1 sandwich

Millet Burgers

Allow millet to cool before working it into patties or it can burn your hands. Use a one cup scoop-style measuring cup for the burger size. Mold a tight patty. Almond butter can be used in place of peanut butter. Crumble a Millet Burger patty over a salad for a tasty treat.

Cook 2 cups raw millet in 5 cups water, pure
2 medium red onions (3 cups) diced
2 tablespoons olive oil
2 tablespoons garlic, minced
5 tablespoons Liquid Aminos
1 cup pecans, chopped, toasted (see step 2)
2 cups carrots (2 to 3 large) peeled and shredded

1½ cups chunky peanut butter, natural (drain oil)
2 tablespoons fresh parsley, minced
¼ cup green scallions, minced
¼ teaspoon or pinch of cayenne pepper
1 teaspoon sea salt
Olive oil spray

Directions

1. Bring 5 cups water to a boil. Add 2 cups raw millet and bring up to a boil. Reduce heat, cover, (allow steam to escape) and simmer until plump (approximately 25 minutes). Remove the cover. Stir, while letting the steam and extra water evaporate for about 3 minutes. Set aside, allowing millet to cool.
2. In a small skillet, toast pecans over medium heat, stirring constantly so they don't burn.
3. Sauté the onions in olive oil until they are caramelized (about 10 minutes).
4. Add garlic, sauté for a couple more minutes. Place into a large mixing bowl.
5. Place millet, pecans and remaining ingredients into the bowl. Then mix until everything is well incorporated. Add salt to taste.
6. Turn on broiler.
7. Scoop the mixture into a one cup measure, form tight patties. Gently lay them on a lightly oil sprayed 15" x 10" large Pyrex dish or baking sheet.
8. Broil until brown on top, watching carefully not to burn. Then gently turn them over and broil until brown on the other side. Watch carefully because the broiler cooks quickly. (This can take about 4 to 5 minutes per side.)
9. For the freezer, allow to cool, place patties in individual airtight containers.
10. Name and date label with a marking pen.

Yield 11 Burgers

Note: You can also make this recipe into a loaf, baking it at 350° until brown on top. Cut in squares and serve **Mushroom Cashew Gravy** on top.

Mock Chicken Salad

The mock smoked chicken preferred for this recipe is a soy protein-based product Follow Your Heart brand, which is available in some natural foods stores, but you may use any kind of mock chicken product you prefer. This recipe is able to withstand a few days of refrigeration. It is great as a sandwich or wrap filling, or stuffed in a tomato shell on a bed of lettuce greens.

1 – 10 ounce package mock
   smoked chicken, cut in chunks
1⅓ cup celery, washed and diced
   fine

¾ cup green scallions, washed
   and sliced thin
¾ cup Vegenaise
1 teaspoon Liquid Aminos
1 pinch black pepper, ground

Directions
1. In a food processor pulse the mock smoked chicken until it is chopped fine, and place it in a medium size bowl.
2. Cut the celery and scallions, and add them to the bowl with all the other ingredients and mix thoroughly.
3. Chill and serve.

Yield serves 4

Note: If Vegenaise brand is not available to you, any soy-based eggless mayonnaise can be used, however you may need to adjust the flavors.

Smoky Tempeh Wrap

Wrap variations depend on your creativity. Olive tapenade or the **Sun-dried Tomato Pâté** recipe can be substituted instead of mustard. Olive tapenade may contain anchovies, so read your labels. Spruce up your wrap! Try varieties of greens, sprouts, fresh parsley, cilantro, or micro greens in your wrap, it's entirely up to you. Smoky tempeh is an excellent, flavorful source of protein to build the wrap around.

2 whole wheat or spelt tortillas
   (flour size)
4 teaspoons Vegenaise
2 teaspoons Dijon mustard

2 cups fresh arugula
1 large tomato, sliced thin
6 strips from a 6 ounce package
   smoky tempeh strips

Directions
1. Lay out the tortillas, spread the Vegenaise and mustard out evenly on each tortilla.
2. Arrange the arugula evenly, and then the tempeh. Add sliced tomatoes. Fold and roll up the tortilla tightly, keeping all ingredients evenly distributed throughout.
3. Slice in half with a serrated knife and serve.

Yield 2 wraps

Note: Tempeh is a fermented soy food most popular in Indonesia, as well as in many large cities. Tempeh is made in various forms, such as burgers, cutlets, etc. Because it has a dominant flavor, it must be covered by marinating, or with spices and seasonings.

This wrap tastes great with **Potato Salad** and/or **Coleslaw**.

Tempeh Tuna

When preparing a tempeh dish uncooked, a highly acidic marinade like this one is needed to balance flavors. Like tofu, tempeh absorbs the flavor of the various herbs and spices it's marinated in. The flavors deepen in this recipe as it marinates in the refrigerator. Stuff this mixture into garnished tomato halves, scooped out on a bed of lettuce leaves, or simply served on top of a salad. It is also a great sandwich filling or wrap.

1 – 8 ounce package tempeh, cut into 4 pieces	½ cup Vegenaise
1½ cups celery, diced fine	¼ cup lemon juice
½ cup green scallions, sliced fine	2 tablespoons Liquid Aminos
	¼ teaspoon cayenne pepper

Directions

1. Pulse tempeh in food processor until fine. Put tempeh in a medium size bowl. Add all remaining ingredients and mix together well.
2. Refrigerate in an airtight glass container up to several days, or serve fresh.

Yield serves 4 (2½ cups)

Note: Tempeh is a fermented soy food high in protein, and easier to digest than tofu as it is less processed. It comes in a variety of different flavors, as well as "to go" burgers in the refrigerated section of natural foods stores. The "vegetable" flavor is great for this recipe. Tempeh has a dominant flavor that is best disguised by herbs/spices or marinade. This is a great transitional recipe toward raw. This was a mainstay with me when I was transitioning to a higher percentage of raw foods in my diet.

ENTRÉES

Eggplant Minestrone Stew   Freezer

Garbanzo beans are best when soaked 24 hours, rinsed and drained before cooking.

Cook beans until tender. Pasta should be slightly undercooked and firm as it will continue cooking in the stew. Dried beans stored for a long time take longer to cook.

2 tablespoons olive oil
2 eggplants, medium, (about 2 pounds) or 8 cups peeled, cut into 1" cubes
1 medium onion (2 cups) diced small
4 tablespoons garlic, minced
3 teaspoons sea salt
1 teaspoon black pepper, ground
1 teaspoon lemon juice
7 cups vegetable stock
1⅓ cup garbanzo beans = 3½ cups cooked

1 jar crushed tomatoes, (28 ounces)
1 can fire roasted diced tomatoes (28 ounces)
3 large bay leaves
2 teaspoons thyme, dried
2 teaspoons oregano, dried
1 tablespoon basil, dried
1 cup fresh basil, rough chop, pressed into a measuring cup
1 – 6 ounce package = 3 cups elbow rice pasta, cooked al dente

Directions

1. Heat the olive oil in a large soup pot on medium-low setting. Brown the onions first and then add eggplant. Add salt, pepper and garlic. Cover, stir and cook until brown and tender.
2. Separately cook pasta according to package directions. Reserve.
3. Add the remaining ingredients except for the pasta. Bring to a boil and simmer 2 hours (until beans are tender). Remove bay leaves.
4. Add the pasta and mix throughout. Simmer another 5 to 10 minutes.
5. Allow cooling time before you ladle stew into plastic freezer containers or bags. Name and date label with a marking pen.

Yield 14 cups

> "Eggplant is low in calories and is a non-starchy fruit that is cooked as a vegetable. It contains a large amount of water. It is good for balancing diets that are heavy in protein and starches."
> Foods That Heal by Dr. Bernard Jensen

Eggplant Roll-ups

For variation, you can use different herbs for this recipe, such as dried Herbes De Provence to baste the eggplant. **Mushroom Cashew Gravy** recipe goes good with this dish if you want an alternative to the **Mushroom Marinara Sauce** recipe.

2 eggplants, medium, peeled (see step 2)

1 – 3 ounce package sun-dried tomatoes[1] (soaked for 30 minutes) drain and mince

1 pound tofu, firm (press water out[2])

3 tablespoons Liquid Aminos

2 tablespoons garlic, rough chop

1 tablespoon+1½ teaspoons Italian herbs sprinkled on top of rolls, before baking

½ teaspoon sea salt (mixed in with dried herbs above)

½ teaspoon lemon juice

½ cup fresh basil, minced

Olive oil spray

Sauce: 2 to 3 tablespoons **Mushroom Marinara Sauce** per roll

Directions

1. Preheat oven to 350° F.
2. Slice the eggplant stem to bottom, (not side-to-side) into 14 slices, about ³⁄₈" thick.
3. Spray 2 large cookie sheet pans with olive oil and lay out eggplant slices. Bake for about 30 minutes covered with tin foil. Turn the slices over and drizzle olive oil and [3]dried herbs/salt mixture on top and continue baking about 5 minutes more, until *almost* tender. The eggplant needs to be tender enough to *fold*, but not break apart.
4. Blend tofu, Liquid Aminos, lemon juice and garlic until smooth and add the mixture to a medium size mixing bowl.
5. In a food processor, pulse sun-dried tomatoes until chopped fine. Spoon the tomato mixture into the mixing bowl with the tofu, gently folding in the fresh minced basil.
6. When the eggplant is cool, lay out the slices, spoon 1 heaping tablespoon measure of filling on top of the smaller end of the *un-seasoned* side of the eggplant, rolling it up until the other side is met. Place eggplant rolls in a 9" x 12" oil-sprayed Pyrex baking dish. Bake the roll-ups *seam* side down, so that they do not come apart, for 25 to 30 minutes.

7. Place 2 to 3 tablespoons of the heated **Mushroom Marinara Sauce** on top of each of the eggplant rolls and serve.

Yield 14 rolls

Note: Instead of soaking [1]sun-dried tomatoes, you can also purchase an 8.5 ounces jar from Trader Joes. Drain oil, mince ½ cup and add in step 5. [2]To press out water from tofu, see Chapter Five, p. 87. [3]Assemble rolls so that dried herbs are on top, for presentation.

Fiesta Tostada

This ethnic type dish always works well to introduce raw dishes, especially for those palates that enjoy Mexican style food. This is a good transitional recipe for either cooked or raw choices. For the cooked choice, warm the tortillas, and for the raw choice you may need both a fork and a knife for cutting the crackers.

4 cracker shells (raw) or 8 to 12 corn *tortillas
2 cups **Guacamole**
2 cups lettuce, sliced finely
1½ cups tomatoes, fresh, diced small (drained)
½ cup sun-dried olives, pitted and chopped

6 to 8 tablespoons **Salsa**, "some like it hot"
1 cup **Cashew Sour Cream**
3 green scallions, sliced thin
Garnish: 4 sprigs cilantro
Garnish: 8 cherry tomatoes cut in halves

Directions
1. Place above prepped vegetables in individual bowls.
2. On cracker shells, layer in this order: **Guacamole**, lettuce, tomatoes, olives, **Salsa, Cashew Sour Cream** and sprinkle green scallions.
3. Garnish: cilantro sprigs and cherry tomatoes.

Yield serves 4

Note: *Tortilla amounts vary, determined by tortilla size and appetite.

Raw shells can be bought in the raw foods section of a natural foods store. **Cashew Sour Cream** is listed with the **Spicy Beet Borscht** recipe. Saltiness in sun-dried olives varies, so you may want to adjust the quantity. Some Farmer's Markets sell sun-dried olives. If they are not available use Kalamata olives.

Hearty Hot Chili

Freezer

Soak 1½ cups dried red kidney beans overnight. Rinse and drain. For Stage Two eliminate meatless ground and add more beans, mushrooms and/or vegetables.

3 cups red kidney beans (raw
   1½ cups = about 3+ cups
   soaked)
5 cups water, pure
3 tablespoons olive oil
2 cups red onions, diced (3 small)
1½ cups carrots (2 medium)
   diced small
½ cup red bell pepper, diced
   small
2 tablespoons jalapeño pepper
   (1 medium) minced
2 cups shitake mushrooms (20)
   chopped small (de-stemmed)

2 tablespoons garlic, minced
1 – 12 ounce package meatless
   ground
4 bay leaves
⅓ cup cilantro, fresh, minced
1 teaspoon chili powder blend
1 teaspoon garam masala
¼ teaspoon cayenne pepper
1 tablespoon tarragon, dried
2 – 1 pound-12 ounce cans, fire
   roasted tomatoes, diced
1 quart vegetable stock
2 teaspoons sea salt
1 teaspoon black pepper, ground

Directions

1. In a large pot, cover beans with 5 cups water. Bring to a boil, turn down heat, cook about one hour or until almost tender. (Skim and discard any foam on top.)
2. Drain bean-water and set the pot aside.
3. In a large skillet, add olive oil and onions and sauté until translucent. Add carrots, red pepper, jalapeño pepper, mushrooms and garlic. Stir mixture often.
4. Add meatless ground and herbs to the mixture and sauté for about 5 more minutes. Add the skillet mixture to the beans in the pot.
5. Add remaining ingredients, bring to a boil, and simmer for about 2 hours. Cover with a lid, allowing air to escape. Stir often.
6. Remove bay leaves.
7. For the freezer, allow mixture to cool, and pour chili into an airtight container.
8. Name and date container label with a marking pen.

> "Kidney Beans strengthen digestion, promote elimination, and is diuretic."
> The Tao of Nutrition by Maoshing Ni

Yield 16 cups

Note: Beans may require different cooking times, depending on the age of the beans.

Any store bought package of chili mix works if you prefer not using your own blend of herbs.

Macaroni and Cheese

The variety of vegan cheeses, compared to dairy cheeses, is limited. Quality, flavor and "melt-ability" vary. The trade-off in health benefits is well worth the small sacrifice of abstaining from dairy cheese.

1 box elbow noodles, 12 ounces
2 cups soy creamer, original (Silk brand)
1 – 10 ounce package vegan cheddar cheese, cut small
¼ cup vegan butter (Earth Balance brand)

1 teaspoon sea salt
¼ teaspoon black pepper
Tiny pinch cayenne pepper (optional)
Breadcrumbs for topping of dish (optional)
Olive oil spray, as needed

Directions

1. Cook box of noodles on top of the stove according to directions on the package. Rinse, drain and place in a large bowl.
2. Preheat oven to 350° F.
3. Spray olive oil on the inside (including sides) of a 2 quart medium Pyrex baking dish.
4. In a blender place vegan cheese, butter and soy creamer. Blend.
5. Pour the mixture over the cooked noodles in the bowl, add seasonings and mix thoroughly.
6. Pour mixture into Pyrex baking dish and bake for about 30 minutes.
7. Serve hot.

Yield serves 4 to 6

Note: You can add breadcrumbs to the top of this dish before baking for a toasty flavor and a different texture. If you freeze or reheat this dish, add some more cream to keep it moist.

Marinara Sauce Zucchetti

Zucchini noodles are recommended for this raw tomato sauce. If you do not own a Spiralizer, they can be purchased at a kitchen shop. The Spiralizer is used as a garnishing machine. You can also use a grater when you opt for a raw "spaghetti" meal made from zucchini. The (Spiralizer) zucchini noodle-like spaghetti is more fun to eat.

Zuchetti Noodles
2 zucchini, large, equals 6 cups spiralized (or shredded)

Sauce
10 button mushrooms, medium (4 cups) sliced and marinated. (see step 1)
1 tablespoon olive oil (for marinating the mushrooms)
1 tablespoon Nama Shoyu soy sauce (for marinating the mushrooms)
15 small, ripe, roma tomatoes, quartered (3¾ cups)
2 jars (8.5 oz.) sun-dried tomatoes in olive oil

15 sun-dried olives, pitted, chopped (½ cup)
1 cup fresh basil (4 tablespoons + 1 teaspoon) minced fine
3 tablespoons garlic, rough chop
2 tablespoons capers
1 teaspoon red crushed chili pepper seeds
2 teaspoons sea salt
Garnish: basil sprig
Garnish: pine nuts (optional)

Directions
1. In a large mixing bowl, marinate sliced mushrooms in one tablespoon olive oil and one tablespoon of Nama Shoyu soy sauce. Set aside.
2. Cut tomatoes in quarters and add them to the food processor. Pulse until chopped. Add to the mixing bowl.
3. Pulse sun-dried tomatoes and garlic in food processor, add to tomato blend in bowl.
4. Chop olives and hand fold in minced basil and add them to the mixture in the bowl.
5. Add remaining ingredients, thoroughly mixing until fully folded together.
6. Spoon the sauce over the zucchini noodles and serve.
7. Garnish with a basil sprig and pine nuts on top of sauce.

Yield 7½ cups sauce, serves 4 to 5

Note: You can heat the plates in the oven at 350° before serving, or put the noodles in hot water with the heat turned off for 3 minutes. (Especially during cold weather.) Nama Shoyu is an unpasteurized soy sauce. Use Kalamata olives if sun-dried olives are not available.

Mushroom Marinara Sauce Freezer

This sauce is great for pasta, lasagna or **Neatballs.** You can also substitute *meatless ground for mushrooms, or prepare the sauce without either. If you are adding meatless ground, add 2 cups right *after* step 3, stir for 10 minutes.

3 tablespoons olive oil
2 cups onions (1 large) peeled, diced, small
3 cups button mushrooms (12 medium/large) chopped small in food processor
3 tablespoons garlic, minced fine
1 can fire roasted crushed tomatoes (28 ounces)
1 can fire roasted diced tomatoes (28 ounces)

1 can chunky tomato sauce (28 ounces)
4 medium bay leaves
⅔ cup fresh basil, rough chop
1 teaspoon oregano, dried
1 teaspoon thyme, dried
2½ teaspoons sea salt
1½ teaspoons black pepper, ground
Tiny pinch cayenne pepper (optional)

Directions

1. Heat the olive oil in a 5 quart soup pot on medium-low setting. Sauté the onions until they are translucent.
2. Add mushrooms to the pot and stir until browned and tender.
3. Add the garlic and stir for about a minute.
4. Add the tomato ingredients, bay leaves and dried herbs. Quickly bring the mixture to a low boil. Simmer for two hours, stirring occasionally.
5. Add fresh basil and remaining ingredients, let them simmer for another 10 minutes.
6. Remove bay leaves before serving hot.
7. Ladle one cup of sauce (per serving) over pasta or spaghetti squash.
8. For the freezer, name and date container label with a marking pen.

Yield 8½ cups

Note: Rice pasta is recommended instead of whole-wheat or semolina (follow directions on the package). This sauce is heartier adding either filling. A tiny pinch of cayenne brings out deeper flavors. *Meatless ground may be Yves or Lightlife brand. For Stage Two prepare spaghetti squash as your pasta with **Mushroom Marinara Sauce.**

Neatballs

Neatballs can be served in Pita bread as a **Falafel**.[1] Or served over rice pasta, **Brown Rice**, spaghetti squash and **Mushroom Marinara Sauce**, or as hors d'oeuvres at a party.

1 pound tofu, firm (press water out[2])	2 medium onions (2 cups) sliced, compressed
3 to 4 slices sourdough bread (1½ cups) freshly ground breadcrumbs	3 tablespoons Liquid Aminos
	1 tablespoon curry powder[3]
1⅔ cups walnuts	1 teaspoon sea salt
	Olive oil spray

Directions

1. Mash the tofu in a large bowl until smooth.
2. Place bread in a food processor and pulse to a crumb consistency. Add the crumbs to the bowl with the tofu.
3. Pulverize the walnuts in the food processor until a powder consistency. Add the powdered nuts to the bowl with the tofu and breadcrumbs.
4. Sauté onions in a small hot pan with Liquid Aminos until the onions are caramelized.
5. Puree the caramelized onions in a food processor and then add them to the tofu mixture in the bowl.
6. Add curry and salt to the mixture and mix thoroughly.
7. Preheat oven to 350° F.
8. Roll the mixture into 1 full tablespoon size tight balls and place them on a large 10" x 14" oiled Pyrex dish. Treat them delicately so they hold their shape.
9. Put the Pyrex dish in the oven and double-check them in 15 minutes. Turn them over at 30 minutes.
10. Bake the balls for about 15 more minutes after they have been turned. The total cooking time is about 45 minutes. Serve hot.

Yield 33 balls (party platter size)

Note: [1]**Falafel Pita Pockets** recipe can be found within the Sandwiches and Wraps section.
[2]See directions in Chapter Five, p. 87 for pressing water out of tofu.
[3]Curry strengths can vary. You may want to adjust the curry spice to your taste. This dish is also good with **Confetti Couscous**.

Neat Loaf

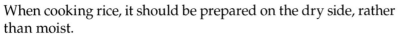

When cooking rice, it should be prepared on the dry side, rather than moist.

Optional: This recipe can be baked the day before and chilled. This allows the recipe to set up, then cut in portions. This is a favorite hit for entertaining and a great freezer item.

3 cups brown rice, (1½ cups raw rice = 3 cups cooked)

1 large onion (2½ cups) peeled, diced small

3 tablespoons Liquid Aminos

2 cups walnuts

2 cups sourdough bread, cut into small chunks (pressed down in cup)

3 tablespoons garlic

1 pound tofu (extra firm) (*press water out)

1½ cups tomato ketchup (Note: additional ketchup is also used below in the recipe)

1 teaspoon black pepper, ground

2 teaspoons coriander, ground

2 teaspoons cumin, ground

¾ teaspoon sea salt

Olive oil spray, as needed

½ cup tomato ketchup for basting the top on Neat Loaf (step 8)

Directions

1. In a medium pot add rice to 3 cups boiling water, cover, turn heat on simmer, turn off heat at 45 minutes. Set aside for 15 minutes to absorb any moisture.
2. In a hot non-stick sauté pan, simmer, mix and stir the onions with Liquid Aminos until caramelized (about 10 to 15 minutes). Set aside.
3. Preheat oven to 350° F.
4. In a food processor, separately (one at a time) pulverize garlic, walnuts, and bread. Empty each of the pulverized ingredients from the processor into a large bowl.
5. *Press moisture from tofu and crumble it into the bowl.
6. Add the caramelized onions, rice, 1½ cups ketchup to the bowl. Add spices and mix thoroughly until fully incorporated and it resembles sticky dough.
7. Spray the inside of a 9" x 13" x 2" Pyrex dish with olive oil and fill it with the Neat Loaf mixture. Pat the mixture down so it is packed tightly and evenly.
8. Bake in the oven for about 30 minutes, until it turns golden brown on top. Remove from oven. Spread ½ cup tomato ketchup on top, bake about 30 minutes more and remove (after verifying that it is mostly dry to the touch). Set aside for 20 minutes before cutting. Neat Loaf is best moist inside, yet dry enough to cut in slices or square portions, and serve.
9. Allow to cool, and then put in airtight containers for the freezer. Name and date label with a marking pen.

Yield 10 slices or squares

Note: *To press water out of tofu, see Chapter Five, p. 87.

Polenta Croquettes

Freezer

This dish can also be served as an appetizer with **Mushroom Marinara Sauce** as dip. For the sun-dried tomatoes I often prefer using the marinated jar from Trader Joe's.

You can also make this Polenta mixture into a loaf.

1½ cups cornmeal, raw, cooked in 3 cups water, pure
1½ tablespoons olive oil
1 tablespoon garlic, minced
2 cups onions (½ large) diced small
2 tablespoons Italian seasoning blend

1 jar sun-dried tomatoes, 8.5 ounces chopped, drain oil (see note above)
3 tablespoons fresh basil (7 large leaves) minced
⅓ cup pine nuts
2 tablespoons Liquid Aminos
2 teaspoons sea salt
Olive oil spray

Directions

1. In a medium saucepan bring water to boil, add cornmeal, cover and simmer for 20 minutes, mixing often.
2. Put the hot cornmeal in a large bowl.
3. Mix and stir onion, garlic and Italian herbs in olive oil until they are translucent.
4. Add all of the ingredients into the bowl and mix until they are evenly distributed. Allow the mixture to cool enough to work with, but not too cool to shape.
5. Preheat the oven to 350° F.
6. Roll ¼ cup measure of the mixture in your hands into a tight log. Place it on a large, lightly sprayed cookie sheet or 10" x 14" Pyrex pan.
7. Repeat step 6 until the whole mixture is rolled.
8. Bake in the oven until lightly browned, about 45 minutes. (No need to turn the rolls.)
9. Serve warm with a side dish of **Mushroom Marinara Sauce**.

Yield serves 4 to 6 (20 croquettes)

Note: If you choose to soak sun-dried tomatoes, drain them and marinate them in **Garlic Olive Oil**, add a couple squeezes of lemon juice, and marinate two hours minimum. This will give them flavor. If you don't have the **Garlic Olive Oil** recipe prepared you can add some minced garlic to olive oil and lemon juice. Drain the sun-dried tomatoes.

Portabello Mushrooms

The Portobello mushroom has a hearty and meat-like texture. Mushrooms are fragile and break easily. Handle them gently at every step.

4 large Portobello mushrooms
1 tablespoon olive oil
1 tablespoon garlic, minced
1 pound tofu, medium/firm
   (*press water out)
½ cup sun-dried tomatoes, drain
   thoroughly (8.5 ounce jar)

1 cup basil, fresh, minced
2 tablespoons Liquid Aminos
2 tablespoons lemon juice
2 pinches cayenne pepper
1 teaspoon sea salt
Olive oil spray

Directions
1. Wash mushrooms by rinsing them gently. Lightly pat both sides dry.
2. Cut off stem and scoop out the black spokes of the Portobello mushrooms, leaving the shell intact. See note below.
3. In a food processor add the remaining ingredients, except basil, and blend.
4. Preheat the oven to 400° F.
5. Place mixture in a medium size bowl and fold in the basil.
6. Spray a large Pyrex baking dish. Bake mushrooms 15 minutes before stuffing.
7. Portion the mixture into 4, and stuff the mushroom shells with the filling.
8. Bake mushrooms about 30 minutes.
9. Optional: To further crisp the tops of the mushrooms, put them under the broiler for 4 to 5 minutes. Watch them carefully so they don't burn.

Yield serves 4

Note: *See directions in Chapter Five, p. 87 for pressing water out of tofu.

Step 2 mushroom trimmings can be sautéed another time, served with vegetables.

Roasted Root Vegetables

If you would like this dish to be crispier, place it under the broiler for a few minutes, but *watch* it carefully as crisp turns to burned quickly!

2 onions, quartered and peeled

2 yams, peeled, halved and cut in medium chunks

2 carrots, peeled and cut in medium chunks

1 beet, quartered and cut into ½" slices

2 turnips cut into medium chunks

1 rutabaga, cut into medium chunks

2 tablespoons **Garlic Olive Oil**

1 tablespoon Herbes de Provence

Season sea salt and black pepper to taste

Directions

1. Preheat the oven to 350° F.
2. Toss all of the ingredients together in a large bowl.
3. Spread the mixture out onto a large 10" x 14" baking dish.
4. Bake covered for about 25 to 30 minutes. Remove cover and continue to bake until tender, but slightly crispy.
5. Add salt and pepper to taste.

Yield serves 4

Scrambled Tofu

Crumbling the tofu makes this scrambled tofu easy to prepare. And, if you want a lighter and fluffier texture you can blend the tofu instead. This recipe is also great in a large tortilla wrap with **Cashew Sour Cream** and **Salsa** as a topping. Curry powder strengths vary, so you may want to adjust the amount to your taste.

1 pound Silken medium/firm tofu, (*press water out)
2 teaspoons curry powder
¼ teaspoon turmeric
1 tablespoon olive oil
1 cup red onion, small dice
1 small clove garlic, minced
2 cups (small box) button mushrooms, sliced

½ cup red bell pepper, stemmed, de-seeded, medium dice
½ cup green bell pepper, stemmed, de-seeded, medium dice
3 tablespoons Liquid Aminos
1 cup roma tomatoes (2 small) medium dice
Tiny pinch black pepper
Optional: tortilla wrap

Directions

1. In a bowl, crumble the tofu to get large size crumbles.
2. Add in the curry powder, turmeric and Liquid Aminos, mix gently to coat the tofu crumbles.
3. In a hot sauté pan, heat the olive oil. Sweat red onions and garlic until translucent.
4. Add the mushrooms into the sauté, cook for about 5 minutes.
5. Add in bell peppers first, then tomatoes, black pepper, and the tofu mixture, and stir gently until all flavors are fully blended and the tofu has a nice even yellow color.
6. Serve immediately, while still hot, with **Crispy Potatoes**.

> "The soybean is valued for its high protein content, but it also has an exceptionally high amount of many other vitamins and minerals."
> Foods That Heal by Dr. Bernard Jensen

Yield serves 2 to 4

Note: *To press water out of the tofu, see directions in Chapter Five, p. 87.

Seitan Stew

Cooking time always varies with the texture and size of the vegetable. In order to make certain that the vegetables are al dente, do not overcook them, as they will also be cooking in the sauce. When you prepare a recipe, always double-check your seasonings to see if it needs more or less of something for your particular taste. Recipes can be followed to the letter, or used as a base for your own creative ideas. This is a great freezer recipe.

2 tablespoons olive oil
1 – 8 ounce package (1½ cups) seitan, cut in bite size pieces
2 potatoes, medium, cut in bite size cubes
2 medium onions (2 cups) medium dice
2 carrots, medium, sliced very thin
3 stalks celery, angle cut, about 1" pieces

2 tablespoons garlic, minced
3 – 14.5 ounce cans fire roasted tomatoes
2 cups peas, frozen
3 bay leaves
1 tablespoon thyme, dried
1 tablespoon oregano, dried
1 cup fresh basil, sliced very thin
Tiny pinch cayenne pepper
Season sea salt and pepper

Directions

1. Heat the olive oil on medium heat in a large pot. Add the onions, carrots, and celery. Sweat the vegetables for 5 to 10 minutes. Stir in garlic.
2. Add the seitan and turn up the heat slightly. Brown the seitan while stirring vigorously. When browned, stir in the potatoes. Cover.
3. Add the tomato products and bring to a boil, then *immediately* turn down the heat to simmer. Add all of the remaining ingredients except the fresh basil, simmer for 45 minutes to one hour, stirring often.
4. Add the basil and seasonings to taste.
5. For the freezer, allow recipe to cool, pour into airtight containers.
6. Name and date the container label with a marking pen.

Yield 10 cups

Shish Kebab

It's fun to set a romantic table with this colorful presentation. Marinate the tofu for 4 hours. Prepping the veggies is simple, but skewering the veggies by hand can take some time. Sometimes an X cut with a knife needs to be made on the corn cuts before they are easily skewered. Kebabs can also be cooked on an outside grill.

6 – 10" wooden or bamboo skewers
1 teaspoon garlic, minced
1 teaspoon ginger, minced
¼ cup Teriyaki sauce
1 pound tofu, extra firm
  (see step 2) (*press water out)
1 red pepper, medium, de-seeded,
  cut 1" square pieces

1 green pepper, medium,
  de-seeded, cut 1" square pieces
1 red onion, medium, cut 1"
  square pieces
2 cups pineapple, fresh, ripe,
  cut 1" square pieces
1 corn on the cob, cut 6 pieces
  (optional in season)

Directions

1. Add garlic, ginger and Teriyaki sauce to a medium bowl.
2. Cut tofu 1½" x 2" x 1" size and place in the bowl to marinate for 4 hours before preparing vegetables.
3. Prep all vegetables according to above directions and place in containers. Prep pineapple by cutting off outside skin and top and discarding skins. Cut into 1" cubes. Place 2 cups of pineapple in container. Set all aside.
4. Arrange varieties of colors of the prep on the wooden skewers.
5. Pour any leftover marinade on top of skewers. Set aside.
6. Prepare **Confetti Couscous.**
7. Preheat broiler and when it is hot, lay out the skewers. *Watch* them carefully, as they need to be turned every few minutes so that they don't burn.
8. Arrange Shish Kebabs, placing them over the **Confetti Couscous** and serve.

Yield 6 Shish Kebabs

Note: *To press water out of tofu, see Chapter Five, p. 87.

Most markets will give free wooden skewers by request from their meat department unless you prefer buying your own. You can also purchase pre-cut pineapple squares in containers. The longer the Shish Kebabs marinate, the richer the flavor.

Squash Enchiladas

Double wrap corn tortillas by heating two together for a heartier wrap. Fill them with the mixture and roll them. Double wraps prevent tortillas from tearing. Choose for yourself whether you like mild, medium or hot enchilada sauce.

1 kabocha squash, about 3¾ pounds (optional) butternut squash
2 tablespoons Liquid Aminos
2 cups onions, diced small
2 tablespoons garlic, minced
1 can olives, chopped (4.25 ounces)
3 cans green enchilada sauce, (14.5 ounces) Hatch brand medium heat

24 corn tortillas (2 packages – 12 each)
Olive oil spray
1 cup red pepper, diced small
1 cup yellow pepper, diced small
¾ cup green scallions, sliced thin
Optional garnish (see step 13)

Directions

1. Preheat the oven to 350° F.
2. Bake the squash in the oven for about 1½ hours or until tender.
3. Cut squash lengthwise and discard the seeds. Put squash in a medium bowl.
4. Sauté onions and garlic in Liquid Aminos. Mix and stir until they caramelize.
5. Add the sautéed mixture to the bowl with the squash and add olives. Mash until all of the ingredients are well mixed.
6. Spray olive oil inside (all sides) of a 10" x 14" Pyrex casserole and pour in ½ can of sauce.
7. Place the remaining sauce in a pot and heat on very low heat.
8. Dip two tortillas into the sauce, drain. Place ⅓+ of the filling inside and roll *gently.* *Do not let the sauce get too hot or it will tear the tortillas. See both notes.
9. Place the tortilla seam side down into the Pyrex casserole dish. Repeat step 8 until all of the tortillas are filled with the mixture.
10. Pour the remaining sauce on top of the enchiladas. Sprinkle the top with the garnish mix.
11. Cover Pyrex lightly with tin foil and bake in the oven for about 30 minutes.
12. Serve hot and top with 1 to 2 tablespoons **Cashew Sour Cream**.
13. Optional: Garnish with a cilantro leaf and halves of 2 cherry tomatoes.

Yield 12 enchiladas

Note: I recommend using tongs to dip the tortillas in the heated sauce. *The tortillas should be heated enough to fold, but not tear. Both the **Spanish Rice** (which can be found with the **Brown Rice** recipe) and the **Guacamole** complement this dish.

Stuffed Baked Potato

Garnishing with a steamed broccoli floret on top of the potatoes makes an inviting presentation.

2 potatoes, russet, washed, brush
   scrubbed
1 cup onions, diced
1 tablespoon Liquid Aminos
⅔ cup soy creamer (original
   flavor)

3 tablespoons vegan butter (Earth
   Balance brand)
½ teaspoon sea salt
¼ teaspoon pepper
Pinch paprika
Garnish: 4 broccoli florets, lightly
   steamed

Directions

1. Preheat the oven to 350° F.
2. Bake the potatoes 45 minutes or until tender. Allow the potatoes to cool.
3. Sauté the onions in Liquid Aminos until they are golden brown.
4. Cut the potatoes in half lengthwise, scoop out the insides and put them in a medium bowl. Add the sautéed onions to the bowl.
5. Mash the insides of the potato with the rest of the ingredients in the bowl, *except* for the paprika and broccoli garnish.
6. Scoop the stuffing back into the potato shells. Sprinkle the tops with paprika.
7. Finish by browning the tops under the broiler. *Careful* that they don't burn!
8. Garnish the potatoes with the broccoli florets and serve.

Yield serves 2 whole or 4 halves

Note: Earth Balance brand tastes very much like butter; however, you can use any soy margarine available.

Tacos

This is a simple, fun meal for company. Set a colorful table, fill your bowls with the ingredients and everyone can serve themselves, or you could hostess.

This is a Stage 1 (processed) version and **Tempeh Tacos**[1] is a Stage 2 (whole) version.

2 tablespoons olive oil
2 cups onions, diced
1 tablespoon garlic, minced fine
1 – 12 ounce package of meatless tofu
1 package 1.4 ounce taco seasoning (Bearitos brand)
2½ cups lettuce, shredded, press firmly in a measuring cup

2 cups tomatoes, diced fine, drain (or use **Salsa**)
1 cup green scallions, sliced fine
1 can chopped olives (4.25 ounces)
12 corn tortillas
1 **Guacamole** and **Cashew Sour Cream**[2]

Directions

1. Shred lettuce, dice tomatoes and scallions and place them in containers until use.
2. Prepare Guacamole, Salsa and Cashew Sour Cream.[2]
3. Preheat oven to 350° F. then wrap tortillas in tin foil and heat for 20 minutes.
4. In a large skillet, add olive oil, onions, garlic and sauté until golden. Add meatless ground tofu and mix together and continue browning.
5. Add package of taco seasonings, mix and stir. Serve hot.

Assembly

Place a small portion of each ingredient onto a warmed tortilla, starting with lettuce, meatless taco mixture, tomatoes, or **Salsa,** olives, scallions, **Guacamole,** etc. Top off with [2]**Cashew Sour Cream** recipe, fold over the tortilla and serve.

Yield serves 4 (12 tacos)

Note: [1]To make **Tempeh Tacos** use 1 – 8 ounce package of tempeh, crumbled (instead of the 'meatless ground' tofu) and follow steps 4 and 5 in the directions.

[2]**Cashew Sour Cream** can be found with the **Spicy Beet Borscht** recipe.

Tempeh Stroganoff

This saucy tempeh dish tastes great served over **Quinoa, Brown Rice** or noodles.

2 tablespoons sesame oil
8 ounces tempeh, cut ½" x ½" x ¼" cubes
10 shiitake mushrooms, medium size (de-stemmed) sliced
3 teaspoons garlic, minced
4 tablespoons Nama Shoyu soy sauce
2 cups onions, diced small
½ red pepper, diced bite size
½ yellow pepper, diced bite size
2 teaspoons Herbes de Provence
1 cup vegetable stock
2 cups asparagus (1 bunch) cut diagonally, small
1 cup cashews, raw
1 cup water, pure
Season sea salt and black pepper, ground

Directions

1. Heat sesame oil in a large saucepan on a medium flame and add the tempeh and mushrooms. Do not stir for 5 minutes. Let the contents get brown, stir gently to continue browning on all sides of the tempeh. Add two teaspoons of garlic and one tablespoon of Nama Shoyu and stir.
2. After tempeh is browned evenly, add the onions, red and yellow peppers and herbs to the pan, mix and stir gently until they are translucent.
3. Add the stock and asparagus to the pan and bring to a boil, cover, and simmer 10 minutes on low heat. Asparagus are best cooked al dente.
4. Blend the cashews, water, remaining garlic and Nama Shoyu in a blender until smooth and creamy. Add sauce to mixture in saucepan and mix well. Season.
5. Serve the tempeh dish warm. Serve over noodles or grain of your choice.

Yield serves 4

Udon Noodles–Tofu/Broccoli/ Spicy Ginger Peanut Sauce

This recipe makes a delicious entrée or side dish served hot, or re-served cold. There is economical and nutritional value in peeling the broccoli stems and cutting and slicing them, utilizing the whole vegetable rather than just the florets when preparing broccoli.

Noodles–Tofu and Broccoli

1 – 8 ounce package Udon noodles, (follow directions on package)

2 tablespoons toasted sesame oil

1 pound tofu, firm, cut into ½" square cubes (*press water out)

¼ teaspoon garlic, minced

¼ teaspoon fresh ginger, minced

6 medium (1 cup) shitake mushrooms, sliced

½ cup red bell pepper, small, ¼"–½" dice

2 cups broccoli florets, pressed tightly in a measuring cup

2 medium carrots (1 cup) shredded

2 tablespoons Nama Shoyu soy sauce

½ cup mung bean sprouts

3 whole green scallions, sliced thin

2 tablespoons peanuts (dry roasted) chopped

Directions

1. Prepare **Spicy Ginger Peanut Sauce**. Reserve until step 6.
2. **Noodles–Tofu and Broccoli:** Cook Udon noodles according to directions (slightly tender). Rinse and drain. Reserve until step 6.
3. In a large sauté pan, sauté tofu in sesame oil. When lightly browned, add Nama Shoyu soy sauce. Brown all sides over medium heat. Gently move tofu to one side of the pan.
4. Add garlic, ginger, mushrooms, red bell pepper and broccoli. Cover with a lid and cook until slightly browned (al dente).
5. When the broccoli is slightly tender toss in carrots, stir around a few times. Cover. Immediately turn off the heat.
6. In a large bowl quickly combine the Udon noodles and the vegetables (reserve tofu until step 7) with the peanut sauce until the noodles are evenly coated.

7. Serve immediately, placing tofu cubes on top. Garnish with bean sprouts, scallions and toasted peanuts, or store in an airtight container in the refrigerator and serve chilled.

Yield serves 6

Note: *To press water out of tofu, see Chapter Five, pg. 87.

> "All the foods in the cabbage family, including broccoli, are best if eaten with proteins, because the combination helps drive amino acids to the brain. Broccoli is high in vitamins A and C, and is low in calories. It is beneficial to the eliminative system."
> Foods That Heal *by Dr. Bernard Jensen*

Vegetable Stir Fry

1½ **Brown Rice** recipe serves 6
4½ tablespoons sesame oil
1 pound extra firm tofu, cubed ½"
   (*press water out)
1 cup red onion (½ large) sliced thin
2 cups (8 medium) shitake mushrooms, de-stem and slice
2 cups celery (2 stalks) cut diagonally, sliced thin
1½ tablespoons ginger, minced
1 tablespoon garlic, minced
¾ cup baby carrots, cut diagonally ¼"
1 small red pepper, de-seeded, sliced thin strips

2 cups broccoli (1 small head) cut into florets
2 cups cauliflower, broken into florets
2 cups eggplant (1 small) ½" cubes (sprinkle salt on eggplant to draw out water)
½ teaspoon sea salt (salt and pepper seasoning for tofu step 1)
½ teaspoon white pepper, ground
1 medium head bok choy, sliced diagonally into thin strips
10 asparagus spears, sliced diagonally
5 large cloves garlic (3 tablespoons) sliced very thin (step 5)
3 cups bean sprouts

Sauce

2 teaspoons wasabi powder
1 tablespoon hot & spicy
   **Szechuan sauce (optional)
7 to 8 tablespoons Nama Shoyu
   soy sauce (to taste)

4 tablespoons seasoned rice
   vinegar
Thai basil, 30 small leaves,
   sliced fine (use regular basil
   if Thai basil is not available)
Garnish: black sesame seeds

Directions

1. In a medium skillet, heat 1½ tablespoons of sesame oil over medium-high heat, 3 minutes, add tofu and seasonings, brown evenly while continuously shaking pan.
2. Reserve *tofu for later use. Keep brown rice and tofu warm until the stir-fry is ready for serving together.
3. In your wok, or extra large non-stick skillet, heat 2 tablespoons of remaining sesame oil on medium heat. Add onions, eggplant and mushrooms. Do not stir for 4 to 5 minutes, letting the mushrooms and onions brown. Add minced ginger and garlic.
4. Add carrots, celery, broccoli and cauliflower. Do not stir. Turn up heat, 5 minutes, let vegetables brown, al dente.
5. Add bok choy, asparagus, red pepper, garlic slices and bean sprouts.
6. Turn up heat to high, add remaining tablespoon of sesame oil. Brown 3 minutes, stirring vigorously, flipping vegetables in pan and tossing gently, 3 to 5 minutes.
7. In a tiny bowl mix together sauce ingredients. (If you like spicy add **Szechuan sauce.)
8. Turn down heat to simmer, add sauce and stir for 2 minutes.
9. Turn off heat and serve with **Brown Rice**. Place the warm tofu on top of the vegetables.

Yield serves 4 to 6+

Note: *To press water out of tofu, Chapter Five, p. 87.

GRAINS

Brown Rice

If you have an abundance of (uncooked) grains, store them in the freezer, as they do not freeze, they just keep cold. This way grain bugs can't get into the grains.

1 cup brown rice, rinsed
2 cups water, pure

Directions
1. Pour the rinsed rice into a saucepan and pour the water over it.
2. Bring the water to a boil. Cover (allowing steam to escape) and turn the heat down to simmer until the liquid is absorbed (usually about 45 minutes).
3. Rice can be seasoned many different ways. Just make sure not to add salt while cooking or the rice will not plump up like it is supposed to.

Yield serves 4 (side dish)

Note: If you want to make a simple **Spanish Rice** after the rice is cooked, add ½ package (1.4 ounce size) of Taco seasoning to the rice and one tablespoon of vegan butter (Earth Balance brand).

Buckwheat 'n' Beet Greens

This simple recipe is a hearty, healthy breakfast. Any vegetable of your choice can be substituted, steamed and blended. Toasted buckwheat is also known as kasha. See optional toasted buckwheat recipe below, as either variety can be prepared. Rue McClanahan, T.V. star of *Golden Girls* loved toasted buckwheat and toasted pumpkin seeds for her breakfast.

Buckwheat
1 cup buckwheat
2½ cups water, pure
1 tablespoon vegan butter
1 tablespoon Liquid Aminos

Beet Greens
1 bunch beet greens, washed
   thoroughly, cut small
1½ cups water, pure (reserve ½ cup
   broth for blending, see step 4)
1 tablespoon vegan butter
1 tablespoon Liquid Aminos

Directions

1. In a small pot boil 2½ cups of water and add buckwheat. Stir, and turn down the heat to simmer.
2. Cook with a lid, allowing steam to escape if necessary, for 20 to 25 minutes, until tender. Stir occasionally.
3. While the buckwheat is cooking, separately steam the beet greens in 1½ cups of water. Reserve ½ cup broth water for the blender.
4. In a blender add ¼–½ cup of beet greens broth, (depending on your desired consistency) vegan butter, Liquid Aminos and blend until smooth.
5. Add vegan butter and Liquid Aminos to the buckwheat and mix thoroughly.
6. In individual bowls add buckwheat with the blended beet greens on top and serve.

Yield serves 2 to 4 (3 cups Buckwheat, 1½ cups Beet Greens)

Optional Toasted Buckwheat

Note: If you are preparing toasted buckwheat, use 2½ cups water, because the toasted makes up a moister type cereal (more like an oatmeal consistency). Kasha will also take less cooking time than the raw buckwheat (about 15 minutes to cook). For the preparation of raw buckwheat use two cups of water. I often prepare blended beets or zucchini squash.

> "Buckwheat strengthens stomach, stops dysentery, lowers blood pressure and strengthens blood vessels."
> The Tao of Nutrition
> *by Maoshing Ni*

Confetti Couscous

Every dish should be this quick and tasty. It would give us more time to play!

1 cup couscous
1¼ cups water, pure
2 tablespoons non-dairy butter (Earth Balance)
1 tablespoon +1 teaspoon Liquid Aminos

⅓ cup red cabbage, minced
¼ cup red pepper, de-seeded, chopped fine
⅓ cup parsley, fresh, minced

Directions

1. Prepare all vegetables and place them in a medium bowl.
2. In a small pan bring 1¼ cup water to a boil. Add couscous, stirring quickly. Cover with a lid and immediately remove from heat. Allow the couscous to stand for 5 minutes and then add butter.
3. Add couscous to the bowl and fold in red cabbage, red pepper and parsley.
4. Serve hot with **Shish Kebabs** or any recipe of your choice.

Yield serves 4

Cornmeal Mash

> "Cornmeal strengthens the stomach and spleen, benefits the heart, is a diuretic and stimulates the flow of bile."
> The Tao of Nutrition by Maoshing Ni

This goes very well served as a breakfast. For a sweet breakfast, add some raisins or maple syrup and cinnamon. For savory meals, season with Liquid Aminos or salt to your taste. If you are making the **Polenta Croquettes** adjust the cornmeal mash to 1½ times this recipe.

4 cups water
1 cup cornmeal

4 tablespoons vegan butter (Earth Balance brand)
Season sea salt

Directions

1. Place the cornmeal in a medium saucepan with 4 cups of water. Bring the mixture to a boil and then simmer it with a cover on. Stir frequently so that the mixture does not stick on the bottom of the pan. The cornmeal is done when it becomes thick and slightly stiff (about 8 to 10 minutes).
2. Add the vegan butter and serve warm.

Yield serves 4

Millet

Millet is a high-quality grain, valued for hypoglycemic conditions, as it releases natural sugars slowly into the bloodstream. This grain is served as a cereal, or in the same way that any grain is served. Prepare this recipe when making **Millet Burgers**.

2½ cups water, pure
1 cup millet, rinsed and drained
2 tablespoons vegan butter (Earth Balance)

Directions

1. In a saucepan add water and millet. Turn the flame on high to start. As soon as it boils, turn the heat down to simmer. Cover with a lid, allowing the steam to escape.
2. Cook millet for about 25 minutes, until it is light and fluffy.
3. Add vegan butter and season.

Yield serves 4 (3 cups)

Note: Millet can be prepared savory style by either adding sea salt or Liquid Aminos, or it can be made sweet by adding raisins or dates, agave nectar or maple syrup. Try this recipe with **Cashew Mushroom Gravy.**

> "Millet stops vomiting, relieves diarrhea, consolidates or astringes the stomach and intestines, clears heat, promotes urination and soothes morning sickness."
> The Tao of Nutrition by Maoshing Ni

Quinoa

Grains such as quinoa, millet and rice make up very nice versions of how you would prepare a potato salad. They are called grain salads and are great for leftover grains.

1 cup quinoa
2 cups water, pure
2 tablespoons vegan butter (Earth Balance)

Directions

1. On top of the stove, add quinoa and water to a medium pan.
2. Bring to a boil, and simmer with lid on (about 20 minutes), until the grain becomes light and fluffy.
3. Add vegan butter (optional) and season to taste.

Yield serves 4 (3 cups)

Note: This recipe is also a delicious cereal served with fresh almond or seed milk. Unless you're preparing this as a breakfast cereal, you may not need to add the vegan butter. Either prepare it sweet by adding maple syrup or savory by adding Liquid Aminos. Quinoa has a light texture with a tasty nut-like flavor. It is very high in protein.

Crispy Potatoes

Any type of potatoes or yams can be used for this recipe. Served with breakfast or dinner, it is a simple recipe to prepare. Leftovers would make a great potato salad.

2 cups potatoes, scrubbed, un-peeled, cut into bite-size pieces
1 tablespoon **Garlic Olive Oil**

1 teaspoon Herbes De Provence
Season sea salt and black pepper to taste

Directions

1. In a large skillet, on medium low heat, add *garlic oil, potatoes and herbs.
2. Cover with a lid, and cook for about 10 to 15 minutes, until tender and crisp.
3. Season with salt and pepper and serve.

Yield serves 4

Note: If you do not have the *Garlic Olive Oil** recipe stored in the refrigerator, add one tablespoon of olive oil and one half teaspoon of minced garlic to the skillet with the potatoes in step 1.

Jazzy Jerusalem Artichokes

Trader Joe's markets, as well as other natural foods stores, sell sun-dried tomatoes in a jar.

3 cups Jerusalem Artichokes, raw, scrub/washed, cut bite size
1 cup sun-dried tomatoes (jar 8.5 oz.), drain excess oil.
1 tablespoon garlic, rough chop
4 tablespoons lemon juice
2 tablespoons cilantro, fresh, minced
2 tablespoons capers
Season sea salt

Directions

1. Thoroughly scrub/wash Jerusalem Artichokes and cut them in bite size pieces and put them in a medium bowl.
2. Place sun-dried tomatoes, garlic and lemon juice in food processor and pulse until minced and mixed thoroughly. Place mixture in the bowl.
3. Fold cilantro and capers into mixture, covering Jerusalem Artichokes with sauce.
4. Season to taste.

Yield serves 4

Marinated Kale

For this dish, add the **Spicy Ginger Peanut Sauce**. For a raw version, omit steps 1 and 2. Instead, marinate the raw kale in step 3.

1 bunch of kale, washed, cut in small bite size pieces

Directions
1. Place the cut kale in a steamer pot with water.
2. Bring the water to a boil and then turn it down to simmer and cook for about 10 minutes, or until the kale is tender. Drain thoroughly.
3. Put the kale into a bowl and add ¾ cup ***Spicy Ginger Peanut Sauce** and mix lightly.
4. Transfer the kale mixture to a glass airtight container. Allow the kale to marinate for several hours periodically shaking the container so that the marinade and kale mix throughout.
5. Chill before serving.

Yield serves 4

Note: *The **Spicy Ginger Peanut Sauce** recipe yields 1½ cups. Since this recipe only calls for ¾ cup, you can: 1) make up half of the peanut sauce recipe, 2) make one extra bunch of kale and utilize all of the sauce, as it will keep for several days, 3) you can also serve this sauce over any steamed vegetable.

> "Kale is very high in calcium, vitamin A and iron. It is good for building up the calcium content of the body, and builds strong teeth. Kale is beneficial to the digestive and nervous systems.
> Foods That Heal *by Dr. Bernard Jensen*

Mashed Potatoes

For variation, you can also prepare yams the same way as mashed potatoes.

4½ cups quartered potatoes (13 small) cut in quarters
3 tablespoons vegan butter (Earth Balance brand)
1¼ cups soy milk
¼ teaspoon black pepper, ground
¾ teaspoon sea salt

Directions

1. In a medium steamer pot, steam potatoes until tender, about 10 to 15 minutes.
2. Place potatoes in a food processor, adding butter and soy milk and pulse until desired texture is reached. For creamier potatoes add more soy milk.
3. Serve hot.

Yield serves 4

> "The potassium in the potato is strongly alkaline, which makes for good liver activation, elastic tissues, and supple muscles. It also produces body grace and a good disposition. Potassium is the 'healer' of the body and is very necessary in rejuvenation. It is a good heart food also, and potatoes can be used very well in all cases of heart troubles."
> Foods That Heal *by Dr. Bernard Jensen*

Almond Milk

This recipe can be used just like milk on cereals, in warm beverages, as a base for fruit smoothies, or just served in a glass. Its taste is similar to dairy milk, with all the benefits, and no harms. As milk, it is best served chilled.

1 cup raw almonds, soaked overnight, rinsed 2 to 3 times, drained = 1⅓ cups

4 tablespoons maple syrup (grade B is recommended)
5 cups of water
1 teaspoon vanilla flavoring

Directions

1. In a blender, blend the above ingredients until smooth.
2. Strain the milk, and pour it into a glass container to chill in the refrigerator.

Yield 5½ cups

Note: Soaked almonds can be dried thoroughly and kept in the refrigerator for up to one week, without spoiling. They are handy to have on hand for milks or nut cheeses and other high protein snacks. Leftover almond pulp can be frozen and used for making raw crackers in the dehydrator.

"Almonds ventilate lungs, relieve cough and asthma, transform phlegm and lubricate intestines."
The Tao of Nutrition by Maoshing Ni

FRUIT SMOOTHIES

Avocado Ambrosia

This recipe can be served as a dessert in a parfait glass garnished with a mint sprig and strawberry, or it can be served as a breakfast smoothie.

1 coconut, young baby, cracked open, coconut milk and coconut meat

1 medium avocado, pitted and peeled

3 tablespoons agave nectar

2 strawberries (1 each glass) as garnish (optional)

2 sprigs mint (1 each glass) as garnish (optional)

Directions

1. Open the coconut with a cleaver, hitting all sides of the top to create an opening large enough to scoop out the inside coconut meat with a spoon.[1]
2. Pour the liquid from inside the coconut into the blender, then scoop out the coconut meat. See note below regarding [2]trimming.
3. Place it in the blender with the avocado and agave nectar. Blend until smooth and creamy.
4. Chill or serve immediately.
5. Garnish and serve.

Yield serves 2

Note: [1]A picture of how to cut a coconut can be found in Chapter Five. Be mindful that all coconuts are not created equal as their meat contents vary in amount and thickness.

Use accordingly to produce a creamy texture and rich flavor.

When the coconut is spooned out of the shell, it may often come out with some dark brown skin around the outside of the white coconut meat. [2]Trim this off with a small paring knife before blending. Create your own smoothies with coconut and colorful, exotic fruit blends.

Nut/Seed Milk Basics

This is the place where I encourage you to play with a recipe. All you need is the basic idea of what a nut or seed milk is; some ingredient suggestions, and you're off and blending! Adjust the amounts of water, nuts, seeds, sweeteners and spices to your taste. Use raw, organic nuts and seeds. *Always rinse and drain seeds and nuts. They can also be combined with each other. It is optional whether you want to strain your milk.

Nuts
Almond
Hazelnut
Cashew

Seeds
Sunflower
Sesame, hulled or un-hulled
Pumpkin
Hemp (does not require soaking)
*Flax (use soak water in recipes)
   See note below

Sweeteners
Agave nectar
Maple syrup
Brown rice syrup
Other natural sweeteners as you
   discover them

Spices
Cinnamon
Nutmeg
Carob powder

Flavorings
Almond
Butterscotch
Vanilla

Directions
1. With the exception of hempseed, all seeds or nuts should be soaked 3 hours or more. The larger the nut or seed, the longer the soak. Nuts are best soaked overnight for easiest digestion.
2. Drain, and rinse the soaked seeds/nuts.
3. Start them in the blender using only enough water to cover them and get the blender blades turning. They will become a paste.
4. Gradually, as the blades turn, add more water until desired consistency.
5. Add sweetener, spices and flavorings to taste.

Note: *Flax — do not drain soak water; use in seed milk. Flaxseeds become mucilaginous and gel when wet so take this into consideration.

Any of these milks or nut/seed combinations can be made as a base for smoothies.

Strawberry Banana Smoothie

Smoothies can be made with any combination of fruits, including berries and bananas along with juice that complements the flavors. For a richer smoothie add some sesame tahini or almond butter. Or add a few cashews to the blend. In the summer season with the varieties of fruits, you can go wild!

2 boxes (pints) strawberries
2 medium bananas
⅓ cup cashews
⅓ cup water, pure

2 tablespoons *agave nectar or
  2 to 4 dates, small, pitted
⅓ cup peppermint leaves, fresh

Directions

1. Place all of the ingredients into a blender and blend until smooth.

Yield serves 2 to 4 (4 cups)

Note: *Agave nectar or dates may be added, as fruits always vary in sweetness.

Strawberry Plum Smoothie

2 boxes (pints) strawberries
4 plums, small, pitted, large chop

1 cup orange juice
4 dates, small, pitted

Directions

1. Place all of the ingredients into a blender and blend until smooth.

Yield serves 2 to 4 (4 cups)

Note: When fruits are in season they are usually very sweet, however if not, you may want to add dates or agave nectar as a sweetener, to your taste.

Suggestions: 1) Pineapple, mango, banana and coconut milk. 2) Variety of berries, banana and almond milk. With smoothies, everything works. Get creative! If you are out of fresh fruits, make a date, nut, vanilla and water smoothie. Get nutty! Go bananas!

> "Strawberries are a good source of vitamin C, contain a large amount of fruit sugar and are delicious when juiced. They can be considered an eliminative food and are good for the intestinal tract. Because of their high sodium content they can be considered a 'food of youth.' They also have a good amount of potassium."
> Foods That Heal by Dr. Bernard Jensen

SAUCES, SPREADS, DIPS and DRESSINGS

Asian Dressing

This recipe is delicious on an Asian type salad or on a simple bed of salad greens.

Use very little dressing. It is mainly an oil-based dressing, so it will spread. Or use it as a marinade for a side dish, such as raw or steamed string beans or kale. This dressing keeps fresh in the refrigerator for up to a week.

15 dates, small, soft, pitted
2 tablespoons ginger, rough chop
2 tablespoons garlic, rough chop
1 cup sesame oil
½ cup water, pure
1 teaspoon umeboshi plum paste

4 tablespoons seasoned rice vinegar
¼ cup fresh lemon juice
1 teaspoon red crushed chili pepper seeds

Directions
1. Starting with liquids first, put all ingredients except dates and red pepper in a high-powered blender.
2. Blend liquids, add garlic, ginger and plum paste.
3. Re-blend with dates until smooth and creamy.
4. Fold in the red pepper flakes.
5. Serve or store in an airtight container in the refrigerator.

Yield 2½ cups

Note: You will need to use a high-powered blender and its plunger for thick dressings. For step 3, if you do not have a high-powered blender and plunger, put the dates with ¼ cup water (see ingredients list) in a food processor to purée them. Add the puréed dates and the remaining ¼ cup water to the dressing mixture in the blender and give it a final spin.

Bean Dip

This bean dip is also great as a filling for burritos, tostados, or as a base sauce for pizza. It can also be a party dip, or served on top of a salad. Serve it hot or chilled.

Sooryia Townley inspired this easy, economical potluck dish.

1½ cups kidney beans, dried, soak overnight and drain
1 teaspoon garlic, sliced
1 – 15 ounce can pizza sauce
¾ cup tomato, fresh, (1 medium) diced small
½ teaspoon basil, dried
½ teaspoon cilantro, dried
½ teaspoon oregano, dried

1 teaspoon jalapeño pepper, minced
1 tablespoon onion powder
4 tablespoons Vegenaise
½ teaspoon lemon juice
½ teaspoon sea salt
½ teaspoon black pepper, ground
Tiny pinch cayenne pepper for more spice (optional)

Directions

1. In a large pot, cover the beans with water, bring them to a boil, turn down heat to low, then simmer for about 20 to 25 minutes until tender. Drain.
2. Add the beans and remaining ingredients (except diced tomatoes) to the food processor. Blend until smooth. Empty the mixture into a medium size bowl.
3. Gently fold in diced fresh tomatoes.
4. Serve hot for burritos, etc. or chill in the refrigerator.
5. Serve cold on cucumber slices as an appetizer, or with tortilla chips as a party dip.
6. Name and date container label with a marking pen for the freezer.

Yield serves 4 (3½ cups)

Bruschetta

This topping goes great with sourdough toast, especially for an Italian meal. The size of your toast will determine the yield of the servings.

2 cups tomatoes, (4 medium) chopped fine
1 cup basil, fresh, minced
1 loaf sourdough bread, sliced

1 tablespoon garlic, minced fine
1½ tablespoons olive oil
1 teaspoon sea salt

Directions

1. Hand chop, or separately put tomatoes in the food processor and pulse until fine. Drain off tomato juice. Mince basil and garlic.
2. Place all ingredients in a medium size bowl and mix together.
3. Allow flavors to marinate by chilling in the refrigerator.
4. Before serving, stir the marinated mixture and re-drain.
5. Pre-portion and spread over sourdough toasts.

Yield serves 4 (8 heaping tablespoons)

Note: For variation, mix **Bruschetta** topping in with the **Cream Cheese (Basic).**

Caesar Dressing

This is an extremely versatile dressing used in salads, as a dipping sauce, or drizzled over roasted vegetables. The tangy flavor is balanced with the bitterness of the sesame tahini and Dijon mustard. Double the batch and keep some in the fridge. This dressing is great to have on hand and it keeps very well. This dressing especially complements **Caesar Salad**.

⅓ cup olive oil
1 tablespoon garlic, rough chop
¼ cup lemon juice
¼ cup nutritional yeast
1 teaspoon fresh rosemary,
  plucked from stem

1 teaspoon thyme, dried
⅓ cup water, pure
1 tablespoon Dijon mustard
⅓ cup *kalamata olive juice
2 tablespoons sesame tahini
Sprinkle dulse flakes (optional)

Directions
1. Blend all ingredients in a blender until smooth and creamy.
2. Refrigerate or serve.

Yield 1¾ cups

Note: *Kalamata juice is the liquid part of canned olives.

Cream Cheese (Basic)

I recommend a high-powered blender, such as the Vita-Mix, for this recipe. Use the plunger so that you can reach a smooth cream cheese-like texture. Many other blenders require a good amount of water to get the blades turning. The recipe then becomes more like a sour cream than a cream cheese texture.

1⅔ cups cashews
¼ cup lemon juice
1 teaspoon garlic

⅓ cup water, pure
1½ teaspoons sea salt

Directions

1. Blend all of the ingredients in a high-powered blender until smooth and creamy.
2. Store in an airtight container in the refrigerator to allow recipe to set up.

Yield 1½ cups

Note: This mixture is best when made with a thicker consistency. Varieties of cream cheeses can be made with additional ingredients and flavors.

Options: (can be added together or separately)
    2 tablespoons cilantro, minced fine
    2 tablespoons sun-dried or kalamata olives, pitted and chopped
    2 tablespoons chives, sliced fine
    2 tablespoons sun-dried tomatoes, chopped fine

Creamy Cilantro Dressing

This dressing can be tossed with cold pasta or served over a bed of salad greens.

4 tablespoons Vegenaise
1 teaspoon garlic, minced
1 teaspoon ginger, minced
¼ cup + 1 teaspoon *lemon juice
3 teaspoons agave nectar

2 tablespoons fresh cilantro,
 minced fine
½ cup pre-marinated olives,
 spicy, pitted, chopped

Directions

1. With a whisk, vigorously mix all of the ingredients in a small bowl and serve.

Yield 1 cup

Note: *Lemon strengths will vary due to some lemons being more tart than others. When it comes to measurements of variables, adjust the flavors to your personal taste.

Dill Chives Cream Cheese

This simple recipe is delicious served as an appetizer on top of cucumber rounds or stuffed in celery. Crackers and bagels beg for this non-dairy version of cream cheese. Allow the recipe to set up for several hours in the refrigerator to resemble a cream cheese texture.

1 teaspoon garlic, rough chop
1⅔ cups cashews
¼ cup lemon juice
⅓ cup water, pure
1½ teaspoon sea salt

1½ tablespoons dill, fresh, minced
3 tablespoons fresh chives, sliced fine

Directions

1. Except for the dill and chives, add the above ingredients into a high-powered blender and mix until smooth and creamy.
2. Pour mixture into a small bowl and fold in the dill and chives.
3. Chill in an airtight glass container in the refrigerator to allow the cheese to set up.

Yield 1½ cups

Note: To gain the desired texture of 'cream cheese' you will need to use a plunger with your high-powered blender.

Garlic Olive Oil

This is a basic garlic flavored olive oil that I find handy for keeping in the refrigerator for sauté cooking or raw preparation. For a basic salad dressing, estimate the amount of dressing you need, pour out enough garlic olive oil, and add lemon juice to taste.

2 tablespoons garlic, large, peeled, rough chop
2 cups olive oil

Directions
1. Place the chopped garlic and the olive oil in a blender. Blend until they are completely mixed together and smooth.
2. Pour the mixture into a glass bottle and store in the refrigerator until use.

Yield 2 cups

Note: **Garlic Olive Oil** is mentioned in other recipes. This recipe has an extended refrigerated shelf life.

> "Garlic has long been considered a medicinal plant. It is high in iodine and sulfur. The body converts garlic to alkaline ash in the process of digestion. It can be mixed with parsley and used in the treatment of high blood pressure."
> Foods That Heal *by Dr. Bernard Jensen*

Guacamole

This is also a base for the **Tostada Fiesta** and **Tempeh Taco** recipes. It is most delicious when served freshly made, as the color oxidizes within hours, even with lemon as a preservative. For variation, add lime instead of lemon juice. Try adding salsa.

3 medium/large avocados, pitted and peeled
1 tablespoon garlic, minced fine
2 tablespoons lemon juice
2 tablespoons onion, minced fine

⅓ cup fresh cilantro, minced fine
2 tablespoons *salsa (optional)
1 teaspoon sea salt
Pinch cayenne pepper

Directions

1. In a bowl, mash avocado with a masher or fork to desired texture.
2. Add the remaining ingredients to the bowl, and mix thoroughly.
3. Chill in the refrigerator or serve immediately.

Yield 2 cups

Note: *For variation, add some **Salsa** and adjust seasonings to taste. Salsa can also be store-bought, kept refrigerated and used to add a unique flavor to other recipes.

> "Avocado at its peak contains a high amount of fruit oil. Fruit oil is a rare element, and it gives avocado its smooth, mellow taste and nut-like flavor. Fruit oil also gives the avocado its high food energy value. Unlike fruit, it contains very few carbohydrates."
> Foods That Heal by Dr. Bernard Jensen

Italian Dressing

If you can chill this dressing overnight, it will allow the flavors to deepen. Depending on the portion size of your salad, mix the dressing in salad and serve. Always add dressings to salads just before serving. This dressing keeps very well in the refrigerator.

1 teaspoon fresh chervil or parsley, minced

2 teaspoons fresh tarragon, minced

2 teaspoons shallot, minced fine

1 teaspoon garlic minced fine

½ cup olive oil

2 tablespoons strawberry vinegar

1 tablespoon balsamic vinegar

1 tablespoon lemon juice

1 teaspoon agave

2 teaspoons Dijon mustard

½ teaspoon salt

¼ teaspoon black pepper

Directions

1. Whisk together all ingredients in a small bowl.
2. Chill, allowing the flavors to deepen, and serve.

Yield serves 4 to 6 (¾ cup)

Miso Ginger Dressing

Miso is a valuable food for good health because it replenishes the intestinal flora (friendly bacteria). In a dressing it adds delicious flavor to the health picture.

1 teaspoon garlic, rough chop
1½ teaspoons ginger, small chop
3 tablespoons white miso
1 tablespoon sesame oil
3 tablespoons sesame tahini
3 dates, medium, soft, pitted

2 tablespoons lemon juice
1 teaspoon umeboshi plum paste
¾ cup water
⅛ teaspoon sea salt
Tiny pinch cayenne pepper

Directions
1. Blend all of the ingredients in a high-powered blender until smooth and creamy.
2. Serve or chill in an airtight container for several days.

Yield 1¾ cups

Note: This recipe has a refrigeration shelf life of several days. It is delicious served over salads or steamed vegetables. There are different kinds of Miso paste with various flavors made from different varieties of grains and ranging from white to yellow to brown in color.

Mock Bleu Cheese Dressing 1

This dressing has the closest similarity to bleu cheese that I have found. Make this dressing in advance of serving and the flavors will marinate and deepen.

1 – 6 ounce package Soy Bleu (Sunergia foods: see Brand Name Resource Guide)
1 tablespoon garlic, chopped
4 tablespoons olive oil
3 tablespoons + 1 teaspoon lemon juice
⅔ cup water, pure
1 teaspoon sea salt
1 – 6 ounce package of Soy Bleu, crumbled

Directions
1. In a blender combine the first 6 ingredients and blend (reserving the second package of Soy Bleu).
2. Put the blended mixture into a small bowl and crumble the second package of Soy Bleu. Fold mixture together so that the texture resembles the dairy version.
3. Refrigeration allows the flavors to marry, creating a richer flavor.

Yield about 1½ cups

Note: An even simpler way to prepare a bleu cheese dressing is by adding olive oil to your salad, then crumbling the Soy Bleu on top, mixing it throughout. Season to taste.

Mock Bleu Cheese Dressing 2

2 cups Vegenaise
1 – 6 ounce package Soy Bleu Cheese, crumbled by hand

Directions
1. Add the crumbled Soy Bleu cheese to a small bowl.
2. Mix in Vegenaise until both ingredients are fully incorporated.
3. Chill in the refrigerator, or serve immediately.

Yield 2½ cups

Note: Vegan cheeses cannot be expected to taste the same as dairy cheeses do in flavor, but the health benefits outweigh this small trade-off. Vegan recipes stand on their own for taste.

Mock Liver Pâté

This pâté has a look and flavor similar to liver, and can be served with Matzos for the Jewish holidays. There were times when guests didn't know it was not liver, or if they did know, it didn't seem to make any difference. The dish was well complimented.

2 tablespoons olive oil
1 large onion (2 cups) diced small
2 tablespoons + 1 teaspoon garlic, minced
10 medium button mushrooms, sliced
1¼ cup walnuts
½ cup frozen peas (Stage 2) or
　1 – 15 ounce can of peas (Stage 1)
2½ teaspoons sea salt
¼ teaspoon black pepper, ground
Tiny pinch cayenne pepper

Directions

1. On top of stove, in a medium sauté pan, mix and stir onions and garlic in olive oil until golden brown.
2. Add mushrooms to the sauté pan and cook until the mixture is slightly browned.
3. In a small pan bring water to boil, add peas and simmer for 5 minutes. Drain.
4. In a food processor pulse walnuts until textured powder, add mixture, add peas and remaining ingredients and blend (in the food processor) to form a paste.
5. Empty the food processor mixture into an airtight glass container and refrigerate.

Yield about 2 cups

Note: Some chefs use string beans instead of peas.

Mushroom Cashew Gravy

This rich gravy sauce can be served on top of your favorite pasta, over steamed vegetables or a baked potato. Remember, re-heating nut sauces makes them thicker.

2 tablespoons safflower oil
1 small onion (1 cup) chopped small
2 tablespoons garlic, minced
1 tablespoon shallot, minced
2 cups button mushrooms (8 medium) sliced

4 tablespoons Liquid Aminos
¾ cup cashews
1¼ cups water, pure
¼ teaspoon Herbes De Provence
¼ teaspoon sea salt
2 pinches black pepper, ground

Directions

1. In a medium size sauté pan over medium to low heat, sauté onions, garlic and shallots until slightly caramelized. Add mushrooms and Liquid Aminos.
2. While you are sautéing, in a blender, combine cashews and water and blend together until the mixture is very smooth and creamy.
3. Add the cream sauce to the mixture in the sauté pan and mix thoroughly.
4. Remove from heat and quickly serve or store in an airtight glass container. It will keep well in the refrigerator 3 or 4 days.

Yield 2½ cups

Note: This gravy will thicken very quickly if left on the burner and can easily burn on the bottom. This simple and tasty gravy also goes great served over **Millet Burgers** or **Neatballs**.

Pimento Cream Cheese

This cream cheese recipe holds great stuffed in a cucumber shell (cut cucumber length-wise and scoop out the seeds) and wrapped in a first layer of Saran Wrap and an outer layer of Aluminum Foil overnight. Remove wrapping and using a serrated knife cut thin slices and garnish the platter and serve as an appetizer. Or spoon the filling inside a tomato shell, and serve on a bed of green, leafy lettuce.

1 cup red pepper (½ large) rough chop
1 teaspoon garlic, rough chop

1 cup cashews
⅓ cup lemon juice
1 teaspoon sea salt

Directions
1. Blend all of the ingredients in a high-powered blender until smooth and creamy.
2. Allow for set up in the refrigerator to resemble the texture of cream cheese.

Yield 1 cup

Pimento Dressing/Dip

This colorful dressing is a hit whenever it is served. This recipe contains no added oils, other than the natural oils in the cashews. The best presentation for this dressing is to serve it on top of the salad rather than mixed throughout.

2 cups red pepper (1 large red pepper) rough chop
1 tablespoon garlic
1 cup cashews

½ cup lemon juice
¼ cup water, pure
1¾ teaspoons sea salt

Directions
1. Blend all ingredients in a high-powered blender until smooth and creamy.
2. Drizzle 2 tablespoons on top of the salad or refrigerate in a glass container.

Yield 2 cups

Note: The deeper, more colorful red pepper will make the dressing a more brilliant color. This dressing has a good refrigerated shelf life. Serve **Pimento Cheese** with **Antipasto**.

Pine Nut Dressing

This dressing has a very good refrigerator shelf life of several days. It complements the **Caesar Salad** or any salad of your choice.

1 tablespoon garlic, rough chop
1 – 8 ounce package pine nuts, raw

1 cup water, pure
⅓ cup lemon juice
½ teaspoon sea salt

Directions

1. Place all of the above ingredients in a blender and mix until a creamy consistency.
2. Pour into a container and chill or serve.

Yield 2 cups

Note: You can also toast pine nuts in a saucepan on top of the stove for a toasty flavor.

> "Pine Nuts lubricate lungs, stop cough, lubricate intestines, promote body fluids."
> The Tao of Nutrition *by Maoshing Ni*

Salsa

I sometimes mix salsa with the **Cashew Sour Cream** and serve over a baked potato. Salsa is also used for the **Tacos** and **Fiesta Tostada** recipes.

1 cup tomatoes (1 medium) minced
½ cup orange pepper, diced fine
½ cup yellow pepper, diced fine
1¼ teaspoon jalapeño pepper, minced fine (heat strengths vary)
1 teaspoon garlic, minced
¼ cup red onion, diced fine
2 tablespoons cilantro, minced fine
1 teaspoon sea salt
Pinch cayenne pepper

Directions

1. Place the first six prepped ingredients into a medium size bowl.
2. Except for the cilantro, blend ¼ of the salsa mixture and mix together in the bowl. Then fold in the minced cilantro and seasonings.
3. Chill and serve.

Yield 1¼ cups

Note: Salsa can be added to salads or vegetables for flavor. I often keep store-bought salsa in the refrigerator as a staple to flavor recipes if I don't have the fresh ingredients or the time.

Sesame Lemon Dressing

This recipe is delicious on an Asian type salad, or on a simple bed of salad greens. This dressing can also be used as a marinade for either raw or steamed kale.

½ cup sesame oil
⅔ cup lemon juice
½ cup water, pure
1 tablespoon garlic, rough chop
1 tablespoon ginger, peeled, rough chop
1 teaspoon agave nectar

2 tablespoons white miso
2 tablespoons umeboshi plum paste
6 dates, medium size, pitted
Tiny pinch cayenne pepper
1 tablespoon black sesame seeds

Directions

1. In a blender place all of the ingredients, except the black sesame seeds and blend until smooth and creamy.
2. Fold the black sesame seeds into the dressing.
3. Refrigerate in an airtight glass container.

Yield 2 cups

> "The lemon is rich in alkaline elements. Fresh lemon juice is an outstanding source of vitamin C. Lemons are high in potassium, rich in vitamin B, and may be considered a good source of vitamin G."
> Foods That Heal *by Dr. Bernard Jensen*

Sour Cream 'n' Chives

Perfect for topping enchiladas or a baked potato. Be creative and make varieties of versions of sour cream by adding different herbs such as basil, etc. This recipe could also be served over a salad.

1 teaspoon garlic
1 cup cashews
4 tablespoons lemon juice

¾ cup water, pure
½ teaspoon sea salt
⅓ cup chives, sliced fine

Directions
1. Place ingredients, except chives, in a blender and blend until smooth and creamy. Place mixture in a small bowl.
2. Fold chives gently into mixture.

Yield 1½ cups

Twisted Sour Cream 'n' Chives

Variations of basic recipes are a great way to use up any leftovers and put different flavors into a dish.

½ cup black olives, chopped fine
½ teaspoon jalapeño pepper, de-seeded, minced

Directions
1. Prepare **Sour Cream 'n' Chives** recipe above.
2. Fold the black olives and the jalapeño pepper into the mixture.
3. Keep chilled in the refrigerator, stored in an airtight glass container.

Yield 2 cups

Spicy Ginger Peanut Sauce

Almond butter can be used instead of peanut butter if you prefer. This tasty recipe is a companion with **Udon Noodles and Broccoli** and the **Marinated Kale** recipe, as well as any steamed green vegetable of your choice.

1 cup peanut butter, unsalted
1 tablespoon fresh ginger, grated
½ teaspoon shallot, minced
1 tablespoon garlic, minced
¾ cup water, pure

3 tablespoons Nama Shoyu soy sauce
3 tablespoons seasoned rice vinegar
¼ teaspoon red crushed chili pepper seeds

Directions

1. In a blender or food processor, combine all ingredients together until smooth and creamy.
2. Serve over selected recipe choice.

Yield 1½ cups

> "The peanut improves appetite, strengthens spleen, regulates blood, lubricates lungs, promotes diuresis and aids in lactation."
> The Tao of Nutrition *by Maoshing Ni*

Sun-dried Tomato Pâté

This pâté can be used as a spread on crackers, cucumber rounds, celery sticks or a sandwich. It can also be a filling in rolled collard leaves or Belgium endive. If soaking sun-dried tomatoes, soak for 15 minutes and use the soak water instead of adding the pure water in the recipe. This pâté has a very good refrigerator shelf life.

1 cup walnuts, soaked, rinsed and drained dry = 1⅓ cups
½ cup sun-dried tomatoes, packed tight (or ½ cup tomatoes in 8.5 ounce jar, drain)
1 teaspoon olive oil

¼ cup basil leaves or 6 medium leaves (packed tight in a measuring cup)
*4 to 6 tablespoons water, pure
¼ cup lemon juice
1 tablespoon garlic, rough chop
1 teaspoon sea salt
Pinch black pepper, ground

Directions

1. In a food processor, place all of the ingredients and blend until smooth.
2. Store in an airtight glass container in the refrigerator.

Yield 1½ cups

Note: *There should be enough water so that the nuts are very finely chopped and the pâté is smooth and moist, not wet. If you choose to soak sun-dried tomatoes, drain them, add a couple squeezes of lemon juice, and marinate them in the **Garlic Olive Oil** for 2 hours. This will give them flavor. If you don't have the **Garlic Olive Oil** made up, you can add some minced garlic to olive oil and lemon juice.

"Walnuts tonify the kidneys, strengthen the back, astringe the lungs, relieve asthma, lubricate the intestines, aid erratic or rebellious Chi (energy) and reduce cholesterol."
The Tao of Nutrition by Maoshing Ni

Tahini Dressing

This simple recipe is a popular dressing for salads and vegetables. It takes just a few minutes to prepare and has a refrigerator life of several days.

1 teaspoon garlic, rough chop
¼ cup + 2 tablespoons sesame
    tahini

1 tablespoon + 2 teaspoons
    lemon juice
¾ teaspoon sea salt

Directions

1. Place all of the above ingredients into a blender with ¾ cup of water.
2. Blend until a smooth and creamy consistency is reached.
3. Serve or chill in the refrigerator for up to several days.

Yield 1 cup

Note: The lemon flavor fades after refrigeration. Refresh the lemony tang by adding some fresh lemon juice (to taste) before serving. For variety, try **Miso Ginger Dressing**.

> "Sesame seed (brown) nourishes the liver and kidneys, lubricates intestines, blackens gray hair, tonifies the body overall and benefits skin."
> The Tao of Nutrition by Maoshing Ni

Tarragon Vinaigrette

¼ cup + 1 tablespoon olive oil
⅛ cup balsamic vinegar
⅛ cup seasoned rice vinegar
1 teaspoon shallot, rough chop
1 teaspoon garlic, rough chop

2 tablespoons agave nectar
½ teaspoon Dijon mustard
2 tablespoons tarragon, dried
Tiny pinch sea salt and black
    pepper

Directions
1. Place all of the above ingredients into a blender, except the tarragon herbs, and blend until smooth.
2. Pour mixture into a small container.
3. Fold in tarragon herbs, mix and serve, or chill in the refrigerator.

Yield ⅓ cup

Thousand Island Dressing

This is your basic, traditional thousand island salad dressing. It's great on sandwiches, such as a Reuben or as a dip. Have some on hand for a quick flavored kick on vegetables, raw or steamed.

⅓ cup little pickles or gherkins, whole
⅔ cup Vegenaise
⅓ cup ketchup

Directions
1. Pulse the little pickles or gherkins in the food processor until fine.
2. Place in a bowl and mix well with the other ingredients.
3. Chill in an airtight glass container and serve.

Yield 1 cup

Note: This dressing can also be made adding lemon juice to taste, omitting the gherkins.

You can either/also mix together pickle relish, ketchup and Vegenaise.

Tofu Feta Cheese

This recipe goes great with the **Greek Peasant Salad**. The Greek style serves one solid piece of the Feta Cheese on top of individual salads. It crumbles easily. This recipe needs to be made in advance so that it marinates thoroughly.

½ pound tofu, firm, (*press water out), slice lengthwise into 4 pieces

1 cup lemon juice
2 tablespoons sea salt
½ cup water, pure

Directions

1. Combine lemon juice and sea salt. Dilute this mixture with a bit of water to create a brine-like liquid. Make enough to cover the ½ pound brick of tofu and let it marinate in the lemon brine at least 24 to 48 hours.
2. For a smooth feta cheese, put the tofu in a food processor and blend until smooth. For crumbles, crumble it by hand.
3. Store in the refrigerator before use.

Yield 4 slices

Note: *For instructions on pressing water out of tofu, see Chapter Five, p. 87.

You can purchase Soy Feta Cheese manufactured by Sunergia Soyfoods. Before serving, be certain to press brine-liquid out of the Tofu Feta Cheese.

DESSERTS

Cashew Lemon Icing

This recipe can also be served as a topping on a fruit breakfast or any dessert.

2 cups cashews
¼ cup water, pure

½ cup lemon juice
¼ cup agave nectar

Directions
1. In a high-powered blender, mix all of the ingredients thoroughly until smooth. Use the plunger to achieve the creamiest texture.
2. Spread the icing evenly over the dessert of your choice and refrigerate, allowing it to set up for 24 hours before serving.

Yield 1⅔ cups

Cashew Vanilla Cream

This simple cream is for topping any dessert, or it can be served with a mixed fruit bowl for breakfast. This cream is delicious and can be added to fruit smoothies!

2 cups cashews
1 cup water, pure

4 tablespoons agave nectar
2 tablespoons *vanilla flavoring

Directions
1. Place all of the above ingredients in a high-powered blender and blend mixture until it is a creamy and smooth texture.
2. Serve, or store in an airtight container for several days.

Yield 2 cups

Note: *For a richer, deeper vanilla flavor use the vanilla bean instead of vanilla flavoring. One vanilla bean brings out the deep, awesome vanilla flavor whenever it's used. However, it is a very costly item that is usually saved for special occasions, like bringing the boss home for dinner! This recipe has a good refrigerated shelf life.

Chocolate Mint Mousse

This simple, delicious, dessert takes only minutes to prepare. My son Stewart says he doesn't like tofu, yet when I make him desserts like this, he always asks for more! Non-dairy chocolate chips are generally found in natural foods stores.

1 – 9 ounce package semi-sweet chocolate morsels (about 1 cup)
⅓ cup +1 tablespoon maple syrup
1 pound tofu, Silken (Silken brand works best for puddings) (*press water out)

2 tablespoons coconut oil
4 drops peppermint flavoring, or to taste (use a high-quality food grade)
Garnish: berries and a mint sprig

Directions
1. In a medium saucepan, melt the chocolate in the maple syrup on a very low flame on the stove.
2. Place all ingredients into a blender and blend until smooth and creamy.
3. Chill in parfait glasses and allow the mousse to set-up. After it sets up, add a couple dollops of **Cashew Vanilla Cream** on top to each glass.
4. Garnish and serve.

Yield 2½ cups

Note: *For directions on pressing the water out of tofu, see Chapter Five, p. 87.

Caution: Hot ingredients can break a glass blender, so be careful. Grade B maple syrup is the best nutritional quality to purchase. **Cashew Vanilla Cream** goes great as a topping, or you can also try it swirled into the **Chocolate Mint Mousse**.

You can also serve this dessert as a candy, using small molds for their shape. Refrigerate or freeze the candy.

Chocolate Orange Cranberry Cheesecake

This cake has the texture of cheesecake. The crust is made with dried cranberries, and the filling is chocolate and vanilla/orange, with a frosting of **Cashew Vanilla Cream.** A high-powered blender and plunger are required for the filling texture.

Crust

10 dates, small, pitted
1 cup dried cranberries (do not re-hydrate)
¼ cup pecans
¼ cup walnuts
1½ cups coconut, dried, shredded
5 tablespoons water, pure
1 tablespoon coconut flour for dusting
    cake pan

Filling

1½ cups cacao nibs or 1 – 8 ounce package
    (various brands differ in sweetness)

2 cups cashews
1 cup water, pure
¾ cup maple syrup
2 tablespoons coconut oil
1 teaspoon orange flavoring
1¼ teaspoon vanilla flavoring

Frosting

1 cup cashews
½ cup water, pure
1 teaspoon coconut oil
2½ tablespoons maple syrup
1 tablespoon vanilla flavoring

Directions

1. In a food processor, add all crust ingredients. Mix until it resembles moist dough.
2. In a 7" spring release cake pan, dust the surface and sides with the coconut flour. Press the crust dough down very tightly, lining the bottom and sides to the top.
3. In a blender, combine filling ingredients, blend and pour filling into the cake pan. Chill 15 minutes.
4. Blend frosting ingredients in a blender and gently frost the cake.
5. Refrigerate 24 hours *minimum*, to allow the cake to further set up.
6. Take a knife and go around the sides of the cake pan to loosen and release.
7. Release cake and slice with a serrated knife using a cake spatula for serving.
8. Optional: Garnish each cake plate with an orange slice.

Yield 1 – 7" cheesecake serves 12 to 16+ (depending on how thin they are cut)

Note: This cheesecake is very rich and filling, so keep your slices thin. The cheesecake flavors marry over time, and further enhance the recipe.

Kids Kandy Yums

These candies look pretty served on a plated paper doily, and are a treat for kids of all ages. Marzipan is a raw Italian almond paste that can be purchased at a natural foods store. Whenever working with dates, it is a good idea to frequently wash and dry your hands. This technique will speed up the prep time. This recipe freezes great!

38 dates, medium, pitted (Barhi or any soft date)

¼–½ package Marzipan (8.8 ounce package)

¾ cup coconut, dried, shredded

38 pine nuts

Directions

1. Cut Marzipan in bite size pieces to fit inside the dates.
2. Stuff the dates with Marzipan.
3. Roll each date in a bowl of coconut.
4. Garnish each date with a pine nut.
5. Refrigerate or freeze in an airtight container.
6. Name and date (no pun intended) container label with a marking pen.

Yield 38 pieces

Lemon Blueberry Cheesecake

A Vita-Mix blender is ideal for this recipe because lower-powered 'generic' blenders just won't give you a smooth enough consistency for the filling. If using another blender, be sure to stop the blender and hand-mix/stir the contents from time to time throughout the blending process. This is an easy, yummy cheesecake to prepare.

Crust
⅓ cup water, pure
1 cup walnuts
1 cup pecans
1 cup dried figs, stems removed
2 tablespoons coconut flour, for dusting

Filling
2 cups cashews
1 cup *lemon juice
⅔ cup + 1 tablespoon agave nectar
2 tablespoons coconut oil
2 tablespoons vanilla flavoring
½ cup water, pure

Topping: 1 box blueberries, fresh, whole, rinsed and drained (see step 2, filling directions)

Crust Directions
1. In a food processor, pulse the walnuts and pecans until fine. Place in a large bowl.
2. Blend the figs with ⅓ cup pure water in the food processor until smooth and mix thoroughly with the nuts.
3. In a 7" spring release cake pan, dust the surface and sides with coconut flour. Press the crust dough down very tightly, lining the bottom and sides to the top. Set aside.

Filling Directions
1. Blend all of the ingredients in a high-powered blender until smooth and creamy.
2. Pour mixture into crust. Blend ½ box of blueberries with ½ teaspoon of agave and mix with remaining blueberries. Cover cheesecake with the blueberry mixture.
3. Refrigerate a *minimum* of 24 hours and serve when the cheesecake sets up firmly.

Yield 1 – 7" cheesecake serves 12 to 16

Note: *Meyer lemons are less tart.

This is a very rich dessert. Serve in small slices; you can always offer seconds to your guests.

Coconut flour can be found in natural foods stores. (It adds flavor to the cake and non-stick to the cake pan.) Any raw, good tasting powder can be used in its place.

Rainbow Parfait

Parfait desserts make a great presentation. For any leftovers the chef eats the bonus snack. Fruits prepared this way are also excellent for smoothies. Below, I am giving ingredients according to layers. [1]The blueberry mixture goes in the 1st and 3rd layer.

[1]1st layer

2½ cups blueberries, fresh

2 teaspoons coconut oil

4 to 6 tablespoons agave nectar (amount is determined by the sweetness of the berries)

Directions correspond with each bold numbered layer

1. Blend the above in a blender and divide *half* the mixture between 4 parfait glasses. (Spoon approximately ¼ cup in each glass.)

2nd layer

1 cup strawberries, fresh

½ cup cashews

3 tablespoons agave nectar

1 teaspoon coconut oil

2. Blend, spoon out 2nd layer, dividing the mixture between 4 parfait glasses. (Spoon approximately ¼ cup in each glass.)

[1]3rd layer

3. Add the remaining blueberry mixture to the 4 parfait glasses.

4th layer

4. Blend 1 cup fresh pineapple chunks. Make sure there is enough space left for the 5th layer (or blend 2 cups pineapple for layers 4 and 5). Divide mixture in 4 glasses.

5th layer

5. If you are blending pineapple for both the 4th and 5th layers, *either* increase the amount of pineapple (step 4) or blend one pitted soft persimmon to add to the last layer, finishing the layering process to the 4 parfait glasses.

6. Allow dessert to set up overnight in the refrigerator. Garnish with strawberry fans and mint leaf sprigs.

Yield serves 4

Note: Any colorful combination of fruits can be used. If persimmons are not in season, use another colorful, custard-like fruit, such as mango, or increase the amount of pineapple. Sapote and cherimoya are also delicious custard-like fruits. They lack the color intensity, but they make up for it in flavor! Natural sugars in fruits may often vary, so adjust the sweetness to your taste.

Sesame Candy

EnerG brand makes a product called, "Pure Rice Bran" which is used as a binder in this recipe. Rice bran is made from the outer hull of brown rice and contains essential B Vitamins. This recipe is a "kid candy," big and small, with a fabulous freezer life.

1½ cups sesame seeds, whole
2 cups sesame seeds, ground to
   sesame meal
½ cup sesame tahini
¾ cup maple syrup

1 cup rice bran
2 teaspoons vanilla flavoring,
   pure
¾ cups coconut, shredded

Directions

1. Combine sesame seeds, sesame meal, sesame tahini, maple syrup and rice bran together in a medium size mixing bowl.
2. Add in vanilla flavoring and mix all ingredients together thoroughly.
3. Roll mixture into balls measuring 1 tablespoon each and roll the balls in coconut.
4. Place them in containers for freezing.
5. Name and date your container label with a marking pen.

Yield 45 balls

Note: Especially for kids (unless you are entertaining), you don't need to roll the balls, nor cover them in coconut. The sesame candy can be cut in squares and spooned from the container and served. In this way, it's more casual, with less preparation time.

If you do roll them, wash your hands frequently or your hands will get sticky. Or freeze the mixture 48 hours first. Freezing them in advance of rolling them makes them roll faster.

Tangerine Ice Cream

Kids big and small will scream for tangerine ice cream! Before serving, allow about 10 minutes for the ice cream to set out and become creamy.

2 cups tangerine juice, (9 medium) freshly squeezed

1 cup cashews, raw (nuts are not soaked for this recipe)

¼ cup agave nectar

1 tablespoon coconut oil

Directions

1. Juice tangerines and measure 2 cups of juice.
2. In a blender, combine all ingredients and blend.
3. *Pour mixture into ice cream maker and set timer for one hour.
4. Put the ice cream in airtight plastic containers for the freezer.
5. Name and date the container label with a marking pen.

Yield serves 4

Note: *If you do not have an ice cream machine, freeze the blend in plastic containers. See steps 4 and 5. For making ice creams and sorbets I started out using a less expensive ice cream maker which works perfectly fine if that is your budget. Because I was trying to focus on the transition to raw foods I invested in a commercial machine. They can sometimes be bought used and found online at resale sites such as Craigslist.

> "Tangerines are high in vitamin C. The thin membrane that covers the segments contains a digestion-aiding factor, and should always be eaten."
> Foods That Heal by Dr. Bernard Jensen

Tangy Lemon Tango Sorbet Freezer

Ice creams and sorbets can be made 24 hours before, as a dessert for an evening meal or party. They are totally guiltless and can be enjoyed to your heart's content.

1 tablespoon fresh ginger, minced
½ cup water, pure
2¼ cups agave nectar

3 cups cashews, raw
4 cups Meyer lemon juice, fresh
   (Meyer lemons are best)

Directions
1. Peel and mince ginger and place all ingredients in a blender and blend thoroughly.
2. *Place half of the blended mixture in an ice cream maker for 1 hour. Then empty the sorbet into an airtight container for the freezer. See step 4.
3. *Place the remaining mixture in the ice cream maker for 1 hour, creating a double batch of this tangy dessert. Pour the sorbet into containers and repeat step 4.
4. Name and date your plastic container label with a marking pen.

Yield 8½ cups

Note: *If you don't have an ice cream machine, freeze the blend in plastic containers. See step 4. To make ice creams and sorbets you can freeze the mixture after it is blended, however the machine gives it a creamier texture and a richer flavor. If you plan on eating an abundance of raw foods I recommend buying a commercial machine. Sometimes they are advertised *used* for sale on bulletin boards in natural foods stores. They sell fast!

Tutti-Frutti Ice Cream   Freezer

This simple, healthy, summer treat is especially wonderful for kids of all ages! If you don't have an ice cream machine, omit step 3. For a creamier texture, take out ice cream 20 minutes before serving.

5 peaches, medium, ripe
2 nectarines, medium, ripe
1 cup cashews

2 tablespoons agave nectar
1 tablespoon coconut oil
3 drops *peppermint oil

Directions
1. Gently wash and remove pits of all fruits and cut in quarters for the blender.
2. Blend fruits and add remaining ingredients until smooth and creamy.
3. If you have an ice cream maker, empty blender into the machine and run for 1 hour.
4. Place ice cream mixture in airtight containers for the freezer.
5. Name and date plastic container label with a marking pen.

Yield 3½ cups

Note: Seasonal fruits vary in sweetness, so you may need to adjust the sweetener. Stocking your kitchen with high-quality flavorings or *food-grade essential oils will give you a variety of ideas to expand your creativity in developing unique and fun recipes.

Wendel's 'Other Love' Chocolate Pudding

My husband enjoys this daily! This recipe stores great in the refrigerator for several days and is also a terrific party food. Wendel often likes to add a bit of vanilla and varieties of berries to create some different ways to enjoy this healthy dessert.

2 cups cacao nibs
1 cup cashews, raw
1 cup agave nectar
3 tablespoons coconut oil

2½ cups water, pure
2 pinches of cinnamon
Garnish: 3 berries and sprig
of mint

Directions
1. Add all ingredients to your blender and pulverize until entirely smooth and creamy.
2. Store in an airtight glass container for at least 24 hours for the chocolate to set up.
3. Add 1 to 2 dollops of **Cashew Vanilla Cream** on top.
4. Garnish and serve.

Yield 5½ cups

Note: Cacao is raw chocolate before it's processed. This bittersweet chocolate becomes sweet by adding a sweetener. The book *Naked Chocolate* by David Wolfe describes the extraordinary health benefits of cacao. It's a hit in our house! (Every night!)

Yummy Yam Pie

For best digestion, nuts should be soaked overnight, rinsed, and drained dry. Nuts can be stored in the refrigerator for a few days until use. Instead of marshmallow crème you can use the **Cashew Lemon Icing**.

Crust

⅔ cup almonds, raw
⅔ cup pecans, raw
½ cup cherries, dried (do not re-hydrate)
⅔ cup coconut, shredded
10 dates, small, pitted
3 to 4 tablespoons water, pure (add water depending on consistency)
1 tablespoon coconut flour for dusting spring release pan

Filling

4 cups garnet yams, peeled and cut in pieces
⅔ cup maple syrup
2 teaspoons cinnamon, ground
1 pinch nutmeg
4 tablespoons *psyllium powder
1½ tablespoons coconut oil
⅔ cup diced fresh pineapple, small dice
1 cup marshmallow crème (vegan)

> "Sweet potato (Yam) strengthens spleen and stomach function, tonifies Chi (energy), clears heat, detoxifies, increases the production of milk."
> The Tao of Nutrition by Maoshing Ni

Directions

1. For the crust, pulverize all of the crust ingredients in a food processor until it forms a sticky mound and the mixture still has texture.
2. Dust a 7" spring release pan with coconut flour on bottom and sides.
3. Form crust into the pan, pressing tightly on bottom and sides to the top. Set aside.
4. For the filling, place all of the filling ingredients except pineapple and marshmallow crème in a food processor and blend until very smooth and creamy. Put into a medium size bowl. Fold in *drained* pineapple pieces. Do not add juice.
5. Pour the yam filling into the pie crust. When half of the pie is filled, add ½ cup of marshmallow crème into the center, and finish layering the filling into the pie. Frost the pie with the remaining ½ cup of marshmallow crème.
6. Allow the pie to set up in the refrigerator for a minimum of 24 hours before serving.

Yield 1 – 7" pie

Note: *Psyllium powder is used as a thickener to absorb moisture from the yam filling. Marshmallows come in two varieties that I have found. One is packaged, with the look of a marshmallow and the other is a product called Ricemellow Crème, manufactured by Suzanne's. It is made from brown rice syrup and soy protein. Both types are found in natural foods stores.

Caution: regular marshmallows contain animal gelatin.

Chapter Seven
Is There A Doctor In The House?

How often does it happen that we can be privy to knowledge from a variety of medical and naturopathic experts about their health philosophy? I consider the information in the following medical/nutritional interviews so valuable that I created a separate chapter for them.

Experts don't always agree on health subjects. However, since each reader may come from a unique dietary background and nutritional goal, the following information in these interviews can give you *food for thought* to be assimilated and digested over time.

If you decide to choose the vegan way, the only transition step is simply to start becoming vegan. You can then explore and discover what works for you — a vegan starch-based diet, a no oil diet, or raw vegan diet. The choice is yours.

NAME	OCCUPATION/INTERESTS	PAGE
Ellie Bloomfield	Medical Doctor	208
Caldwell Esselstyn	Medical Doctor, Author	210
Joel Fuhrman	Medical Doctor, Author	214
Michael Greger	Medical Doctor, Director of Public Health and Animal Agriculture — Humane Society of the United States	216
John McDougall	Medical Doctor, Author	220
Pam Popper	Naturopathic Doctor, Nutritionist	223

ELLIE BLOOMFIELD, MD, Glendale, CA

When I was at medical school, the Food Guide Pyramid[1] had carbohydrates at its base and then protein, which was mostly dairy and meat. Vegetables were the second smallest group, just before oil. It was a model of a balanced diet that wasn't based on any real nutritional data. For instance, the daily protein requirement was based on calf-feeding studies. And fiber was completely missing.

In medical school our only nutrition class was mostly about all the horrible things that can happen to you with severe deficiency diseases, like scurvy, or niacin deprivation with the four "Ds": dermatitis, dementia, diarrhea and death. That's the kind of thing we had pop quizzes on. If you didn't have beriberi or kwashiorkor, you must be healthy.

There was no instruction on how to help people adopt a more healthful way of eating, which happens to be what you need the most when you're a practicing MD. Nothing. Nada. Not one word.

Some time ago Dr. Dean Ornish developed a program for patients that were told they needed bypass surgery. It included a vegetarian, high-fiber, low-fat diet, plus exercise and stress reduction. He ran it head to head against cardiac bypass surgery, and proved his program was equal in efficacy. And it cost less, so the insurance company Mutual of Omaha started covering it in their policies. Unfortunately, none of the other major insurance companies followed suit. Even though it would cost the general public and even the insurance companies less for the Ornish program, there are still far more procedures than Ornish programs, probably because there are more interventional cardiologists and cardiovascular surgeons than there are doctors who can do Ornish programs, or even know how to get patients into one. It's not a conspiracy or anything, it's just that professionals believe in what they know how to do. In this country, the organized professions are the squeaky wheel that gets the grease. It would take a long time to educate as many doctors to do Ornish programs as we're training to do the procedures. There's also our tendency to want passive, quick fix solutions to our health problems. Bypass surgery or angioplasty takes under a day to do, plus under a week in the hospital, and then a few brief follow-up visits. The Ornish diet is forever, and takes a lot of coaching and support.

Also, it's hard to get good data on whether nutrition can affect the diseases we're getting. Most studies gather data by asking people to report what they have eaten in the past. Folks don't really remember, or they see their dietary habits through

---

[1] Food Guide Pyramid is now My Pyramid currently published by USDA.

very rosy glasses, so self-reported dietary intake is pretty unreliable. This may be why so many recent epidemiological studies of nutrients have such counter-intuitive results. Diet is so complex an issue. Right now, if an individual subjectively feels better on a vegan diet and worse eating dairy and meat, then that's about as reliable a conclusion as any big National Institutes of Health (NIH) study.

But there have been some positive changes. The Food and Nutrition Board (FNB) guidelines now put fruits and vegetables at the base of the food triangle. Next are starches, not just bread and pasta but also corn, potatoes, and whole grains. After that comes protein, which includes not just meat, but also beans and legumes. At the very tiny top come the fats, oils and sweets.

So a good question is, if we don't need much fats and sweets, why do we eat them so voraciously? It's probably because salt, sugars, and oils are the three scarcest foods in Nature. Until very recently, getting fats required going out to kill something, or you got oils through a very laborious process to extract them from nuts or olives. To get salt, you went to an ocean to make salt from sea water, or bartered if you had no ocean. The only sweets available were honey, or fruits and berries in season, which were much, much, smaller then, so you had to gather a lot of them. So our craving for fats, sugars and salt helped us survive, to be really motivated to go through all that effort.

The food industry is well aware that fat, sweet, and salty sells. I heard a lecturer put things into perspective, during the few hours of nutritional instruction we did receive. He said that if you froze someone in 1940 and then woke her up again in 1980 and gave her an Oreo cookie, she would probably gag on it and spit it out! He explained that over the years the amount of fats and sugars in Oreo cookies has just gone up and up and up, and people have bought more and more and more. If you're a food company with shareholders and executive bonuses, the profit motive beats good nutrition every time.

America's worst health challenge today is the chronic diseases, and they are all more prevalent in industrialized countries, where the diet is rich in fats, sugars and salt. It makes sense to try to limit them, in any diet, from vegan to a Standard American Diet (which is appropriately abbreviated as "SAD").

Using raw foods also makes sense. Our biology is probably better set up to get our essential fatty oils, for example, by eating nuts or seeds the way they are in Nature. You may have noticed that raw nuts take longer to get rancid; their anti-oxidants are natural preservatives. Peanut butter and roasted peanuts go bad sooner (because they are not nuts but actually legumes). But I've had raw cashews around for a long time, and they taste fine. The best packaging for food may be the natural state it had when we were hunter-gatherers, when we were working hard to get just a little salt, fat and sugar — not just opening a package to get a lot of them.

CALDWELL B. ESSELSTYN, Jr., MD,
Cleveland, OH

Author: *Prevent and Reverse Heart Disease*
Interview by Brian von Dedenroth — Journalist

I was raised on a beef and dairy farm in upstate New York. My diet was standard American, with a heavy emphasis on cheese, dairy, and lots of meat. My father had his first heart attack at age 43 in 1945, when few appreciated the relationship between nutrition and atherosclerotic heart disease. Actually there was an increasing awareness about this in the 50s and 60s, but I personally began to experience an interest when I had been on the staff at the Cleveland Clinic for ten years. I was chairman of our breast cancer task force and head of the section on thyroid and parathyroid surgery.

As chairman of our breast cancer task force, I became increasingly disillusioned with the fact that although I was committed to help women resolve their breast cancer issues, no matter how many of these operations I was performing I was doing absolutely nothing to help the next unsuspecting victim. Nobody had any proven idea of the causation of breast cancer.

In 1982 I made an epidemiological survey of breast cancer. In Kenya, breast cancer was 20 times less frequent than in the US. In rural Japan, in the 1950s, breast cancer was infrequent. Yet when Japanese women migrated to the US by the second and third generations, still pure Japanese American, they had the same rate of breast cancer as their Caucasian counterpart.

Even more powerful, is the data on cancer of the prostate. In the entire nation of Japan in 1958, 18 men, autopsy proven, succumbed to cancer of the prostate. By 1978 that number had climbed to 237 which still is absolutely nothing compared to the over 30,000 that will perish in 2008 in America. The interesting thing about prostate cancer is this: of men at age 50 in both this country and in Japan who have died of unrelated causes, 50% have non-invasive cancer of the prostate at autopsy. Over the next 25 or 30 years, because of the American diet, a significant number of men in the US will develop invasive prostate cancer, whereas in Japan, as long as they eat their native diet, the cancer remains non-invasive.

It seemed to me that my bones would long be dust before I could produce a study identifying the relationship between breast cancer and nutrition. It was much more compelling to look at heart disease, the leading killer of men and women in western civilization. My review revealed heart disease was virtually non-existent in multiple cultures that subsisted on plant-based nutrition such as the rural Chinese, the Papua Highlanders in New Guinea, Central Africa, and the

Tarahumara Indians in northern Mexico. A cardiac surgeon in those areas might as well plan on selling pencils. This is powerful information. By culture, heritage and tradition these cultures, free of cardiovascular disease, subsist largely on plant-based nutrition.

In the autopsy results of our American G.I.s in Korea and Vietnam, 80% at an average age of 20, already had gross evidence of coronary disease. In similarly investigated Korean and Vietnamese casualties, the same disease was rarely encountered. If you look at more recent studies of the American civilian population, those between the ages of 16 and 34, who have died of accidents, homicides and suicides, everybody has it.

In the spring of 2007, when I was moderating a panel at the Milken Global conference in Los Angeles, one of the panelists was Dr. Lewis Kuller, a physician in the Department of Public Health, University of Pittsburgh — School of Medicine. As a result of his ten year cardiovascular health study, he made the following comment on the panel. "All males by age 65 and all females by age 70 who have been exposed to the traditional western diet have cardiovascular disease and should be treated as such." That is a testament to how destructive typical animal-based nutrition is. Nobody escapes.

With cardiovascular disease being the leading killer of men and women in western civilization and anticipated to be the number one global disease burden by 2020, it was anticipated that if you could get people to eat to save their heart they would also save themselves from obesity, diabetes, hypertension, strokes, heart attacks, as well as these common western cancers of prostate, breast, colon, ovaries and uterus.

I changed my own diet in April 1984. When my wife Ann and I were at a surgical meeting banquet in New Haven, Connecticut, the waitress brought out a dish with roast beef absolutely draped all over the sides of the plate. I looked at Ann and said, "This is it!" That was my epiphany. Ann said, "If you are not going to eat your roast beef, then I'll take it." Ann's mother had died of breast cancer at age 52 and two weeks after the New Haven experience, her sister was diagnosed with breast cancer. After that news, she looked at me and said, "I'm with you." I knew that I wanted to do this with a group of patients but before I could do that, I first had to do it myself. My total cholesterol was 185 mg/dl and three months later it was 155 mg/dl. I was very disappointed; I wanted to be like a rural Chinese. In addition to my already in place plant-based diet, I then also eliminated every kind of oil. My cholesterol dropped to 119 mg/dl, and now I knew how to do it: eat nothing with a mother, nothing with a face, no dairy and no oil.

There are profoundly favorable changes that occur within three weeks of starting a plant-based, no oil diet. The inner lining of the arteries, the endothelial cells, respond by once again manufacturing nitric oxide. Nitric oxide is the strongest vasodilator in the body. For instance, if someone with heart disease has a pet scan, which shows an area of the heart muscle poorly purfused with blood, and we put them on plant-based nutrition, within three to six weeks the area that was previously not well purfused is fully recovered. The endothelial cells that line the arteries are no longer being injured with every meal. Their capacity to manufacture nitric oxide has been restored, and the blood vessels going to the heart once again can dilate. With dilatation there is a huge increase in flow. That area of heart muscle that was previously deprived now has the flow it requires.

That's an example of just how fast a patient can recover using plant-based nutrition. It also explains why we are able to get rid of heart pains (angina) in these patients so rapidly.

There is wonderful research from the University of Maryland, Australia and Columbia, South America, utilizing the brachial artery tourniquet test. It is a very sensitive test for the endothelium and its capacity to manufacture nitric oxide. Dr. Robert Vogel, of the University of Maryland, took young students to a fast food restaurant. Half of those students ate corn flakes and the brachial artery test remained normal. The other half ate hash browns and sausages, and within 120 minutes following the meal, the food had so injured the endothelium, they could not make sufficient nitric oxide to pass the brachial artery tourniquet test. This profound example has been repeated with dairy products and oils. Every time you eat oil, dairy and meat you are injuring delicate endothelial cells. These series of injuries to the endothelial cells continue to mount. If you spread all the endothelial cells in a normal person one layer thin, they would cover six or eight tennis courts. With decades of nutritional injury, those eight tennis courts of endothelial cells are down to one to two tennis courts, and heart disease is established. The exciting news is endothelial cells recover and their capacity to make nitric oxide is restored with plant-based nutrition.

The original patients in my study were terribly ill. Most had failed their first or second heart bypass or they had failed their angioplasty, they were too sick for these interventions or they had refused any procedure. Five of the patients had even been told by their expert cardiologists that they had less than a year to live. Incredibly, all five of those patients lived beyond 21 years. Patients who are fully compliant in adopting a plant-based diet can halt this disease and achieve selective disease regression.

I have told you that typical animal-based nutrition immediately injures our endothelium cells by ages 18 to 20, and cardiovascular disease is established. We can make a strong case that every time children eat school meals; they are injuring their blood vessels. Of course, it is happening at home as well, but by starting at the school level you make the point with the parents. Why not start with children and prevent disease?

Cardiovascular disease is also responsible for dementia. In 2001, at the stroke meetings in Miami, Meagan Cleary and her team from the west coast reviewed over 11,000 MRIs of the brains of Americans. At age 50, they noted tiny white spots on the MRIs. These are little strokes. It is not a problem, because there is a lot of reserve in the brain. But if you continue into your 60s, you find yourself commenting, "sweetheart where did I leave the car keys?" If you continue eating this way, by your mid-70s you say "sweetheart where did I leave the car?" By your 80s you say, "Are you my sweetheart?" Fifty percent of Americans have dementia by age 85. This is one of the most profound reasons to think about switching to plant-based nutrition.

The medical community is not in the dark about the cause of atherosclerosis and heart disease. Practically all physicians recognize this disease is because of the western diet. Yet most physicians do not appreciate how profound the capacity of nutritional change is in halting this disease.

Look at the sudden decrease in deaths from strokes and heart attacks in 1939 when the Germans occupied Norway. The Germans took away their cows, pigs, horses, sheep, goats, and chickens for their army. What happened while this population was now subsisting on plant-based nutrition? The deaths from heart attack and stroke in Norway plummeted from 1940 through 1944. As soon as the war ended, there was immediate restoration of heart attacks, strokes and deaths that occurred with the resumption of animal-based food.

Just as most people know not to put their hands in poison ivy, we need to get to the point where every person understands that when you eat ice cream, a cheeseburger, steak, French fries and oils, you are injuring the lining of your blood vessels.

About the protein issue: Let's start with the animal kingdom, of which we are a part. What are the biggest, strongest animals? The elephant, the hippo, a giraffe, a bull: If you want to be big and strong you eat what the big and strong eat. What do these animals eat? Grass. Name anybody who has been eating a well-rounded plant-based diet who has any protein deficiency. It doesn't happen. There are many world-class athletes consuming plant-based nutrition.

Everything we ask our patients to do in the book[2] that I wrote based on over 20 years of research is evidence-based. This research indicates that by eating plant-based you make yourself heart attack proof and practically stroke proof, obesity proof, type 2 diabetes proof and hypertension proof. You also minimize the likelihood of accelerating the possibility of producing cancers. It is really a wonderful win/win situation. As we become more familiar with the multitude of ways of preparing these foods, we end up with delicious meals that enhance our well-being rather than destroy it.

I think what holds people back from changing their eating is they are not given the correct information and knowledge. That information and knowledge is the essence of my book.

---

[2]   *Prevent and Reverse Heart Disease* by Caldwell Esselstyn, MD.

JOEL FUHRMAN, MD, Flemington, NJ
Author: *Eat to Live* and *Disease-Proof Your Child*
Interview by Marilyn Peterson

Dr. Fuhrman

As a practicing physician and nutritional educa-
tor, I've spent 20 years of my life teaching people
about the relationship between nutrition and disease
based on the results of the 30 to 40,000 medical
journal studies I've reviewed.

I advise people on what they need to do to
achieve good health, and that doesn't necessarily
mean a vegan diet. People can eat mostly raw food
with some cooked vegetables, perhaps having a
serving of animal products once or twice a week,
and that can still be a healthy diet.

My role as a professional is to tell people how
to make a "flexitarian" diet, either choosing what
amount of animal products might be acceptable in the diet if they want that, or
creating a vegan diet, ideal for health, and instructing them on the nutritional
advantages of moving toward veganism and toward more raw foods. My role is to
present nutritional science rather than to promote veganism.

I think it's important to justify and support people making even gradual changes
to what we see as ideal. You never know, some people will take longer to get there
and so there has to be a lot of different approaches in the way in which we try to
entice, teach, motivate and educate people to make improvements in their health
and move toward a plant-based diet.

I think that my message will have a better effect at moving the community
toward the vegan diet, or toward a diet that is better for the environment and
better for people's health, if it doesn't come from a person who has an underlying agenda of vegetarianism or veganism. If people want to learn more about the
advantages of being vegan then that would be ideal, and there are reasons for
that besides the obvious health issues. But I think that what I personally choose
to do for moral or ethical reasons isn't what my image as a physician specializing
in nutrition is all about.

I have just one agenda, one purpose, and that's to have each individual person's
needs met so they can achieve the best health possible for them. Then I can give
people information that will most effectively motivate them to make the changes
necessary to improve their health. Some people can make the change toward veganism all the way and other people can do it in more gradual steps, reducing animal
products to more sensible amounts from 40% of the typical American diet down to
10% (of calories), or a diet with higher amounts of vegetables.

People have been misinformed and incorrectly educated. People graduate from school and the most important and most critical information that they could have learned about — health — they know nothing about. I marvel at the human body's ability to reverse even very serious conditions and its ability to maintain itself. That is so important for people to learn.

Nutrition shouldn't be a belief system, and it shouldn't be put into our social consciousness in schoolrooms based on wrong information that has led us down the path to dietary suicide. What is popular for political, economical and social reasons in this country is a diet that results in degenerative diseases. That's why it is so important for me to take a stance on what a good diet would be, and to explain to people the factors that have governed their thinking in the past and why those factors are not based on science.

For example, the importance of dairy products in the diet has been sold to us and advertised so much that we accept it as a truth without knowing the science behind why that may not be the best source of our calcium. We have to go back and tear down that house and rebuild it anew. It's important for me that people can come to me for unbiased, unaffected advice, not based on any predisposed notions, which is a fair interpretation of the scientific literature. You don't want to have the milk industry doing studies and interpreting those studies and saying how good milk is for us. We want to have an independent person with no ties to the milk industry determining those studies, don't we? Equally, we don't want to have a person espousing the benefits of vegetables and the damaging effects of animal products if their sole agenda is an anti-animal consumption agenda.

We want an impartial opinion and I try to give people one. I want to make scientists and the community of people who read my information, realize that they will get good information from me based on science. Should they choose to pursue their diet in one direction or another, at least that choice is not colored or affected by bad science.

I even see inaccurate, biased research being done by some authorities in the vegan community whose agenda sometimes affects their interpretation. Exaggerations and distortions that polarize the country just give people a reason to reject information, and if we want to move society, our message will have a better effect if it is based on years of scientific scrutiny. We have to attack this problem of America's dietary suicide in a different way.

MICHAEL GREGER, MD, Washington, DC

Director of Public Health and Animal Agriculture —
Humane Society of the United States
Interview by Brian von Dedenroth — Journalist

"I try not to be a hypocrite. Therefore, I follow the same diet I recommend to my patients in clinical medicine, a plant-based diet. This is a diet centered on fruits, vegetables, whole grains, legumes (beans, peas, and lentils), nuts, seeds, and all that good stuff."

Brian: How has your experience as Director of Public Health for the Humane Society of the United States and as Farm Sanctuary's Chief Medical Investigator informed and changed your eating behavior?

Michael: A combination of factors influenced me. One element was my experience and contact with farm animals. I didn't grow up on a farm, I had pets but I never had any relationship with farm animals other than through my eating utensils.

Brian: When did things change for you and what tipped things in this direction?

Michael: I remember a National Geographic picture that haunted me and just sticks in my mind, of a puppy in a cage, in a dog meat market somewhere. I felt repulsed, thinking: "How can they eat a dog?" Being the critical thinker I like to think I am, I had to challenge myself for consistency, I had to ask myself: "What is the difference? Where can we really draw the line?" This is what began my thinking about the animal welfare standpoint.

Brian: You grew up on the typical western diet?

Michael: Yes, the only way I knew was a typical western diet; eating meat three times a day.

Brian: It surprises me to hear that at an early stage in your medical career you attributed the diseases you saw in the hospital with an animal fat-centric diet rather than other confounding factors.

Michael: Walk down any hospital corridor and it is just one after another; heart disease, cancer, stroke, diabetes; you can't get away from it. Someone once said 'Learning medicine in a hospital is like learning forestry in a lumber yard.' In medical school they don't really emphasize any kind of prevention whatsoever. Less than a third of medical schools have a single course in nutrition. It's all drugs and surgery and what can we do to band-aid people together. The National Geographic picture started me on the transition, but it was really visiting Farm Sanctuary, meeting the animals in person, that led me to completely change my diet.

Brian: Let me sum this up. You saw a National Geographic picture back in high school where they were eating dogs. The common thread of animal consumption caused you to start considering your own diet. Then in medical school, you started seeing patients whose diseases were a result of their animal-based diet. How did all of this affect YOUR diet?

Michael: Before medical school I was already eating this way, so this goes back to 1990 when I cut all the crap out of my diet. First I started as vegetarian, and then became vegan.

Brian: Tell me about Farm Sanctuary and meeting the animals. What was it that triggered you to say, "I'm doing the right thing and I need to tell other people to do this as well?"

Michael: Cows are just like big puppy dogs, they are fuzzy and warm. The animals made it real. I had the choice; to eat the animals or help them out. It wasn't a hard decision to make.

Brian: Why do you think it's such a hard decision for most people in this country?

Michael: My sense of what is holding people back is that they don't have the same relationship with farm animals that they do to the companion animals in their lives. Once in a while we will see a movie about *Babe* or something. For an example of this attitude, when there was a beef recall, I had reporters ask me, "What do you mean they kill dairy cows at a dairy cow slaughter plant? Dairy cows make milk, they don't make hamburger!"

People are ignorant about how agriculture works, and the industry exploits that ignorance with these bucolic images of "Old McDonald's Farm." The current meat and dairy industry recognizes that if people were to know the truth, they would be turned off. If you ask the average person who participates in these national surveys, they think it's okay to eat meat. However, 80 to 85% of the people don't think it is okay to treat animals the way industrial animal agriculture treats them. Across the board, when it comes to the most grievous acts of cruelty, the battery cages, the gestation crates, the veal crates, people are almost universally opposed to animal cruelty.

As a physician, I know these products are killing people. The number one cause of death, every single year, since 1919, in both men and women is heart disease. Heart disease risk is largely determined by one's LDL (bad) cholesterol level, and that in turn is principally determined by saturated animal fat intake.

Brian: Let me throw this one at you. I'm John Q. American. I'm 35 to 40 years old. I have no history of heart disease. My cholesterol is fine. I love my bacon double-cheeseburger and a good juicy steak from time to time. As long as I'm buying organic humanely raised animal products, why should I care? I'm not one of these people you saw in the hospital suffering from a disease.

Michael: If you were to get hit by a bus tomorrow and we did an autopsy, we would see atherosclerosis already in your arteries. These chronic diseases, like heart disease and cancers, can take decades to accumulate, and it may take decades to reverse as well, so we need to start eating healthy as early as possible.

Brian: How do you explain that this is going to be you in ten to twenty years, if you last that long?

Michael: It's like when I get a smoker in my office and they're saying, "Look I smoke two packs a day, I don't even cough, I don't have emphysema, I don't have lung cancer, what's your problem?"

I try to relate to them stories of the people I've seen drown to death in their own fluids from lung cancer, gasping for air. I have them follow me around a hospital ward. People have the sense that dying of heart disease is quick and painless, you fall over in bed, and it's short and sweet. Perhaps only half just drop dead, where their first symptom of heart disease is their last. The rest can be disabled, incapacitated, can't even walk up the steps, have crushing chest pains all of the time, and have to under-go these horrible operations. It's not the way you want to live.

Brian: Let's say, I'm hearing what you're saying Doc, so I'll cut down on the animal products, I'll even eat vegetarian BUT I love my eggs and my cheese. I can't give up cheese. Cheese is beautiful. I'm going to be a lacto-ovo-vegetarian. Talk to me about how that might affect my health.

Michael: By adopting a partial vegetarian diet, because you don't want to give up dairy, is like smokers who cut down to a half a pack a day because they don't want to give up smoking. That is definitely a step in the right direction and will certainly be beneficial to their health. But for those who *really* care about their health, I can't pretend that it is going far enough, in terms of chronic disease prevention, to be a part-time vegetarian. I tell them all about the many alternatives to cheese and eggs. If they can't get rid of cheese, shave a little Parmesan for flavor. But it is these cardiologist's wet-dream entrées like "double-cheese pepperoni pizza," that are clogging up people's arteries.

At Cornell, where I attended college, the vegetarian option was deep-fried cheese. We were trying to get them to do more vegan options and they said, "Look, no one ever eats our vegetarian options, so why would we make more options?" If you are concerned about cardiac health, full-fat cheese is essentially the worst.

Brian: How is our health affected by the antibiotics we ingest by consuming these animals treated with these drugs?

Michael: The meat industry is putting everybody at risk. With Mad Cow Disease, basically if you don't eat beef, you don't eat products that contain beef, and you don't get a blood transfusion from a meat eater, you won't get Mad Cow Disease. But that is not necessarily true with other farm animal diseases.

Animal agriculture results in 18% of carbon-equivalent greenhouse gas emissions — that's more than all planes, trains, and automobiles combined. It's the same thing with these emerging infectious diseases coming out of factory farms.

Brian: What is the current threat to human health from diseases derived from animal agricultural practices?

Michael: There are highly disease-causing strains that predominantly come out of factory farming conditions and have the potential to trigger truly catastrophic pandemics beyond what we have seen in the past.

Brian: Okay. No more meat or poultry for me. I'm going to eat fish from now on. It's good for me, loaded with Omega-3s. I've read about it and seen it on the news. Fish is the way to go. Right?

Michael: Fish are worse. In terms of the environment, half the fish consumed are now from aquaculture, which is harmful to the environment. People are eating fish for their health, thinking they are getting the Omega-3 oils but only certain fish have that and you can get them (Omega-3s) from other sources. We humans don't make these Omega-3s (essential fatty acids). Guess what, the fish don't make them either. Fish eaters get it from eating fish that ate algae. Aquaculture fish are fed other aquaculture farmed fish, cattle meat, bone and blood meal. You do not get Omega-3s in fish that are farmed this way.

Brian: Give me the "riding off into the sunset on a humanely treated horse" statement encapsulating why people should adopt a plant-based diet.

Michael: As far as a plant-based diet, why do my patients stick with it? They stick with it because they feel so much better.

Why don't people give it a chance? What I tell people is, "Look, you don't have to eat this way your whole life if you don't want to, but give me three weeks, give me a month." Afterward, even if I told them to go back to meat, they wouldn't because they feel so much better. If you have been putting crappy gasoline in your car and then you put in the good stuff, you say, "I am never going back." What could be more convincing than their own body telling them that? It's not just about listening to me.

Also it helps to be familiar with these issues. Look at some of this footage on how farm animals are treated and what more do you need? If animals are the reason why you want to do this, and you want to do more, and you find yourself blocked, then go on the Internet and go to a video site on factory farming. You will see footage that will stick with you forever; for example, the eyes of that pregnant sow in a metal crate. She can't even turn around for months. And if that doesn't do it for you then how can you really in your heart care about animals?

If their parents and grandparents are healthy and they don't see the consequences of meat-laden diets, tell them to volunteer at a hospital or nursing home. Look at a couple of people on ventilators or unsuccessfully recovering from open heart surgery and look at their lives, at how much freedom has been taken away from them. I think many people just need something concrete like that, for reality to soak in.

JOHN McDOUGALL, MD, Santa Rosa, CA
Stories of Hope
Interview by Mark Viergutz

Mark: What did you eat as a child, growing up?

John: Everything bad, the typical Standard American Diet.

Mark: Were you in Hawaii when you learned about, and started thinking about the various diets and lifestyles?

John: Yes, that's when everything changed. I had suffered poor health up until then, including a massive stroke. I had surgery for abdominal stomach troubles and a stroke at age 18. My whole bad health thing basically urged me to write and to talk to people about what foods do.

The first revelation in Hawaii, being a practicing doctor, was that I began seeing that people didn't get better. No matter how hard I tried with the pills that I gave them they didn't improve much and that was very frustrating. And the second thing that happened, concurrently, is that I was able to observe the first, second, third, and fourth generation Filipinos, Japanese, Chinese, and Koreans that I was taking care of. The first generation had exemplary health, and they were always trim and they lived into their 80s and 90s. They were fully functional. They were not on prescription medications. Characteristically, they lived on their native diet of rice and vegetables. But the kids became *westernized* and they got fat and sick, and developed diseases that I was trained to treat. After that, it became a research project for me, and has been going on from 1976 to this day.

Mark: When you first became a vegetarian, what did your diet consist of initially?

John: Well, it was a transition for us. Over a two-year period of time we went from regular beef, to range-fed beef, to chicken and fish, dairy products and eggs, and then to non-egg, non-animal diet with oil. Then we gave up the oil. We've been eating that way 99.99% of the time, since about 1977.

Mark: When you say you gave up the oil, you use no oil at all for cooking?

John: That's correct. People think a vegetarian diet is a very healthy diet but it can get very sickly as far as a diet. A vegetarian diet like most people are eating today can be dripping in oil and soy products. That's not healthy. My diet is better described as a starch-based diet. People are always having a hard time understanding that concept but it's important that they do. I consider myself vegan but I don't want my diet to be associated with a typical vegetarian, fattening, greasy, diet.

Mark: When you began eating a primarily starch-based diet, and feeling the effects, can you explain the influence this had on your perspective of health and nutrition?

John: It went the other way around. I discovered my patients weren't getting well. At the same time I discovered, from my experience with the Asian population, that sickness was not inevitable. That came first and then our personal transition came afterward. It was not a vegetarian diet that changed my practice; it was more my practice changing my diet.

Mark: How are you finding the acceptance, among the medical community about that?

John: Much better. There are so many powerful financial influences that keep things going in the wrong direction. I do see some changes among my colleagues. I feel my colleagues are waking up and saying, "Hey, you know, I didn't go to medical school for seven years to become a drug salesman." Additionally, they're starting to understand that the rich western diet is what creates all the "business."

Mark: Are you finding, among the general population at large, more of an acceptance of a starch- and plant-based diet?

John: Oh, I think so. Statistics show that more and more people are becoming vegetarian. And it's happening because they're being forced into it. One reason is that we have new information and technology sharing the truth quite rapidly in terms of the Internet. We live in an information age. The truth does rise to the surface and I think that's important.

Another thing is that this is becoming too big. People, organizations, government, and so on, have no choice but to realize the truth because of two things that march side by side. One is the destruction of human beings. We have a population of six and a half billion people on this planet. Over one billion of them are overweight or obese and over one billion of them have high blood pressure. Eight million a year die of heart disease. It's an epidemic of sickness that is getting worse and worse as more and more populations in different countries become involved with a rich western diet.

Mark: When you're working with the patients, helping them to change their diet and move toward a vegetarian diet, what sort of advice do you give them?

John: Well, that's the heart of the difficulty. The problem is *getting them to do it*. This is something that I've been working on every day, to try and get people to rethink what's going on. Our efforts have taken the direction of things like books, TV shows, radio shows, DVDs, live-in clinics on weekends, and adventure trips to Costa Rica. We can do all kinds of things to try to change people's minds. It's an ongoing process that doesn't happen overnight. There are extremely few people who change their diet overnight. When they finally say this is what I want to do because it's right, it's the truth, and it's much preferred over what I used to do, then they make a change.

Mark: Well, how about once you've had somebody who's made the transition to becoming a vegetarian, and is now considering becoming vegan?

John: These people have at least gone through some process of change but they're often quite reluctant. For example, to get people to give up their cheese is a real effort.

I have all kinds of discussions, articles I've written on the problems with dairy, the problems with eggs, and once they learn that, it helps.

They are in a situation where they're still constipated, they're still fat, they're still greasy, and they're still sick. They are vegetarian, and they say, "I've developed this new way; why am I not getting results?" You explain, basically, that dairy is liquid meat, and the oil is going to keep you fat, and eggs are full of cholesterol. It eventually gets through and they take the next step.

Mark: Are you doing new research in any direction?

John: Right now I have a 501c3, a non-profit, tax-deductible organization, and have raised about $650,000 for a project to find a dietary treatment for multiple sclerosis, which we're trying to get worked out with the university. That's the latest project I'm involved in.

Mark: On the subject of high fructose corn syrup, do you think something should be done about the amount that's in the products that people consume?

John: High fructose corn syrup acts differently in the body than other sugars. It raises cholesterol and triglycerides more than any other sugar and causes the production of fat. We have a whole list on our website of canned and packaged products which have things in them that are free of harmful ingredients. Mary has probably published over twenty five hundred recipes and many of them are on the website. We don't use packaged foods very often. Most of what we use is really simple food.

Mark: Of course a main concern for people is the time element in the preparation.

John: Our last cookbook was called, the *McDougall Quick and Easy Cookbook*.

Mark: Where do you see vegetarianism going in the future?

John: I'm optimistic. I really am.

The Internet is so good at teaching, we have thousands of patients who have changed their diet, gotten off their medications, changed their whole life, and they are all telling the story. There are hundreds, if not thousands of other health advocates that are out there trying to tell the story. People are listening, and they're changing, and they get the results that they ought to be getting on weight-loss and on getting their health back. The message is spreading. And it's vital that it spreads.

Basically, what it's come down to, and it's escalating because of third world countries becoming wealthy enough to eat all this rich food, we're just basically eating the planet to death. It's happening so quickly, far, far more quickly than anybody had ever predicted. We just have to get this fixed. There's no other option.

Mark: So, you see that as being more of a direction you're taking with your efforts to promote the diet you believe in.

John: Well, that's the thing that gets me out of bed in the morning. In other words, that's what really makes me want to continue doing this work. The problem is they're eating the *planet* to death, which is ruining the future for my grandchildren, and their children, and so on. Because of that, I've been reinvigorated to tell the story. And with great enthusiasm, and taking all kinds of risks and adventures on it because this is bigger than somebody dying of a heart attack.

Mark: Oh, much bigger. Exactly. Is there anything else you'd like to add to cap this off?

John: Just one comment: I hope that Marilyn can express in the book that a starch-based diet is the best of all. You have to have the starch to get the calories, clean calories. Raw food is fine and certainly an all-raw vegan diet is better than the Standard American Diet. But somehow it's not what people should be eating instead of a starch-based diet. Some fruits and vegetables can be raw, but raw brown rice, raw potatoes are pretty tough. It's impossible; you just can't do it. If you look throughout all recorded history, at all populations that have crossed this earth, they've all lived on starch-based diets, except for those in the extremes of the environment, like the Eskimos.

If you want to explore some of the issues, like the oil issue, you can go to my website and look under a section called *Hot Topics*. It tells you why these free oils are so hazardous. You will find all the research, all the logic behind it at: *www.drmcdougall.com*.

Dr. John McDougall is the author of *Maximum Weight Loss, Digestive Tune Up, McDougall's Medicine: A Challenging Second Opinion* and *The McDougall Quick and Easy Cookbook* and more.

DR. PAM POPPER, Worthington, OH

Naturopathic Physician and Nutritionist
Founder and Executive Director of *"The Wellness Forum"*
Interview by Marilyn Peterson

My intention was not to become vegan: that is not how I started. I came to the realization that my eating habits were terrible when I started reading articles and magazines that said that the way you eat affects your health. I was eating a pound of shortbread cookies with three pots of coffee a day. Every educated dietician knows that is not a good idea, so I was very lucky that this terrible diet of mine had not resulted in health problems *yet*.

I am almost 51 years old and I am absolutely sure that if I hadn't changed my ways that by now serious, terrible things would have happened to me. It was just the logic of all of this that made me do some independent research. I just wanted to improve my health and my children's health.

I really wasn't sick, and I really wasn't overweight, but I was over-fat, and I was tired all the time. Even the cookie eating and coffee drinking wasn't working so much anymore. I remember loving weekends so that I could sleep in the afternoon.

What a way to live your life, where you are looking forward to sleep. So the first thing I noticed was instantaneously my energy level was starting to improve. That was a positive thing, and also at the same time, I was burning off fat with exercise, cleaning out my gastrointestinal tract. My body wasn't used to handling high fiber foods. I can see where a lot of people could experience this on their own without any help and could say this isn't too much fun and I think I will quit.

I was pretty determined as I saw the super logic of it so I stuck with it because I knew it was the right thing to do. The energy I was feeling told me that it was the right thing to do. The discomfort didn't last a real long time, it was uncomfortable for a couple of months and after that it was astounding. My whole complexion changed. I used to not leave my house without make-up on my face. Now I wear a little eye make-up and I don't wear any make-up on my face and I don't have to. My hair got nice and shiny and thick, and overall you could tell I was healthier just by looking at me.

I call myself a recovering garbologist, which appropriately describes what I used to be, and I went off the deep end, which describes my personality. I remember coming home one day and just deciding that we are getting rid of all of the bad food in the house. So I got rid of all of the bad food in the house and there was nothing in my house to eat. I remember my youngest kid saying to me, *what are we going to eat?*

I told him I haven't gotten that far yet and that he will have to give me a little bit of time to figure that out. I know what we are *not* going to eat, but I don't know what we are going to eat. That is what part of my business is all about, helping people facilitate that transition and not have to do what I did, which is an awful lot of trial and error of not knowing what to do. I rattled around until I figured it out. I have a Bachelors, Masters, and PhD in Nutrition and a degree in Naturopathy, which is the practice of natural medicine.

Thank God the first books I read were written by Dr. John McDougall and not Dr. Atkins, because it just as easily could have been. I started reading these various books by Dr. McDougall, and I read Dr. Dean Ornish's book and I started seeing this incredible connection between optimal diet and health and eating more plant foods and less animal foods. One day I went to a lecture where I really heard how bad animal foods were for you, and I gave up everything but fish. That happened about 14 years ago. I was an occasional fish eater, once in a while I would eat a little goat cheese or something and that went on for many, many years.

About three and a half years ago I woke up one day and realized that months and months had passed since I had eaten fish; I didn't miss it, I didn't care and I realized that I was a vegan, and have been ever since.

My intention at the beginning of the process was not to become vegetarian or vegan. My intention really was just to improve my diet and improve my health. What I have found when people come to see me is that some of them are very, very sick and a vegan diet is appropriate and I talk to them about it. For a lot of them, we just want them to start on the journey to better health, and a lot of them will end up vegetarian or vegan, not because they intended to, but because it becomes your lifestyle. You don't have to worry about a whole lot of things like mercury in fish. A lot of things concern me that don't pertain to me health-wise, that is kind of reassuring.

Most people get up every day and they are not happy with what they do, I get up every day and I can't wait to get into work. I love what I do and part of what makes me love it is seeing positive results in people and how they thank us so much for turning them on to eating this way. I feel better and look better and I am not afraid about my health anymore.

I'm a vegan; I love it. It works for me!

Dr. Pam Popper is the founder and Executive Officer of The Wellness Forum (*www.wellnessforum.com*).

Chapter Eight

Vegans Up Close and Personal

This chapter offers real-life perspectives relating to the transition, with interviews from a wide variety of vegans — celebrities, restaurateurs, health practitioners, presenters, teachers, students/interns, authors and food writers. The stories are wonderful, entertaining, informative, and come at the subject from many different angles.

This bouquet of stories has been picked to bring out a variety of transition experiences that will hopefully benefit the reader, no matter what path in life each person is following. I find threads of my own story woven throughout the tapestry of their stories.

Additional interviews can be read on my website: *http://www.veganbitebybite.com*

NAME	OCCUPATION/INTERESTS	PAGE
Zel Allen	Author	228
Matt Amsden	Author, Chef, Restaurateur	229
Matthew Cheek	Student	232
Brian Hines	Author	233
Howard Lyman	Author, Speaker, Former Cattle Rancher	234
Nicholas Palomino Mendoza	Student, Aspiring Writer	237
Lillian Muller	Author, Actress, Cover Girl (Playboy Magazine)	240
Eva Stefurak	Mother, Cooking/Raw Foods Teacher	242
Martha Theus	Author	245
Soorya Townley	Massage Therapist	247
Will Tuttle	Author	249
Mark Viergutz	Food Writer, Photographer	253
Tatiana Wrenfeather	Nutritional Counselor/Detox Coach	255

ZEL ALLEN, Granada Hills, CA
Author — *The Nut Gourmet*
A No-Stress Vegan

I grew up in an era where women were happy to be "homemakers." My mom loved to cook. She prepared many Jewish dishes using kosher meat, rib steak and lamb chops. Roasted chicken and broiled fish, hot dogs and beans were sometimes a Saturday night dinner. Dairy products were a major part of our diet. One could not have borscht without sour cream or bread without butter. Cottage cheese and fruit was a familiar lunch or a light summer dinner. Milk was not homogenized then, so bottles of milk had to be shaken. If you wanted the cream; you would just pour off the top four inches where the cream collected. As important as meat and dairy were, my parents also bought many fruits and vegetables. They shopped often and always had a refrigerator full of produce.

My treat was a cup of tea with milk and I also had my share of ice cream cones. My mom always said that I was a "good eater," but maybe a little too good. I was pleasingly plump throughout my childhood, the teen years, and during most of my adulthood. Not obese, but 15 to 30 pounds more than my present weight.

My transition was a gradual process. I was battling bladder infections and candida. The more antibiotics I was given, the worse I felt. The urologist didn't have any idea those antibiotics were feeding the candida. Because of the antibiotics, I was experiencing stomach pain and enormous discomfort from the bloating and gas. I became very lactose intolerant, but didn't know it. My internist began running me through all sorts of tests — upper and lower GI and a Barium Enema X-ray. I was feeling pretty miserable. Finally a friend suggested I might be lactose intolerant. Without hesitation I was ready to abandon dairy products and within a few days I was healing.

I ditched allopathic medicine and made an appointment with an OMD (Doctor of Oriental Medicine) who used American herbs for healing. She was a great help and suggested I might do better if I switched to a vegetarian diet. I had already been rid of dairy for several months. Next to go was the meat, then the chicken, and last was the fish. The transition for me was over a period of two years with no ill effects or discomforts. In fact, I was delighted with the weight loss of 30 extra pounds and I have kept them off with no problem. I loved being thin for the first time in my life. In addition to all the other benefits, I no longer crave sugar or sweets.

While I was working on articles for our web magazine *"Vegetarians in Paradise"* I began reading research about the awesome health benefits of nuts. I found tons of conclusive studies that showed eating small quantities of nuts several times a week could help to lower LDL and total cholesterol. That was the spark that lit the flame for *The Nut Gourmet* cookbook. In the process, I am glad that I took the time to read extensively and educate myself about the health benefits of a vegan diet and learning about the nitty-gritty of basic nutrition in order to assure that I was eating healthfully.

I am grateful to the web, the library, vegan festivals, cooking classes, vegan restaurants and seminars that support me while I continue to learn. I also found joining a group with other like-minded people to be supportive for me.

I didn't stress about being the perfect vegan. I just started traveling the path and I got there step by step.

MATT AMSDEN, Santa Monica, CA
Restaurateur, Raw Food Chef, Author — *RAWvolution,*
Owner of RAWvolution, and Euphoria Loves
RAWvolution café in Santa Monica, CA

I didn't grow up vegetarian or vegan. I was eating a Standard American Diet (SAD) all my life until I turned twenty-one. Then I went from eating at McDonald's to 100% raw virtually overnight. What triggered the change was an interview I heard on the radio with David Wolfe. After listening to the interview I read a couple of his books as well as other books, and I was really motivated to change and I did it straight away. I have been raw vegan for about nine years now (2007).

What David Wolfe was talking about in that particular interview on the radio was really from a nutritional base. That appealed to me and I would say that my initial impetus to become vegan/raw was based on health and nutrition. But then as I learned more it became other things as well, like compassion for animals and the environment. I very quickly realized that we are a part of it as well.

The benefits that raw foods have over cooked vegetarian food are usually three main things. First, water content. You can eat a ton of cooked food and not only is the food not contributing to the water intake for the day; it's also dehydrating you further in your body's attempt to digest it. Raw food contains all the natural water that it started with. When you are cooking food, the steam that you see is the water leaving the food. The second would be enzymes, which are talked about a lot in raw food literature. Enzymes are responsible for every metabolic process that happens in the body and cooked food destroys 100% of the enzymes while raw food has all of them intact. That's pretty substantial. Nutrition is the third thing. Cooked food can have 85% less nutrition than the same food eaten in its raw state. The fact is that you're getting so many more vitamins and minerals eating the same food raw as you would if eaten cooked.

I guess the karmic aspect of eating depends on most people's philosophical or spiritual beliefs. As for me, I can choose to eat something that doesn't include killing a living creature or I can eat things that do. For me it is a pretty clear choice. A lot of people would have a harder time eating meat if they actually had to kill the animal themselves. In fact, I would venture to say that most people wouldn't be able to do it, especially in such a way where they do it without being upset. When a tiger kills something, it's just a part of its physiology and it's geared to do that mentally and physically, but we humans don't typically enjoy death. It's more natural for people to encourage life. I feel really good that I'm able to eat without causing death. And I definitely believe in karma and the karmic effects of eating or not eating living creatures or contributing to their death by supporting an industry that operates that way.

Karma is really just a way of saying cause and effect. Cause and effect is not a new age concept; it's an undeniable fact of existence. If you do one thing, something happens; you do something else and something else happens. I guess everyone does have a different opinion of what things are good and what things are bad, but there is an effect. Most people are eating cooked food, most people are not eating organic food, most people are eating non-vegetarian food or animal products, and we have the world that we have today, which is a failing ecosystem. We've done more damage to the planet in the last hundred years than has ever been done in history. There are wars, there's poverty, unhappiness and depression. Maybe if we tried something else we'll get another result. What's for sure is that if we keep doing the same thing, we're going to get the same result.

In my opinion the raw diet is the thing that everyone's been looking for. People are always hearing about diets. Oh, this is the new way to lose weight, or this is really going to make you feel good. This isn't a product and this isn't a diet. This is a way of life that makes sense. It's based on science, it's based on common sense, and it's how every other animal on the planet lives with the exception of domesticated pets. They are the only animals that don't eat a raw diet, and they're the ones that experience diseases the way that people do, so it's pretty obvious what the correlation is. Eating raw is easy to do; it's getting easier and it's great. The food tastes fantastic, super fresh, and you feel great from eating it. There's no down side.

Better things always cost more. You spend a little more money for a little while, and eventually you end up eating less food anyway. If you want to eat the best food in the world, and I don't see why you wouldn't, you should be okay with spending a little more on it, at least for the time being until everyone does it, and it's just the way things are.

I think the transition or change (to raw food) should be adopted as you're comfortable. Certainly be in the process of moving forward, if you have decided that's your goal. Always move toward the goal but don't be attached to how it happens. In other words, it's all about including more raw food even if it's a small amount.

If it was more than yesterday, it's a great step. You can constantly be in the state of moving forward and before you know it you're doing a lot better.

It's also a self-fulfilling prophesy because the more raw food you eat the better you feel. When you naturally feel better you don't need a lot of discipline. It's easy for people to realize, "Oh wow, when I eat that I feel great and when I eat this I feel kind of crappy." Of course you're going to go eat more of what makes you feel good for the most part and really research what support systems are out there. There are food delivery services, there are restaurants and there are books. You can get any supplement and food product delivered to you in the mail. There's really a lot of help out there.

I absolutely think it is possible for most anyone to live this kind of lifestyle and eat organic foods. And the more you buy organic, the more you support organic agriculture, the more accessible it becomes for everyone and it should be the case that it's cheaper than conventional food. Right now, when we buy organic food, we're paying for what we're not getting; the chemicals. If everyone started eating organic today, it would become cheaper from supply and demand. Also, non-organic agriculture has an unfair advantage because conventional produce is subsidized where organic is not. Beyond that it's not just a matter of what's expensive, it's an investment in your health and you can't afford *not* to eat organic food.

If you want to save a little money and eat pesticides then that's one choice, but I think a better choice is to invest in your health because the return on that is incalculable. Basically you're going to pay *now* or pay later. So, pay a few cents more for organic which oftentimes turns out to be the same price when you calculate how much you can sink into health insurance and medical bills. Not only that, you're also going to feel terrible.

A lot of the products that go into landfills are used cooking implements and the implications of eating meat on the planet. It takes many thousands of gallons of water to produce one pound of meat, much more than it takes to produce vegetables, or grain or other vegetarian choices. Most of the grain grown on the planet goes to feed livestock, which goes to feed people, so it's just shortening that chain, getting closer to the source of your food.

Rawfoodism and veganism are following the same pattern that trends follow when they get a lot of media attention and a lot of high-profile people get interested in it. It is being talked about a lot and people are trying it out. Trends can last decades and the best ones do. A trend that is sustainable to the planet, fantastic for people nutritionally, and tastes good; there's no reason why it shouldn't stay around.

MATTHEW CHEEK, Los Angeles, CA
Why Vegan?

I consider myself incredibly fortunate to have been brought up in a household that, although not entirely vegetarian, treated kale, broccoli, and spinach as main courses, and things like millet and quinoa as daily food staples. In fact, I owe much of my extraordinary physical, spiritual, mental and emotional well-being to the dietary patterns I developed early on. However, I didn't realize how important my food paradigm would be until my freshman year in college.

As a student of philosophy, both then and now, I commit myself to an undying search for truth; and I seek to understand the systems, spiritual and social, that validate ideas and ways of life as truth. When I started college, I lost a lot of control over what I ate. As a result, my diet was based on what the school provided, and I found myself relying on burgers, pizza, and Mexican food.

Then I discovered John Robbins' book, *Diet for a New America* and learned the major arguments against the consumption of animal products as well as how deeply what we eat affects the rest of the world. Environmental, socio-economical, humanitarian, nutritional, and ethical ideas flurried around my head before slapping me in the face with the resolution that I was not meant to ingest things that were harming my body, my fellow beings, and the world at large. I immediately phased about 90% of all animal products out of my diet, save a cheese pizza now and then. A year and a half later, after reading a few more books on the subject, it was time to become pure vegan in order to solidify my newfound physical and mental clarity with a higher spiritual connection and solidify my lifelong commitment to a better way of life.

It might sound strange, but I found my first transition into vegetarianism, and my later switch to veganism not the least bit difficult. After learning the conditions under which the consumption of animals takes place and seeing how clearly it is connected to social conditioning, negative karmic energy, and the overall corruption of the mind, I knew my actions needed to defend my ideals for a better world. So when people ask me why I am vegan, I maintain a holistic response: *because of everything.*

I live vegan to defend my body from unwarranted nutritional devastation, to rid the environment of the toxic abuse that animal harvesting causes, to stand up for widespread truthful knowledge about how each and every decision that we make on a daily basis, right down to the things we put in our mouths, affects every living being on this planet and symbolizes how we see ourselves fitting within the grand scheme. I made the switch for my own well-being just as much as I did for yours, for my future children, and for every being that suffers unnecessarily from severely antiquated and morally unjust patterns of consumption. And I have never felt better!

BRIAN HINES, Salem, OR

Author — *Life is Fair,* and *God's Whisper –
Creation's Thunder*

Growing up in rural central California, foothills of the Sierras, my boyhood should have followed the usual trajectory of (1) BB gun, (2) pellet gun, (3) .22 rifle, then (4) deer rifle. I got up to the pellet gun stage. One day, shortly after I'd gotten the gun, I was wandering around shooting at birds with a neighbor boy. I'd never hit anything alive until then. I remember aiming at a songbird in a bush. I pulled the trigger. The bird fell to the ground dead. Instantly I felt terrible. Actually, I still do. I never shot at another animal again. This is interesting, since I was only ten or eleven, or thereabouts, and had never gotten any exposure to anti-hunting or anti-meat eating ideas. This could have been a foreshadowing of my subsequent vegetarianism.

I've been a vegetarian since 1969 when I was 21, to the best of my recollection (like they say, "If you remember the 60s, you weren't there"). Being part of the San Francisco Bay Area "Flower Child" scene, after psychedelics and Jefferson Airplane, I took up yoga and meditation.

My yoga teacher encouraged vegetarianism. I adapted to a meatless diet pretty easily, but was still eating fish when I went home for a college Christmas break. My mother cooked some frozen prawns for me. I took the plate in hand, sat down at a table, and looked at what was on it in fresh-eyed amazement.

I thought: *That curled-up creature was once alive and now it's not — because of me.* Bingo! From that moment on I became a meatless, *fishless* vegetarian. Thirty-eight years later, I still am. However, if I'd been asked to bet on this prospect when I was a teenager, I'd have laughed off such a ridiculous notion.

My mother believed in Dr. Spock, or at least her interpretation of his child-raising philosophy, which meant letting me choose on my own what I wanted to eat. This turned out to be very limited; plain hamburgers (just a patty and a bun, plus salt) and equally plain salads (lettuce and dressing) being a large part of what kept body and soul together for many years. So I was an unlikely vegetarian, as up into my twenties I didn't like many vegetables. Barbeque beef sandwich, French fries, vanilla coke — that was my idea of a perfect restaurant meal until yoga and meditation attuned me to the health and moral consequences of my diet. I felt stronger, leaner, and lighter as I reduced my meat intake. Equally importantly, I stopped feeling like the animal world was clearly divided into (1) humans and (2) all other creatures.

I don't think you can eat meat with a clear conscience unless you view animals as *something other* — without the same desire for life, liberty, and the pursuit of happiness that we people have. The prawn I was about to eat was experiencing whatever prawns experience until it was killed, packaged, and frozen. That could have been its one and only chance to live. Maybe reincarnation is a fact, maybe not. I don't know. But this part of life/karma is undeniable: I wanted to eat meat; meat producers responded to my want; animals were killed as a result. As soon as this became clear to me, I had to remove myself from the demand-supply chain, from being the cause that became the effect — the killing of animals.

HOWARD LYMAN, Ellensburg, WA
Author — *Mad Cowboy* and *No More Bull!*
Speaker, Former Cattle Rancher
Interview by John McDougall, MD

"Public enemy #1" — this is what cattlemen had dubbed Howard F. Lyman, a successful rancher himself until age 40. After he appeared on the Oprah Winfrey show in April 1996 to discuss Mad Cow Disease, both he and Oprah were sued by a group of Texas cattlemen for publicly disparaging a perishable commodity.

But Howard has done much more than tick-off ranchers. For the past 15 years, he has been educating the public on organic farming and making informed food choices. As a Washington, DC lobbyist for small farmers, he helped pass the Organic Standards Act, and today he heads the Humane Society's "Eating with Conscience" campaign. Below, Howard discusses the trial and what he's been doing since.

McDougall: Why were you sued by the Texas cattlemen?

Lyman: John, the only thing I called for in that show was that we stop grinding up cows and feeding them to other cows. When I said that, twenty million viewers understood exactly what I was saying. Had I said we have to stop feeding "bovines to bovines," or "ruminate protein" to "ruminates," the cattlemen wouldn't have been pissed off.

I also said that if we didn't stop feeding cows to cows, in ten years we could have an event that makes AIDS look like the common cold. That's because England had just announced that Mad Cow Disease could spread to humans.

Several months later, the US in fact banned cows from eating cow parts, goats and sheep. But this ban doesn't go far enough. Today, cows can still be fed cow blood as well as other animals, such as horses and pigs, which may have eaten other diseased animals. (Mad Cow Disease started in England when cows were fed sheep infected with scrapie.) In fact, about 75% of the 95 million beef cattle in America are routinely given feed that includes animal parts, aka "protein concentrates."

McDougall: What were some of the highlights of the Amarillo, Texas trial?

Lyman: One of their expert witnesses admitted on the stand he was being paid $150,000 to $200,000, and he testified for ten minutes. I do believe the cattlemen spent more money in this trial than what they were suing us for. Another man from the Chicago Board of Trade testified that the Oprah show had driven the futures market in beef way down. But the same day of the so-called "Oprah drop" he had said something completely different on Chicago TV. In an interview, he said the market had been driven down by high grain prices, not the Oprah show. And we replayed that videotape. At first, I thought they were going to win. The largest employer in Amarillo is a cattle slaughter facility and the income of everyone on that jury, in one way or another, depended on the cattle industry. You never saw so many hats, boots and belt buckles in all your life. We asked for a change in venue, and the judge denied it out of hand. But I think the jury believed in the right of free speech as much as we did. After six weeks of trial, they came back in less than six hours and found us not liable.

McDougall: And that should have been the end of it?

Lyman: It should have been. But the cattle ranchers have appealed, with a ruling expected spring 1999. Also, 130 feedlot operators have filed another suit. I believe when we win the appeal, the second suit will be thrown out and this chapter will come to an end.

McDougall: Don't you think they've brought a lot of negative publicity to themselves?

Lyman: Oh, I think they not only shot their foot off, they shot their head off. The cattle industry today is dying, and I think this was the worst publicity it could have ever received. Remember, US per-capita consumption of beef used to be 95 pounds annually, and today it's down to 65 pounds. Meanwhile, the trial has given me a much bigger forum and media profile; I'm broadcasted on 3,000 radio shows a month.

McDougall: It's a dying industry in the United States, but not around the world.

Lyman: That's right. But remember that the United States is a major exporter and our lifestyles influence what other countries eventually consume.

McDougall: Why did you stop cattle ranching 20 years ago?

Lyman: In 1979, when I had 7,000 head of cattle, 12,000 acres of crop and 30 employees, I became paralyzed from the waist down because of a tumor in my spinal cord, and I was told I had a one in a million chance of walking again. My doctor said that the tumor cells were being stimulated by the chemicals we were using. And that was the first time in my life I really looked seriously at how I was farming. I was buying hundreds of thousands of dollars worth of chemicals (pesticides, fertilizers, beef hormones and antibiotics) that were killing the birds, the trees, and making the soil sterile. Incredibly, I walked out of the hospital, but I walked out a much different individual.

McDougall: Where did things go for you from that point?

Lyman: I knew that what I'd learned at Montana State University was nothing more than brainwashing: "better living through chemistry." So I started reading other things. I started out with Rachel Carson's *Silent Spring*, and then Frances Moore Lappe and others.

When I told my banker we wanted to become organic farmers, he laughed and said, "You want me to lend you money, you're not going to spend with my other customers: the chemical dealer, the pharmaceutical dealer, the fertilizer dealer? There will never be a day like that."

And so in 1983, I sold most of my farm to pay debts. And I organized Montana farmers and even ran for Congress. In 1987, I started working in Washington, DC for the National Farmers Union, which represents small family farms. After five frustrating years there, I started traveling again and talking to people about clean air, clean food, and clean water.

McDougall: You went a lot further than that. You went from trying to grow clean beef to trying to convince people not to eat beef.

Lyman: When I became an advocate of organic farming, it was for environmental reasons. But then I realized the health reasons. I used to weigh well over 300 pounds. My blood pressure was sky high, and my cholesterol was over 300. I would sit down and have lunch, and I swear to God my nose would bleed.

So I gave up meat. Now in Montana, you're better off caught riding a stolen horse than admitting to somebody you don't eat meat. So I didn't tell anyone, even though I ate just lettuce and dairy products for a year. I lost some weight and my blood pressure and cholesterol came down slightly. But cutting out all animal products did much more for me than giving up just meat. After I did that, I had more energy, my blood pressure went to normal, I lost 130 pounds, and my cholesterol went from 300 to 135.

McDougall: How'd you get involved with the Humane Society?

Lyman: In 1994, they asked me to run their "Eating with Conscience" campaign. I travel about 100,000 miles a year getting people to ask these questions: Who produced my food? What did they use on it? What's it doing to me, the environment, and the animals? What it comes down to is that the way we're producing and eating our food is absolutely not sustainable.

McDougall: It seems logical that the Humane Society would be interested in not eating animal products. How much of the Humane Society can see things from that point of view?

Lyman: The amazing thing is that of the 200 employees in the Humane Society of the US, the umbrella organization, 25% of them don't eat any animal products; half don't eat meat. They've increased their membership from 2.5 million in 1993 to 5.8 million members today. So I would say the organization is growing, the awareness is growing and the focus is on doing better.

McDougall: That's all good to say. But there seems to be a big backlash, especially when you see Atkins, who recommends an all-meat diet, on the bestseller list. So really, Howard, where do you think things are going?

Lyman: If you look at the Zone diet and all other fad diets out there, they are telling people "your bad habits are okay." And people love to hear that.

But, John, look at it like this. Each year in the US, one million more people give up meat. And ask yourself: If we are not becoming effective, why did the cattlemen sue us? I think the sales of the meat and dairy industries are dropping like a rock. So I think we're winning.

Re-printed for *Vegan Bite by Bite* with the courtesy of
Dr. John McDougall and Howard Lyman
Sept/Oct '98 interview

NICHOLAS PALOMINO MENDOZA, Los Angeles, CA
From Noxious To Nutritious

Ham and eggs, pancakes and sausage, bacon, egg and cheese burrito; this was breakfast. For lunch: beef sandwich, ham and bologna sandwich on white bread, hot dog, chicken soup, or McDonald's. Carne Asada tacos, chicken tamales, plain hamburger, spaghetti and meatballs or sausage and cheese pizza was dinner.

I had quite the potpourri of flesh-based daily meal options as I grew up a second generation, lower-middle class, Mexican-American on Chicago's south side. My selection of drinks was even less wholesome as I grew up in the midst of what I like to call the "Kool-Aid culture." Every Saturday morning, my fellow babies of the eighties and I watched as Kool-Aid, Hi-C, Juicy Juice and other food-colored, sugar waters were ingrained in our subconscious as viable and healthy drink options. If we wanted to be *really* healthy we could always drink milk. Back then, it "did a body good" and I grew up under the impression that if I didn't drink it my bones would become brittle. To top off this already noxious diet, I absolutely loathed any green vegetables and my dinner table memories include bawling my eyes out as my mother tried to force green beans down my throat. I refused to eat salad, any type of bean or raw nut. My idea of vegetables extended only as far as fried potatoes. I would occasionally eat fruit as a dessert but only strawberries and oranges. My taste buds developed to tolerate no more than the meals mentioned above. I was quite convinced that this was all I would need to eat for the rest of my life.

I continued this diet until I was 23 years old, straying no further than the occasional pre-steak dinner salad. It was at this time that I met people who were more conscious of their eating decisions. A few of my friends had recently become vegetarians and were disgusted by my carnivorous choices. They started voicing their opinions and talking about how completely unnatural it was for humans to eat animals. They spoke of the cruel practices used daily in slaughterhouses, using terms like "rotting flesh" and "decaying corpses" and were visually disgusted any time we would eat out together. They also discussed the karmic implications that came with eating meat. They explained that eating death and pain at every meal would only ensure that I live a painful life and die young. This viewpoint shocked, offended and scared me all at once. I began exploring the idea of karma, along with the practices that are commonplace among the meat and dairy industries. Subsequently, I vowed to stop eating red meat and soon after, I met my lovely girlfriend and nutritional mentor, Katie.

Katie was attending James Madison University and majoring in dietetics. She had just become vegan (after enduring a similar dietary upbringing) and was reaping the benefits and loving life. We shared what we knew about the karmic implications of a meat-eater's diet and she made me aware of the health issues and environmental problems that the meat and dairy industries contribute to. It wasn't long after she shared this information with me that I stopped eating meat altogether. Before this, I had never paid any attention to what I had been putting into my body, thus greatly impairing the essential link between body and mind.

Furthermore, I never put any thought into the cause of the various types of cancers, strokes and other diseases (heart-disease, high-cholesterol, diabetes) that "ran in the family." Once I understood the effect of the toxicity of one's diet, I made the connection between my family's shared diet and the life-crippling diseases that they have also historically shared. I told myself that I would do anything to break this vicious cycle.

Thereafter I started eating fish and a lot of Asian and Indian cuisine due to their vegetarian-friendly menu options. My taste buds were in a different world and my palate was forced to broaden. I tried foods that I never knew existed and ordered dishes that I never dreamed of trying. This time in my life was pivotal as my spiritual and physical development was exponentially improved in comparison to the rest of my life. I re-enrolled in college and began working out daily. My willpower and self-confidence were at an all time high. I had only one problem, I found myself too frequently substituting fish where I normally would have eaten red meat or chicken. So the next dietary step that made sense was to stop eating fish, bringing an end to my fish-filled meal choices. This made way for the discontinuation of all dairy and poultry products in my diet (shortly after I stopped eating fish, I also stopped eating eggs). This was an enjoyable challenge as I was again reinventing my taste buds and palate.

I found new and exciting foods that I would have never tried and also began cooking vegetarian dishes, something that I never saw myself doing. Cooking was an extremely rewarding part of the transition and it gave me a new appreciation for what I was eating. I had also learned not to overeat by familiarizing myself with portion sizes while cooking and listening to my body when it told me I was full. Even a salad for dinner became a viable and filling option and my new love for greens and other plants was stimulating my appetite. I continued working out and reached the point where my body and mind were feeling more invigorated and nourished than ever before.

I knew that ceasing to eat cheese and becoming a label-reading vegan wouldn't be simple because cheese was now my new "meat." Cheese had become a staple at every meal, due not only to its delicious taste, but also because of the many different varieties of cheese available. I still felt, however, that I needed to stop eating cheese in order to fully remove myself from any ecologically harmful and destructive practices.

It was around the same time that I also began feeling alienated from my family (and even some cheese eating vegetarian friends!) at the dinner table. This made it even harder to become vegan, as it seemed that they could not understand my diet and would get worried that I wasn't getting enough protein. They also expected me to be what I call a "convenience vegan" and eat anything that wasn't straight up meat, i.e. dishes prepared with chicken or beef stock, butter and eggs or egg whites. They joked about how I would never last and asked questions like, "What can you eat?" I stood my ground and simply responded calmly, "Everything besides meat, fish, poultry and dairy." Answering this question so many times helped me grasp how limited people's diets are when they do eat meat. I also realized how reliant on the slaughtering of animals meat eaters are. Being reliant on something that you cannot control or even explain the process of, something as important as your daily nutrition, seems strangely unnatural.

I explained to my family (and vegetarian and non-vegetarian friends) that being vegan is a lifestyle that doesn't just come and go, and furthermore, I told them of the positive influence that vegans have on society, simply by refusing dead animal products.

I felt that Katie was my "partner in crime," so to speak, especially considering that around the same time my roommate tried to go cold-turkey vegetarian about three or four times and failed after a day or so each time. This, along with the scathing criticism of my family, was very disheartening. Weaning myself off cheese and other casein-filled products I could finally proclaim myself a vegan.

I found a strong and sudden intimacy in the idea that I was sustaining a diet that consisted only of things that came from the earth. This was a huge step in my life, as never before had I challenged something like my eating habits, which are not only inherited and hard to change, but also a key part of one's survival. I learned that my taste buds recycle every two to three weeks and this helped me realize how mentally dependant I (and every other meat eater) was/is on meat and cheese.

I read *The World Peace Diet* and decided to never look back as I fully realized the mental, physical and planetary implications that come with eating any and all animal products. I found changes in my body as my skin cleared up and started to glow and my hair and nails grew more rapidly. Any depression or random sadness that I had experienced in the past had become inconsequential if not completely absent. I also noticed that, after a month or so, my family was in awe of my will-power and, in fact, started researching vegan and vegetarian diets in order to help themselves in overcoming and preventing the various medical ailments that have been common to other aging family members.

I am extremely proud to say that I have made the full transition and am now an active member of the vegan society. I am more than willing to inform and educate meat eaters, especially those that I consider my friends and family; with statistics, opinions and non-meat options. I feel that I have found my calling and will continue living with a passion centered on the idea that by changing our societal eating habits we can have a positive affect on a world that is in great need of help. I feel rejuvenated and more quick-minded than I ever have in my life. It is through myself and other vegans that the dream of a cruelty-free society lives on.

LILLIAN MULLER, North Hollywood, CA
Actress and Cover Girl
Author — *Feel Great, Be Beautiful over 40!*
Interview by Marilyn Peterson

Lillian Muller has been on nine *Playboy* covers, is the most published Playmate of the Year in *Playboy Magazine* history, and has starred, guest starred and co-starred in thirty films and television shows all over the world.

Growing up on our mini farm in Norway, I ate a lot of pork, a lot of eggs, and milk right from the cow. That many years ago in rural Norway, organic was a way of life. The animals ate naturally, of grasses. There was no factory farming at that time, not like today. We raised chickens and pigs, and liver, pork chops, bacon and ham were our daily fare. Every Christmas my stepfather slaughtered a pig; our beloved pig, but it was our food supply because we were very poor.

Until I was twelve years old I drank a half gallon of cow's milk daily, but I was nursed on mother's milk until the age of two so that was the saving grace that built a strong foundation for me. I liked fruits and vegetables a little, but not much. I was more into mashed potatoes and gravy.

I arrived in America at age twenty-one and came directly to the Playboy Mansion as the 1976 Playmate of the year. My first boyfriend was Hugh Hefner of the Playboy Mansion, where I lived for one year. There I had 24-hour room service available to me; with all kinds of food choices like filet mignon, king crab legs, salmon and roasted chicken — a high protein diet. Definitely not vegan! I gained twelve pounds in my first six weeks!

A couple of years after I left my Playboy lifestyle, as I was studying acting in Hollywood, some health problems showed up. Anemia, dizzy spells, water retention in my joints; and I was plagued with anxiety and depression.

I became vegan three years after I came to America at age twenty-four. At that time I met a holistic doctor who set me on the path to recovery. That path was strewn with thorns as well as rose blossoms. Once I started to clean up my diet I began breaking out in boils, and had headaches from the toxic load that was being eliminated. I went "cold turkey," or the vegan version of that expression, "cold tofu" — no transition — nothing. I became a fruitarian for one year to detoxify my whole system. In that period of time I lost twenty pounds. All of my baby fat melted away and I became a very healthy 110-pound vegan. In the years to follow, I became more energetic and healthier than ever before!

Since that time I have varied my diet from vegetarian to vegan and fruitarian. On a fruitarian diet it was difficult to maintain my weight as a model and actress with a commercial look. I learned to use foods to adapt to my desired weight. In these last ten years I have cared more about quality of life and longevity than having a commercial look, so I remained vegan, with 85% of my intake coming from raw foods.

Today, I am a 100% raw food vegan, with mainly organic foods. I am also raising a sixteen-year-old daughter who has been a vegan since birth. I had a totally vegan pregnancy with a natural childbirth.

Longevity and quality of life are not my only reasons for being vegan. I don't see how a dead animal can benefit my health. Also, I think it is selfish to slaughter an animal for my taste pleasure. It is barbaric! If people would consider visiting a factory farm or a slaughterhouse, it would be easy for them to become vegan very quickly. When you eat meat, you take part in the killing of that animal through the chain of supply and demand.

Factory farming is polluting our ground water. We could feed the whole planet if we didn't eat animals. The steroids, hormones, antibiotics, uric acid, cholesterol and adrenalin poisoning of the scared animals — with all of these factors, why would I want to eat meat when I can eat so many delicious, healthy vegan foods? There is plenty of selection to choose from.

I would rather extend my life expectancy by 30% and so can you, if you start young enough. It is almost suicidal to eat all these animal products. Do you want to get old before your time and die prematurely?

When I was pregnant I wrote the book *Feel Great, Be Beautiful over 40!* and now I am writing another book. At age fifty-one, I posed for my first pin-up calendar in celebration of turning fifty. My youthful appearance is a direct result of the healthy vegetarian/vegan lifestyle I have chosen for the past twenty-nine years. People will often ask me if I have had a face lift, or chemical peel or liposuction. I have no need for superficial sex appeal; rather I enjoy promoting good health and lifestyle with wisdom.

I use my own experiences so that I can help guide other people to find the best lifestyle for them. As a keynote speaker at various California Health Expos and the Natural Health Group of Los Angeles, I am able to get my message of good health out.

Every day I enjoy being a positive role model for what I have found to be true. At age twenty-four, I was sought out by all the wrong type of men for all the wrong reasons. I was anxiety-ridden, insecure, and fearful. I didn't have much faith in myself. My power came from being a model. I didn't know who I really was, what I really wanted or what life was really all about. These days I have much more peace of mind and inner satisfaction.

Turning fifty was a big turning point for me. I believe when you are a half-century old, you better find your real life purpose and commit to serving it. Procrastination is one of the biggest obstacles we have as people. We always think "next Monday I will start." Turning fifty was a wake-up call to get my priorities in order. I have become more serious about my life. Whatever you feel is your mission in life, do it now — today. You may not have the opportunity tomorrow.

Every day when I wake up I remember this line from the movie *Dead Poet's Society* *"Seize the day and make your life extraordinary!"*

EVA STEFURAK, Haiku, HI
Twinkies and Whoppers Set the Stage for this Vegan Family

Both my husband and I grew up on very basic stuff like milk, cereal, bread, beef, potatoes, carrots, corn and apples. In my case, once my parents divorced, everything we consumed was convenient, like quadruple stacks of bread with deli slices, or three bowls of cereal in one sitting. I remember eating entire meals from the corner store, often comprised of peanut butter cups, soda, a container of chocolate cake frosting and corn-dogs. Though hard to imagine, our diets worsened in the teenage years when we could drive to take-outs and whimsically purchase anything with our own dollars.

My husband remembers his mother regularly coming home from work with "dinner in a bag." They stocked their pantry with discount store boxes of Twinkies and soda. I had been taught that vegetables and fresh foods were best, but rarely saw them. They certainly weren't available to me at the corner store and were discolored and overcooked at school.

Just out of college, my husband and I decided we wanted to have a garden. We also started checking out a variety of cookbooks from the library and bravely tried many recipes. Many cookbooks had tidbits on nutrition, and we became mildly interested in what we were putting into our bodies. Perplexed, we began to evaluate all sorts of diets, like Mediterranean, vegetarian, raw foods, grass-fed meat and poultry, vegan and so on.

With our "test kitchen" and growing nutritional knowledge, we discovered that we truly liked a wide variety of vegetables, nuts, spices, fruits and grains. We also enjoyed meat, dairy (especially cheese and yogurt) and poultry. However, we could not find any organic or grass-fed animal products, and felt we could give them up if we could not get the quality we desired.

Meanwhile, I tested positive for dairy allergies when trying to figure out the cause of frequent and severe migraines. So giving up dairy seemed reasonably beneficial and I began to try dairy alternatives like soy and almond milk, rice cheese and puréed tofu. These were all right, especially since the foods we were preparing were more flavorful, fresh and interesting, and didn't need to be smothered in cheese or finished off with a rich dessert. The best dairy-free recipes turned out to be vegan (which is ridiculously obvious now, but it wasn't back then), so we naturally chose more vegan meals.

After several years of wholesome vegetarianism, an interesting circumstance put us on a major meat-eating, dairy consuming path for nearly three years. We got involved with a pasture-fed, organic animal farm that provided raw, fresh products in our area. Since we enjoyed eating meat and dairy, and had heard of the benefits of raw dairy and grass-fed meats, we eagerly began consuming these difficult to find foods. With whole grains and fresh vegetables alongside, we thought our diet had evolved from processed and refined to healthy, natural and even ideal. We continued to consume raw cheeses, fresh eggs, homemade yogurt, tender meats and hearty stocks made with animal bones for many months. My husband even helped out on the farm, slaughtering chickens.

Without much expectation, two things came together to completely eliminate animal foods from our diet in a very short period of time. Though we were pleased with our choices, and actually thought a morning of sausage, eggs, cheese and butter was healing (no kidding!), our two-year-old daughter developed a menacing rash on one of her cheeks. The rash was troubling to watch as it would grow and recede over several weeks. Finally we decided to try an elimination diet to see if it was food-related. We soon found that dairy — even organic, local, and raw dairy — was causing her reddened patch. All along, our daughter *detested* milk: raw, fresh, chilled or warm, from cow, goat or sheep — we tried them all. Reluctantly, we decided to remove dairy from our household to support her, as she was simply too young to watch us eat cheese and yogurt when she could not.

About this time, we developed an acquaintance with a vegan nutritionist and picked up a book called *The China Study* by T. Colin Campbell. We were both amazed and devastated by Campbell's assertions that animal protein, especially bovine milk protein, drives heart disease and cancer. It was *animal protein*, not saturated fat and cholesterol that promoted *cancer*, not just heart disease. We discussed the topic endlessly with each other and anyone else who would willingly read the book. We even bought a case of *The China Study* books and eagerly distributed them to our friends and family.

We asked our new vegan friend why he chose to omit all animal foods, and to our surprise it didn't have anything to do with animal rights or sentimentality. He was a very credible, research-based thinker, and cited numerous recent studies to back up Campbell's statements. Thus, on the basis that we would *greatly* reduce our chances for major disease, we decided to become vegan. We also discussed a wide range of factors; our children's tastes, our growing repertoire in vegan cooking, as well as our attachment to animal foods. The clear decision to become vegan was the best and we have not once reconsidered.

Interestingly, the only difficulty we've gained with our transition to a plant-based diet is a social one. Mastering delicious vegan dishes is not terribly challenging once you commit to it. We feel neither doubtful nor deprived. Happily, everyone in our family is open to trying new foods. Though we're busy, we give home-cooked meals a special priority. Our grocery budget is large, since we view phytochemicals, minerals and vitamins from organic produce as our true health insurance. The gaping hole left by our carnivore diet quickly filled up with greens, vegetables, nuts and fruits.

We now drink *volumes* of green smoothies. Our daughters, ages two and five, eat more variety than anyone we know (adults included). When we ask our oldest if she misses yogurt or chicken, she says "No, I know you make such yummy food, like flax-banana pudding. Mom's restaurant! And chicken makes your heart really tired when you're old... I don't want that."

In contrast, however, the dynamic with contented meat eaters has been quite entertaining and tricky at times. We've found that once people know you're vegan, they get defensive. If they're a certain type, they might start listing off evidence of human meat-eating evolution. We smile and say, "Maybe so." We even say, "Hey — we used to slaughter our own chickens — we know where you're coming from." This is to say: "Don't worry, we're NOT judging you." We purposely lighten the conversation, stay respectful of each person's path, and *never* suggest or infer that carnivores are wrong, ignorant or insensitive. Only when someone is adamant or truly curious do we open up and discuss our personal story.

Since we're sometimes judged at the outset, a relationship occasionally suffers from the perceived difference. For instance, my husband's parents refuse to eat at vegetarian restaurants, but expect us to manage at their favorite grill house. We suspect they think we are purposely complicating our lives, so they want us to deal with the consequences, instead of meeting us somewhere in the middle. Granted, they surely remember us gobbling down cheeseburgers right alongside them only a few years back. In this small way, being vegan has altered our relationship with them. Perhaps, over time, an equitable understanding will emerge between us. Meanwhile, we'll let them see for themselves as we deal with the consequences of increased health, energy, joy, vitality, immunity and dietary simplicity.

MARTHA THEUS, Los Angeles, CA
Author — "Throwin' Down" Vegetarian Style!

I grew up in the Midwest, yet my mother was from the South. Growing up, I ate traditional *soul food*, which, even though it was tasty, was not the healthiest. I distinctly remember not liking vegetables at all. I was a very heavy meat eater and we also ate a lot of cheese and bread, and even fast food. Later I learned to love the taste of vegetables once I learned how to cook them, or actually, how NOT to cook them. You see, most southern cooking involves *overcooking* nearly everything, including vegetables, so I really didn't have an appreciation for them until I became a vegetarian.

I became a vegetarian in 1985, when I was introduced to a spiritual path by my future husband. One of the tenets of the path is the adoption of a lacto-vegetarian diet because we believe that it is unnecessary to take higher forms of life in order to survive. By adopting a vegetarian/vegan lifestyle, we lessen our karmic load.

Since my husband was already a vegetarian, it was actually quite easy because we were on the same page when it came to our philosophy of life. Our children were born and raised vegetarian and even though they are now in college, they are still vegetarian. Although we always gave them the choice, they understood and respected our spiritual philosophy and throughout their lives have adopted it as their own. It also helped that I created, or should I say "re-created" some of the typical dishes that their friends ate; only I substituted vegetarian ingredients. This way, they didn't feel deprived or too different in any way. It's funny, because many members in our extended family thought that our children would not grow up to be healthy if we didn't feed them meat. It turns out that my son is 6' 5", weighs 195 lbs and is on his college basketball team. My daughter is quite athletic as well and plays rugby on a local club team. Basically, we dispelled the myth that you need meat in order to grow up "big and strong." My children do not know any different since they were born and raised that way.

The one thing I noticed right away when I changed to a vegetarian diet was that my digestion improved dramatically. When I ate meat, I used to get severely constipated and I felt lethargic many times. After adopting a healthier diet, I became more regular and people even commented that my skin appeared fresher and even "glowed."

The idea for my book, *"Throwin' Down" Vegetarian Style!* came about when my daughter entered her third year in college and finally had an apartment instead of a dorm room. She had access to a kitchen and asked me to send her some recipes.

As I gathered the recipes, the book took on a life of its own. I decided to expand it into a manual about not only how we eat, but also the benefits of vegetarianism as a whole. America is in the grip of an obesity/health crisis and, although people are searching for alternatives, many don't know where to look. This is especially true for African Americans since our traditional foods can be very unhealthy. According to the American Obesity Association, 78% of African American women are overweight. Many are on the path to suffering related diseases such as diabetes, hypertension, and heart disease. My mother has all three of these and takes more than 12 medications per day just to maintain moderate health. This was a direct result of her diet and lack of exercise. As an African American woman, I felt this book would be a great resource for those women in particular and would show them how they can still enjoy our traditional *soul food* while using vegetarian ingredients.

My mother was lactose intolerant. In fact, many African Americans are lactose intolerant. Our family eats very little dairy because we just feel better when we don't. Occasionally, I will make dishes with rennet-less cheese, (rennet comes from animal sources) but that's about it. We never have real milk (we prefer soy milk) and we never have real ice cream (we prefer soy ice creams). I also have asthma so I limit the dairy in order to reduce the amount of mucous in my system that can add to asthmatic symptoms. Since we have eliminated nearly all dairy from our diet, we have all noticed a reduction in sore throats and common colds.

My daughter and I eat raw foods as much as possible. I feel that my digestion is better with drinking quantities of fresh vegetable juices that we all enjoy. Every so often, we will have complete meals that are raw to give our bodies a break from cooked food.

This is such an exciting time to be a vegetarian. The entire planet is going through a spiritual evolution and it seems that everyone is becoming more concerned about the environment and personal health. I feel so encouraged by this and also blessed to be able to help in any way!

SOORYA TOWNLEY, Reno, NV
Massage Therapist
"I Walked My Talk And Didn't Cave In!"
My Story

I was born into a family of Southerners who ate meat at every meal. We usually started with fried pork for breakfast. When I was in my middle twenties, I went to a yoga potluck and was introduced to vegetarianism. I think I was so toxic that the aroma of their food sickened me, and after I was served, I actually was afraid to taste anything. Instead, I hid my plate of food under a potted plant and left.

But fate stepped in and I found myself living next door to a pasture near San Luis Obispo. That first morning I accidentally looked deeply into the eyes of a cow. I heard myself say, "I've been eating you — oh I am so sorry!" From that moment on, I never touched another piece of flesh of any kind, not even fish. I guess you could call it going "cold turkey." (That was in 1969.)

After my life-transforming experience with the cow, I promptly walked into my first health food store and bought everything new and strange in sight, including soy granules. It was fun spending hours in the kitchen experimenting with different recipes for my roommates who were surprised that they really liked the food. I included cheese and eggs, so it wasn't that foreign to me. With all the soy "meats" I honestly never craved animal flesh again. Whenever I wanted a BLT I used a bacon substitute from the Worthington product line of vegetarian foods.

For about ten years I kept cheese and eggs in my diet. Then I began changing to soy cheese, but still eating eggs. Eight years ago (1999), I became vegan. My body naturally stopped desiring eggs. In fact, every time I would eat one, I had digestion problems. Then a boyfriend told me eggs are very hard to digest and that was my letting go point for eggs.

People say, "It's flu season." I say, "It's too much dairy around the holidays." I feel sad that friends don't understand what is making them sick. Last summer I tried to eat a meal with cheese because the restaurant accidentally gave me some on my dish. I couldn't eat more than a morsel. It just tasted too gross. Once you get away from it, you can actually taste it's from an animal. I have crossed over the mountain and feel it is impossible for me ever to go back to eating meat or dairy.

ERIKA'S STORY
I am now raising my granddaughter, Erika, who has been a vegetarian all her life, because I raised her mother, Charla, that way. Bless her; she held to it all her life. As a baby, Erika was allergic to dairy so I thought that was a blessing. But my daughter did begin to allow some dairy after a while because, with all the birthday

parties and play dates, it became too difficult for her to be that rigid. And Erika, as she began to mature, wanted to be more "normal."

When my daughter died and I began raising Erika, I inherited a child who was attached to the taste of eggs and dairy. Now that she is older she doesn't seem to be as sensitive so I am allowing both eggs and dairy, as I don't want her to feel deprived. But my goal is to eventually move her away from animal products. I am proud of Erika because she understands what it means to eat meat and she always tells the servers at restaurants she is a vegetarian as well as informing parents when she is a guest in their home. Since she was so young, I didn't want to pursue the vegan path just yet. I didn't want to show her the photos of how badly abused the animals are even for their by-products like milk and eggs. I still want her to have a childhood of not knowing the horrors of the world.

When Erika and I first came to live together, I insisted she drink fresh juice in the morning: I started with cucumber, and then slowly added celery, parsley and sunflower greens. At first she was upset and annoyed. I just kept being persistent about how the juice went immediately into her body cells and would help her brain, teeth and bones.

Sometimes she would yell, "I don't care!" It was a struggle and there were times I wondered if I was doing the right thing. At first, when I added the parsley, she said she felt like she was going to throw up. It took a lot of teaching and coaching to get her to see the benefits. I knew I had won though, when a parent told me Erika proudly shared that at her house she was now *juicing* for her health!

I don't know if it's a coincidence, but she hasn't been ill this last year even once, whereas I remember over the years her being so sick that a few times she was on antibiotics. Erika was always infected with something a couple of times in the winter. Aside from the juice, we eat a lot of raw food, big salads and lots of broccoli, spinach, etc. I have just this week added the Omega 3-6-9 oils to her diet.

What has also been difficult is that Erika lived on a lot of microwave processed foods before, and was used to that kind of taste. She has been upset overall by how different her diet is living with me, but I decided *not* to cave in; I just kept going, feeding her what I thought was best while adding a few foods from her former life. I notice she rarely says anything now. Not like she's resigned, more like she is used to the tastes.

I also make delicious, organic desserts. One day we were at a birthday party and there was this awful white flour, white sugar cake from the grocery store. I whispered to her, "If you don't eat it, we can make a healthy one later." She agreed. When we got home we made the healthier cake together. Once she tasted it, she squealed, "Grandma I get it, we just trade up!" That is our new catch phrase, our little inside joke; we "trade up."

Erika also watches all her friend's parents cave in by giving them anything they want. And she notices how they are all ill frequently. Their parents will say, "Oh Johnny had a runny nose and he was around my kids." It's always about these germs flying around, never a thought about white sugar, meat and dairy. One little girl in L.A. will only eat pasta, steak and peanut butter and jelly sandwiches. Several children had a conversation about her and said that her mom is being manipulated! They actually used that word and understood completely what it meant, and joked about what a "sucker" her mom was to be so afraid to be stronger, and insist her daughter eat healthier.

Erika's Uncle Christopher (my son) says that he respected me for always feeding him so well. He once came home from school, opened the refrigerator and said, "Thumbs up, Mom, for having such wholesome foods for me to eat. When I go to my friend's houses there is nothing in their fridge to eat — it's all junk." I appreciated that a lot. To this day he honors me for being strict with his nutrition. I believe that most kids want their parents to be stronger when it comes to their health, but parents are afraid their child won't love them if they don't cave in and feed them whatever they desire, which is usually depleted, dead food.

I had this experience with Erika: A few months ago I overheard her sharing with a couple of her other nine year-old friends who were sitting in a circle in our living room: "My grandma won't allow meat in our house and she, herself, is a complete vegan." Erika was sitting properly straight and her tone sounded reverent and solid. The children were wide-eyed and listening, like it was a fairy tale. I remember thinking, "Wow! It really is about being an example and all the talk in the world won't give you that." I felt content knowing in that moment that even if my granddaughter doesn't express anything to me up front, she is proud of the stand I have taken.

WILL TUTTLE, PhD, Healdsburg, CA
Author — *The World Peace Diet*
Interview by Nicolette Marais, Journalist

Nicolette: I know from your book, The World Peace Diet, *that you ate a Standard American Diet (SAD) for the first twenty years of your life and that you then began to study the cause and effect relationship between consuming animal products and our human existence. Would you tell our readers why you became vegan?*

Will: I became a vegan because of an intense yearning to reduce cruelty to animals at human hands. As I outline in *The World Peace Diet*, I became a vegetarian at the age of 22 (1975) when I visited "The Farm."

It was this powerful living example of the nearly 1,000 people at this community in Summertown, Tennessee, that provided the context for me to go decisively vegetarian at that time. Following this, I lived in Zen and Tibetan Buddhist meditation centers in both the southeastern US and then the San Francisco Bay Area. My motivation gradually deepened to include spiritual awareness and the understanding of karma as well as compassion for animals, people, and ecosystems. By 1980, I had become vegan because I had become sufficiently aware of the suffering inherent in dairy products and eggs. In 1984, I went to Korea and lived as a Zen monk in a monastery that had been practicing veganism for 650 years. This second living example of a vegan community decisively sealed my veganism, and I've been vegan ever since.

Nicolette: As Marilyn's book focuses on making the transition to a plant-based diet, would you elaborate on how you managed to make your own transition? What did you eat growing up? How long did it take you to make to make the transition? How did you do it?

Will: I was raised in a completely non-vegetarian atmosphere in Massachusetts and never remotely considered it until my last years at Colby College, when I began to learn about "The Farm" in Tennessee, and heard about vegetarianism through books and friends at Colby. For me, the experience of visiting and living in vegan communities was the essential support for my transition.

Nicolette: Do you have any advice to offer to readers who will be making a transition to a plant-based diet?

Will: My advice to readers making a transition to a plant-based diet is to read about and try to deeply understand the interconnections between food choices and animal cruelty, environmental devastation, world hunger, and physical, mental, and spiritual health. This strong foundation is essential to building a vegan life that will withstand the winds of opposition that will inevitably come from friends, family, doctors and other authority figures.

Additionally, it's important to remember that fruits and vegetables are natural detoxifiers and a healthy vegan diet will naturally begin cleaning and purifying the body. Toxins will be released for days, weeks, or even months as part of this beneficial process, and one may feel worse while this is happening. Animal-sourced foods, though basically toxic, have a potent placebo effect because of all of the indoctrination we're subjected to in our culture, so it's essential to remember our reasons for going vegan, and understand that all of our body's necessary nutrients can be obtained from plant-based sources. Animal foods contain much higher concentrations of pesticides, heavy metals, dioxins, hydrogenated fats, and other toxins, as well as saturated fat, cholesterol, acidifying protein, viruses, bacteria, plus grief, terror, and despair.

Nicolette: How did it come about that you (taken from your book) 'spent the past thirty years or so exploring the fascinating connections and cause-effect relationships between our individual and cultural practice of using animals for food and the stress and difficulties we create for each other and ourselves'?

Will: Over the past thirty years, I've been not only studying and experiencing the many implications of vegetarianism and veganism, but also simultaneously studying philosophy and education at the graduate level and teaching and lecturing. At the same time, I've been meditating on a daily basis and contemplating spiritual teachings about the interconnectedness of all phenomena. Startlingly significant relationships between our cultural food choices and our problems began emerging through this process, and fascinating patterns of ironies and understandings. These became the foundation of my book, *The World Peace Diet.*

Nicolette: Another important aspect that is close to Marilyn's heart and which she wants to make an important aspect of the book is karma — the cause and effect relationship of eating animal products. Would you summarize to the reader what this means and why this is important?

Will: Although I never use the word karma in *The World Peace Diet,* the underlying idea of karma is central to the book's thesis, that we reap what we sow. I call it the "boomerang effect," and emphasize the spiritual wisdom that reminds us that whatever we would most like for ourselves we are called to give to others. Sowing seeds of misery, disease, bondage, hopelessness, drug addiction, and despair in the animals we dominate and kill for food, we reap the same for ourselves. As we sow kindness, respect, freedom, and peace for others, we sow the same in our life experiences. In Chapter Three, I illustrate how virtually all of the problems we humans face and are unable to solve, we are inflicting directly on animals. We force obesity, osteoporosis, cancer, and disease on animals raised for food, and reap the same in ourselves; we sow seeds of breaking up their families, addicting them to drugs, imprisoning them, forcing them into child pregnancy, and terrorizing them, and reap all of these in our own lives, as we can see by reading any newspaper on any day. As a culture, we are naïve to think we can routinely sow seeds of pain, terror, theft, disease, confinement, stress, and despair in millions of sensitive beings every day, and find peace and justice for ourselves.

Nicolette: When I think of Malcolm Gladwell's book, The Tipping Point, *I wonder if there will be a tipping point for the idea of a karma-free diet? What are your thoughts on this?*

Will: I think if our culture manages to avoid a suicidal meltdown, then it would seem likely, as Thoreau said, that in our evolution, we will stop eating foods sourced from dominated animals. And as I say in *The World Peace Diet,* we must reach this tipping point or critical mass of veganism, and this transformation of our culture, if our culture is to be successful in continuing on this planet. Imagining our culture as a post-tipping point vegan culture, though, is imagining an almost completely different culture. It would be unrecognizably transformed, like a caterpillar into a butterfly.

Nicolette: Do you have any opinions on eating a predominantly raw/vegan diet?

Will: As Donald Watson, who coined the word "vegan" wrote, "There is only one motivation to be vegan, and that is compassion." I see veganism as a noble and ongoing path of spiritual awakening and purification. In the end, veganism is pointing to a profound personal and cultural transformation where all cruelty and violence are transcended. There is no path higher than vegan. Neither raw vegan nor cooked vegan is higher, and if the underlying motivation is reduced to concern for personal health rather than compassion for others, there is a danger of violence being justified for oneself. I think some important additional dimensions of veganism are buying organic foods and foods that are grown locally as much as possible.

Nicolette: Is there anything else you would want to comment on for the readers about being vegan or about karma?

Will: Though veganism is typically seen as deprivation in our culture — as giving something up — it is quite the opposite. We gain enormously by going vegan — inner peace, joy, freedom from the consensus trance, terrific new vistas of delicious food. And though it is one of the noblest actions a human can take, going vegan is nothing to be proud of. It is our *natural* human seeing when we are able to extricate ourselves from our cultural conditioning. It is simply seeing beings rather than things or commodities when we look at animals, and allowing our natural compassion and sanity to guide us in our actions. We become part of the solution, and realize our purpose: that we're here to bless the world.

Nicolette: How has becoming vegan changed your life?

Will: Becoming vegan was for sure the single best thing I've ever done in my life. It is the foundation of a life of meaning, joy, creativity, inner peace, and spiritual sensitivity. Eating animal foods is, I can now see, a pernicious form of culturally induced slavery that is both pervasive and invisible. I have wonderful health, terrific friends, and richly rewarding experiences every day of my daily life adventure. Being vegan is being free of the un-faced guilt of killing by proxy, and of eating terror, fear, and despair. For me, after 30 years, it's like leaving hell and entering heaven. It never ceases to amaze me how people grumble and resist going vegan so strongly! The door is always open, but few actually seize the day and walk through it into a life of freedom and harmony. My greatest joy is to help others break the cultural addiction and come home to the freedom of compassion and to being a force for kindness in the world.

MARK VIERGUTZ, Ventura, CA
Photographer, Food Writer
A Hummingbird's Confirmation

Having now (Summer, 2007) been a vegetarian for nearly thirty-five years, the last ten of which have been vegan, my recollections on making the transition to become a vegetarian have taken on a little bit of a patina. Fortunately, enough detail remains to still tell the story.

This all began when I was 16 years old. I deliberately selected a specific date to officially become a vegetarian so that I wouldn't forget it. I chose Thanksgiving Day in 1972. On that morning, I came traipsing down the stairs of our apartment and announced to my mother that I wouldn't be eating that bird, today, because I was now — *ta-dah!* — a vegetarian!

"You're whhaaatttttt?!!!," was her stunned, if not entirely unexpected, response.

I suppose I could've waited one more day, but it seemed necessary, at the time, to make a statement of principle by which to abide and hold to. Nevertheless, making the complete transition to becoming a lacto-vegetarian took about six months. I still ate some eggs, mostly in the form of vegetable omelets and occasional seafood, which I'd only taken up eating a couple of years prior.

We were living in Carmel, California, and I was a senior in high school. As indicated, it was 1972, the height of the counter-culture movement; hippies, revolution, and rock and roll. I'd read about vegetarianism, and had the good fortune to live in a time and place where small health food stores and natural restaurants were easy to find. That's when I discovered the then ubiquitous avocado, Muenster cheese, and sprout sandwiches on whole-wheat bread. El Torito, in Cannery Row, also had veggie tostadas on their menu, along with the usual complement of cheese enchiladas, rice, beans, and guacamole. However, I wasn't, as yet, aware enough to inquire about lard, so I'm sure I consumed my share of it with each helping of refried beans served to me there.

Veggie pizzas were also easy to come by. However, the fare in most natural foods restaurants wasn't too sophisticated, consisting, in addition to the aforementioned avocado sandwiches along with variations on that theme, the usual patchouli-scented hippie staples of brown rice, steamed veggies, and salads. I also frequented a wonderful deli right on Ocean Avenue, in Carmel, that had these marvelous dark rye rolls, which I'd get with slabs of cheese.

So, I started out by doing what many novice vegetarians often do: consuming lots of dairy, and, without giving it much thought, plenty of animal fat; primarily in the form of cheese, since I never was too fond of milk. When I finally decided to become *vegan*, winter of 1998, it was after contemplating the realization that consuming animal fat shouldn't really be part of a true vegetarian diet. I then lost fifteen pounds over the first two weeks, without even trying to do so. Cutting out the daily consumption of cheese produced an immediate change in my body. I never looked back.

In fact, it was my love of animals, and the desire to no longer consume them, that happened to be the primary motivation for my conversion to vegetarianism. Unfortunately, at the time, I was *unaware* of factory farming practices and thought that consuming dairy products didn't harm cows, which I used as justification for eating these products. Because I was somewhat aware of the health benefits of being vegetarian, I simply looked upon the transition to becoming vegan as an added bonus.

Along with my vegan diet I also began taking multivitamins regularly, just to make sure I got the proper nutrients. I still do to this day and credit antioxidants for the youthful appearance I've managed to maintain all these years.

Around the same time that I became a vegetarian, either just before or not long afterward, my brother and I had an almost mystical encounter with a little hummingbird which convinced me that there was more to animals than most people were aware of or realized, affirming my conviction that these wonderful creatures (all animals) should never be harmed or eaten.

One afternoon I came home to find that my brother, Dwayne, had rescued a hummingbird from the clutches of a cat. With wet and ruffled feathers, it was still alive, but limp and going into shock. I immediately seized it from him and began barking out orders. "Get me a towel to wrap it in. Heat up some water and put some honey and sugar in a saucer. Add the warm water to it, and bring it to me."

In the meantime, I wrapped the bird up to keep it warm and gently stroked its damp feathers to smooth them back down. As I did this, the bird looked up at me with one eye while its head nestled into the towel. Then my brother brought over the sugar-water solution I had him prepare. Ever so gently, I slipped the edge of the hummingbird's beak into the syrup. Within a few moments a long, thin tongue shot out of the beak into the saucer's solution, and the bird started to consume the liquid. I was thrilled.

All those years of watching wildlife documentaries were now paying dividends because that's how I knew that these birds needed constant infusions of sweet nectar and sucrose to satisfy their enormous energy requirements.

Pretty soon, the little guy started to perk up. After several licks of the solution it began to sit up. Although I kept it wrapped in the towel, the little bird was now holding its head up and looking into my face. It didn't seem to have any fear of me either and let me continue to stroke its head. Finally, my puny patient seemed sufficiently recuperated for me to let it go. So Dwayne and I took it to a large bare-limbed oak tree in a field across from the front yard of our apartment. I placed the hummingbird up on a limb. It just sat there and looked down at us. Then we left.

Our mother's upstairs bedroom had a large bay window overlooking the field we had just returned from so I suggested that the two of us go up there and observe really couldn't have seen much beyond the ...ummingbird suddenly flew up to the window ...m the glass, directly in front of our faces, and ..., before flying away. When it disappeared, I ...k the hummingbird just came to thank us." ...orever changed and strengthened my respect ...*all* creatures big and small; sentient beings ...continue to reflect on, which makes me so ...n to never eat them, or anything made from

, CA

...ducts. There ...and bagels, ...les, typical ...hat my par-ents were healthy, but my mother got sick when she was in her late 50s and passed away at 58 from a brain tumor. My grandmother and grandfather both died from heart attacks, and my dad had prostate cancer. By that time I was a bit more nutrition savvy and encouraged him to eat better, but he wasn't interested.

In 1970 I became interested in yoga. While studying, I read a passage in a yoga book that said, "Yogis don't eat dead flesh." I thought, "I eat dead flesh at every meal." The book suggested that I consider a vegetarian diet but not to tell anybody because people tended to disapprove.

I had never even heard of a vegetarian diet so I became sort of a closet vegetarian. I ate dairy and eggs, but cut out all dead flesh. I did this for three years and finally told my husband — but I *certainly* wasn't going to put my children on this diet. I was sure that if they didn't get their "protein," (meaning meat) that I would be doing them great harm. I remained vegetarian for quite a long time and didn't really miss eating meat. My family thought I was a little kooky and weird. Later, after going through a divorce, I started dating a guy, a carnivore, who was a great cook and I resisted it as long as I could, but in 1974 went back to eating animal products.

After seven or eight years as a meat eater, my immune system was rather weakened by my food choices and I got German measles (at age 42). It had a disastrous effect on my body; I became paralyzed in the hospital for several months. It was a rather sobering period in my life. During that time, I had a spiritual experience that opened me up to recognizing I was a spiritual being having a human experience.

---

[1]   For details on Detox Programs contact Tatiwren@mac.com.

The primary message was that I would be okay and to be open to something radical and different.

I had no idea what that might be, but two years later somebody gave me John Robbins' book, *Diet for a New America*. I was trying to eat better; I didn't want to get sick again, and the doctors warned me that I would have reoccurrences of paralysis (which I have never had). Once I read *Diet for a New America*, I realized that I could become a vegan for the sake of the animals, for the environment, and for my own body temple, my own health. It was a very compelling book, an education, and it made me realize that being vegan is a viable choice.

It took me four months after reading the book to actually get up the courage and make the commitment, and say, "Okay, I am going to be a vegan." It was totally scary, because I was an excellent chef but I always used butter, cream and eggs. I could really cook but had no idea how I would feed myself once I became vegan. So after my commitment to myself, I went into the kitchen and cried my eyes out, got it all out and said, "Okay I will have to *re-learn*, make some changes and teach myself by reading some vegetarian cookbooks." I threw away *Joy of Cooking*, my former cooking bible. I didn't realize at that time that I could have used it and made vegan substitutes for the animal products. I threw out everything that had meat or dairy.

I never put it together that the cute little ducks running around the pond in parks were the same ducks that I was cooking in my gourmet cooking class. I didn't put it together that a leg of lamb was actually the leg of a little animal. When I finally did put it together, after reading *Diet for a New America*, there was no way that I could ever eat another animal. It was a *powerful* book that absolutely changed my life.

The transition for me was daunting and exciting. I knew I was a good cook but this was something I knew nothing about. I started going to health food stores and they had weird things like tofu. I took home some tofu, tasted it and thought, "Oh my God, this tastes awful!" Then I realized that it was just a raw ingredient, like flour, and that I had to start playing with it, messing with it, using seasonings. It was all an experiment. I would get an ingredient that I knew nothing about, take it home and play with it to see what I could do.

I was so moved by John Robbins' book that I was not going to ever go back. Factory farming, the way the animals were treated like commodities, how our water was being polluted and our trees were being cut down, the cruelty and all the deleterious health effects — I was already there. I went "cold tofu," determined to stay on the path. I wasn't getting sick anymore.

I started to do classes at my home. Many people that were ill or had ill spouses were making changes, getting off of their medications. They would say, "I don't think I can become vegan," but when they did become vegan they got healthy. It became an inspired path for me.

At that time I started to hear about raw foods, and I just love salads with delicious dressings. I found the Farmer's Market and bought the top quality produce, learning about why organic is better. I kept educating myself, getting stronger about my beliefs in eating and how to nourish the body. I began playing around with making raw foods, and that resonated with me. It was quite natural, so I started to gravitate toward eating more and more raw foods, finding raw food restaurants, making recipes, and experimenting. I love to experiment. I feel like an alchemist creating magic in the kitchen.

I found the raw transition to be a journey. I had no inkling when I became vegan that there was even a raw lifestyle; that some people ate only raw; it was a revelation to me. I already felt confident about being vegan and began playing around with the raw recipes. I didn't have any cookbooks but I would grind nuts up and make different things with nuts and seeds. By 1995 raw had piqued my interest and I was hooked, convinced that it was probably the healthiest food to eat.

I had a wonderful mentor in Michael Klaper, MD. I felt safe with the information he gave me about how the human body had no requirements for animal protein and so I never worry about that. I get my protein from greens, apples, nuts and seeds. I don't go out of my way to get protein; I just eat what I want to. Every time I get my blood checked all of my levels are pretty much right on. I do take a Vitamin B12 supplement from time to time, but I don't take many supplements.

I would offer to the readers this advice from my experience: Make sure you don't get hungry. When traveling, bring food that is high-quality organic so that you don't have to rely on stopping at a Fish and Chips restaurant, eating something like iceberg salad and French fries. As you are transitioning, go to health food stores for interesting vegan and raw snacks to munch on when you are out on the road.

As a vegan I have never felt deprived. I say, "Thank you, God" for showing me a better way.

I feel eternally grateful!

Life Is Just A Bowl Of Cherish
A brief and entertaining biography of an unusual life journey

MESSAGES FROM CHILDHOOD

THE VISION

When I was a child, around 9 years old, I had a vision. We lived in East Los Angeles, a short distance from the county General Hospital (where my father was a frequent patient). I can remember standing on the bridge facing the gray cement hospital, silently witnessing the cries of suffering patients, seemingly boxed into that gray cement hospital like cattle in cattle cars. In the vision, I saw myself all dressed in white with gold colors over my head and my mission was to ease suffering. For years this bothered me, since I was not a doctor and had no inclination to be one. How could I possibly help ease suffering? Then clarity came; I was to help people stay *healthy*, so they didn't have to go to hospitals.

Marilyn at Age 5

FURTHER CLARITY

Many years later, in my adult life, as my work with vegetarian food took shape; another part of this vision from childhood was clarified. I realized that seeing people crowded into hospitals, like cattle in cattle cars, meant that part of my work was to help prevent the suffering of animals. Now that it's clear and I'm teaching transition, the bridge I was standing on at the time of the vision has significance also. The bridge is a way to cross over, to make the transition.

259

FANTASY FOOD

There were early indicators of my role to come. As a child I used to play in the back alley with containers and substances as if I were a chef. There was a large aluminum bin where people tossed out bottles, jars and cans. I would find a discarded cooking pot and something to stir it with. There were often small amounts of mayonnaise or ketchup, etc., on the sides of the discarded jars. I took delight in combining these with liquids and other "ingredients" from cans, spending hours of time happily mixing concoctions and creating recipes in my imagination. I was never so happy as when I could be in my secret (alley) kitchen cooking up fantasy foods in wild combinations and serving them to imaginary guests.

OPPOSITES ATTRACT

- ✧ Mom: Pioneer in nutrition, natural healing and vegetarian diet. Emotional make-up: Kind, co-dependent, victim/martyr, caregiver

- ✧ Dad: Pharmacist, teacher of medicine, carnivore/sugar addict, in constant physical pain. Emotional make-up: Intellectual, violent, emotionally abusive, raving maniac

SHE

My mother, Sheila, lived in Rhode Island and had two children by her first marriage, Roselyn and Louis. Roselyn was a sickly child with a pale complexion, watery eyes and nose, and no energy. One day, while Mother was with the children at a park, she happened to see a child who looked like the picture of health, with sparkling eyes and rosy cheeks. She asked the child's mother what she was doing to achieve this remarkable result and the woman replied that she had been under the guidance of Dr. Max Warmbrandt[1] in Connecticut. This inspired my mother to take a trip to Connecticut and consult with Dr. Warmbrandt. His advice was to put Roselyn on a three-day fast using only fresh orange juice. The results were remarkable as Roselyn gained color in her cheeks and a twinkle in her eyes. Feeling inspired by these first results, my mother began studying natural health and later became a pioneer in her own right.

After her first husband died, my mother moved to Los Angeles, California, with two small children, my stepsister and stepbrother, and started a new life. There she met and married the man who was to become my father.

HE

My father, a pharmacist, taught medicine. He was steeped in the knowledge and belief of chemical medicines. My father had several degenerative conditions when

---

[1] Dr. Max Warmbrandt, of Connecticut, was a pioneer in holistic health and vegetarianism over 75 years ago. He got remarkable results with his patients using vegetarianism and natural methods.

he married my mother: Encephalitis,[2] Parkinson's disease, arthritis, and (he later developed) bowel cancer. As a result, he became a pharmaceutical addict. He was also emotionally abusive and physically violent, a danger to himself and everyone around him.

HE vs. SHE

My parents' perspectives were polarized opposites and both wanted to be "right." I was a pawn in the middle. One time, when I was about five years old, this was dramatically acted out. The three of us were in the park and my parents were having an argument about feeding me at a time when I was sick. My father pulled one arm saying, "Feed my child!" My mother pulled the other arm, countermanding, "Don't feed my child, she's sick!" Each arm was being pulled in the opposite direction. I was terrified! It felt like my tiny little arms were being pulled out of their sockets.

DOMESTIC VIOLENCE

Domestic violence was an ever-present threat in my home. I was afraid to speak out. Even though my mother somehow managed to give me tap dance, singing and piano lessons, ballet and gymnastics classes, I couldn't be present. I cried often and found no peace. At age seven or younger I was an overeater. I was too young to realize that I was eating over my negative emotional feelings; fear and a desperate will to survive haunting me constantly. I had no place to go where I could feel safe from these pressures. I bought and ate way too much food at school. At home, Mother would say, "Marilyn, are you at the refrigerator again? You can't be hungry!" I was trying to fill myself up to avoid the fear and emptiness. I started losing parts of the whole, bit by bit, until I was in pieces. This chipping away of the true self was eating away at me as I was eating my way through the pantry!

THE MARRIAGE OF THE MARRIAGE

Later, as an adult, I had to determine for myself whether medicine or Nature was the right path for me. I discovered there was a way to marry the two and live happily ever after. Each path had a valuable role to play in supporting health and easing suffering. I carefully chose the best of what each (parent) had to offer. I took my mother's constant, fanatical lecturing about health and transformed it into my own style of giving lectures — and getting paid for it! I also learned about foods as medicine. My father taught me that anger hurts and he modeled suffering. I couldn't stop his suffering but yearned to ease suffering for others. As a young child, I used to sing and dance for the old people's home because I wanted to ease their suffering. When we suffer, we gain compassion for others. It was on my way to visit my father in the hospital that I stood on that bridge in front of the hospital and had the childhood vision of easing suffering.

---

[2] Encephalitis is an inflammation of the brain that also affects the entire nervous system.

FOND MEMORIES

Health was the biggest topic in our house because of my mother's constant fascination (obsession) with it. My mother would take me to chiropractors, and doctors who were on the cutting edge, *without* cutting the patient. Many of these doctors turned out to be prominent doctors in the natural health field, such as Dr. Bernard Jensen who was our family doctor, Dr. Phillip Lovell, Dr. Bragg, Jr., son of Dr. Paul Bragg, author and lecturer on natural healing. I was a patient of Dr. Henry Beiler, author of *Food is Your Best Medicine*. Although it sounds as if I was a sickly child, it was not the case. These were doctors in *preventive* medicine and nutrition. Even as a child, I loved what I was learning about health.

HELD HEALTH HOSTAGE

I was given very strong programming about health as a child. *What* my mother taught was more nurturing than the *way* she taught it. Her "coaching" was inserted at every opportunity. Not bad if you voluntarily signed up for the class but I was drafted against my will.

"Marilyn, chew your food very, very slowly."

"Drink your solids and chew your liquids."

"I can't believe you are hungry, you just ate a little while ago."

"Germs do not live in a clean blood stream."

Maybe other draft dodgers have had some of these experiences: If I didn't eat the vegetables that were put in front of me, I was told that it was okay, just to come back and eat when I was hungry. And when I did come back, the same food was put before me. That was the true hunger test. It really got my goat, no kidding (pun intended).

I can remember a time when my mom gave me a big salad in a bowl to eat for my lunch and I hid the salad, including the bowl in the linen closet. First, I carefully buried the bowl underneath some blankets and said, "Okay, I'm finished." "Where's the salad bowl?" she replied. Reluctantly, I had to uncover my crime. And what is my favorite meal as an adult? YES! You guessed it! A big bowl of salad!

When I was going to junior high school, I can remember I always ate alone at lunchtime. My mom used to give me tomato and onion sandwiches or tomato and pepper sandwiches at times. Either I was embarrassed to eat with other kids, fearing they would think my lunches were weird, or my breath was so bad no one wanted to eat with me. Even though my mom made healthy sandwiches for me, somehow I finagled lunch money to buy junk food. I would keep the sack lunches from home in my locker until the mold smell crept out, identifying my dirty deeds.

THE KING OF GREEN

When I was in my teens, I remember a time when "Gypsy Boots," the "Tarzan" of the health field, and his friends were upstairs in our apartment playing tambourines, dancing barefoot and grating cabbage on a washboard. (We used the washboard as a substitute grater because we didn't have a regular one.) He was a free spirit, progressive, and a symbol of Nature. One might have pictured him in a jungle swinging from a tree with a coconut in each hand and the rope between his teeth. He was very prominent in directing people to the health field and Nature. He later became a TV personality.

Gypsy would hold his birthdays at one of the (Hollywood) studio lots and he would foot the bill for a vegetarian banquet. He was a devotee of fruits and nuts even though, at that time, people may have considered him one of the nuts. I would describe him as a legend in his own time.

TEEN REBEL

My "pioneer" mother became my first teacher in nutrition. In spite of her good intentions, however, she was obsessed with nutrition and forced her views on everyone around her. Those close to her became hostages of this fanaticism. Shortly after our delightful visit from Gypsy Boots, my mother got a strong notion that we should all become vegetarian. This challenged my teenage spirit. She and I had many a heated discussion:

"Marilyn, the best thing for you is to become completely vegetarian."

I would cry, "Please, no more!"

She'd retort, "It's the healthiest diet there is!"

"For you!" the stubborn teenager yelled back. "I need to find out what's healthy for me!"

LUNCH AT MGM

At age twenty, I worked at MGM. There were about sixteen of us girl mail messengers, and one male mail messenger; the future, famous actor, **Jack Nicholson.**

The messengers all loved the healthy lunches my mother packed for me, made up of avocado, chopped olives with lots of veggies and other healthy foods. They would *beg* me to trade with them. Their bologna sandwiches were something I was not allowed to have, so I loved swapping my lunch for this tasty, forbidden food. I thought I was getting a treat but it was actually a trick; they got the treats and I was full of bologna. At MGM, healthy eating had caught on, so the rest of the messengers looked forward to the sack lunches I brought from home and I short-changed myself until I changed in later years.

OVER THE HILL OVEREATER

Not only was I a "junk-food junkie," I was also a big time overeater well into my mid-forties, which I find hard to believe since I still claim to be 35. What I learned about overeating from my experience is that the body is hungry for *REAL* nutrition, and it eats and eats, craving the necessary energy, hoping that it will come from the next bite of food! But the empty calories from processed and depleted foods never satisfy the body's needs. After I became vegetarian and very strict about taking the white out of my diet, (sugar, milk, white flours, etc.) my overeating stopped. The solid, whole food nourishment was there and the emptiness from empty calories was gone. Included in this struggle with overeating, I reluctantly discovered, was the idea that we "eat over our emotions." I had to meet this head-on, examine my own psychology and learn what was eating (at) me.

"I WILL NEVER BE LIKE MY PARENTS!"

(Ha, ha!) When I got married, I received great support from my mother. She bought a blender, juicer and other kitchen gifts and helped me set up a natural kitchen. She was a strong influence. Not knowing how to raise a child, I realized that the only way that made sense to me was the way I had been taught. I felt fortunate that I had Mother for support. On an intuitive level, I knew she was correct because she followed the laws of Nature. I remember thinking, "Nature has been around for a long time and has more wisdom than I could ever have."

I began having challenging experiences raising my children. Now the shoe was on the other foot. My first child, Stacy, was on a doctor-recommended cow's milk formula and had not slept at night in ten weeks. She showed signs[3] of being allergic to cow's milk. I put her on a soy formula and she did fine and slept like an angel! The milk to soy milk transition was a wake-up call for me. Later, my son, Stewart, was very ill but I noticed good results from the natural methods (fresh juices) I was using. Doctors objected to what I was doing and not medicating my son, saying I was living in the *"dark ages,"* but I could see how the children were being helped and the doctors' advice was not part of that help.

I took a stand for what I believed in and decided to raise the children on natural methods. I was excited about this; my husband and mother-in-law were not. I stood my ground, however, and said it was not on the table for discussion. Once my mother's influences kicked in, they stayed. Although I had not yet surrendered to the idea of being vegetarian, I did as much as possible to provide healthy foods for the children. For example, I made baby foods in the blender with fresh fruits and vegetables. I used to tell all the neighbors not to feed my children; I didn't want them eating things that I had already eliminated from their diet for health reasons. One day Stacy came home and said, "Claire gave me ice cream but she told me not to tell you." Stewart would also snitch!

IN RETROSPECT

I will say that because of my mother's fanaticism about the vegetarian diet, etc., there was a time when I threw the baby out with the bathwater, so to speak. I rejected her ways just because it was a concept from *her*; I was still angry with her for having forced her diet ideals on me as a child. If she had just done it and not been in my face about it, she could have given her vegetarian influences without my knowing about it. But once an announcement is made, once someone takes a stand, people

---

[3] Projectile vomiting after bottle formula feeding was one strong sign.

tend to get up in arms about it whether the advice is good or not. We don't want anyone telling us what to eat. It follows, of course, that my children were perfect mirrors of my own childhood attitude. And, like me, they rebelled but made good efforts to use the health teachings in their adult years.

CRASH AND BURN

Married at age twenty-two, divorced and a single mom (of two) at thirty-one, trying to sort out my confusion, I rebelled against my mother's teachings, my father's abuse, and my failed marriage. Alcohol and drugs took the spotlight until I nearly blew out all my systems. It was the mid-sixties; I took a dive into the world of experimental drugs. Those were wild and reckless *experimental* drug days. My emotional and mental balance deteriorated along with the physical. I wasn't a happy camper and even *forgot* how to spell happiness. I gradually became catatonic and suicidal. At this stage, I was diagnosed with a severe case of hypoglycemia.[4]

THE REBEL SURRENDERS

This was the beginning of my own survival, my own journey to health. It was a time of desperation. Finding myself at the bottom with no way out, I screamed, *"God, help me!"* My cry was heard; spiritual books, teachers and guides surfaced to show me the way. Sometimes, while reading these special books, the *Bhagavad-Gita* (The Holy Song of God) is one that comes to mind, I remembered being happy. I rediscovered that inner sanctuary I had taken refuge in as a child. I found peace and solace in the sacred teachings that began unfolding before me.

TREASURES IN THE ASHES

What could a maniac father and a martyr mother possibly give me? As I was lifted by Spirit and slowly awakened from the nightmares of childhood, culling through the ashes of burned out trust and love; I discovered valuable gems that could not have been gained any other (easier) way. Happiness was mine, but at a price; I had to take responsibility for my life, see my parents as teachers, and learn to forgive. I had to outgrow the "victim" role and mature enough to be able to appreciate the script I was given, the obstacles I had to overcome to find the "Golden Fleece," the prize of this harrowing journey. There was no room for growth as long as I held on to anger, blame and resentment.

REFRIGERATOR EPIPHANY

In the midst of personal agony (the end of a two year love affair), I had gone to a party at a friend's house and was in the kitchen by myself when I opened the refrigerator in search of a beverage. Suddenly I saw plastic-wrapped packages of meat, animals cut up and surrounded by their own blood. The visual effect hit me

---

[4] Hypoglycemia, in the advanced stages, is very similar to schizophrenia. Google "Hypoglycemia mimics schizophrenia" for various articles. "Glucose Tolerance in Schizophrenia" by Jack L. Ward, MD.

like a sledgehammer! The sensitivity of my own suffering at that time forced me to relate to the suffering of those slaughtered animals. When I closed the refrigerator door I knew I was a vegetarian from that moment on! Meat, chicken and fish immediately fell away and eggs/dairy were later eliminated as I gained more knowledge and experience in transitioning.

BACK TO THE GARDEN

The emotional poisons of my childhood colored my consciousness and led me to rebellion, but the path back to Nature, to the promise of health was always there. Because I was raised on natural methods from birth, this "Garden of Eden" was my heritage, a path to walk in life. After the hypoglycemic collapse I began to recall

it and travel that path. I knew that healing and transformation was in that garden and if I visited it and followed the laws of Nature, I would reap the benefits.

Recalling my mother's teachings, I consulted with a couple of natural health doctors. Henry Beiler, MD, author of *Food is Your Best Medicine*, was one of my doctors. He recommended a vegetarian diet; Dr. Bernard Jensen, my family doctor and mentor *also* helped me along the road to health. I was no longer eating meat, fish and chicken but continued to eat eggs because of my understanding of the Jewish dietary tradition. Originally I thought that eggs were classified as dairy and not animal flesh food. Everything gradually improved and I regained my physical/mental balance. The (teenage) rebel *did* find out what was healthy for her.

BABY STEPS

At first, I found the vegetarian diet and food preparation difficult to understand. Even with my background and training, it took me five years to master the transition to a vegetarian diet and gradually integrate these lifestyle changes. The changes were small and slow, and they came about *bite by bite.*

BEGGAR'S BANQUET

My lifestyle during this transition did not afford me the opportunity for chef school. Instead I was given times of poverty with little or no food in the house. I discovered the food co-op's dumpster discards and was forced to be creative because of the limitations. My cooking talents came to life as I learned to create a tasty variety from limited resources. I was that child chef again, creating something from nothing in my secret kitchen.

TRANSITION WITHIN TRANSITION

The step from a meat-based diet to a vegetarian diet was one big leap. Several years later, I discovered the harmful effects of eggs. It happened in two stages. First I gave up eggs and years later (1981) after learning that dairy was not healthy, I became vegan.

This is how it happened:

THE BODY/MIND/SPIRIT PICTURE

I was living in the California Santa Cruz Mountains and had heard about a chiropractor who was revered for his knowledge and humanitarian spirit. I had already been to a medical doctor who recommended a supplemental program that I had to decline because it was way out of my financial reach. I didn't have much choice; I told him, at his price I would just have to die and be buried in his office. After this I met a chiropractor, Dr. Ed Jarvis, who indicated that I was in serious trouble with my health and needed to take immediate action. Dr. Jarvis didn't charge me; he was a true humanitarian.

When I saw Dr. Jarvis, I told him, "I'm going crazy!" He seemed to understand my physical condition of hypoglycemia and he recognized something else I didn't understand. He told me I needed to be around very positive vibrations, and that my soul was "screaming to go home." When I heard that, I thought *he* was crazier than I was.

He gave me a Polarity Therapy[5] treatment, balancing the energy systems of the body. He suggested I read *Spiritual Discourses by* Maharaj Charan Singh, which he gave to me. Dr. Jarvis also described the symptoms of schizophrenia[6] as a way of paying off karma[7] and evolving spiritually. Schizophrenia is a process of transformation.[8]

At this point, due to my earlier instant transition experience, I was no longer eating meat, fish or fowl but was still eating eggs and dairy.[9] Dr. Jarvis put me on a new segment of my transition diet program; suggesting that I now eliminate the eggs. Because I had been eating the heavier, dense, egg and dairy products, he suggested cottage cheese in the morning in keeping with a need to feel full and get nourishment. I remembered that my family doctor, Dr. Bernard Jensen, had always recommended fruits for breakfast. I thought I knew more than the chiropractor, and did the transition "*my way.*"

"*My way*" led me to more and more confusion. Because of my hypoglycemic condition, fructose — the natural sugars found in fruit — threw me even more off-balance and I continued, in my dietary ignorance, to struggle with the symptoms of (hypoglycemic/schizophrenic) insanity. I had to learn the hard way what

---

[5]   A holistic energy balancing system based on ancient healing principles.
[6]   Advanced symptoms of hypoglycemia are very similar to schizophrenia.
[7]   Coincidentally, I was working part time at a facility for the mentally ill.
[8]   Page 74 of *The Only Dance There Is* by Ram Dass explains the process of transformation.
[9]   In Jewish tradition eggs are actually considered neutral, neither meat or dairy "Parve."

a vegetarian, specifically a hypoglycemic vegetarian, should eat. All sweets, fruits included, had to go.[10]

FRUITION

As I shopped and examined packages of food I was unfamiliar with, not knowing what to eat or how to prepare them, I realized that there would be others, like myself, experiencing health problems, who would turn to a vegetarian diet for relief and that they too would not understand how to make the transition. I had never heard of vegetarian cooking classes. That's not to say they didn't exist; I just never heard of them. Finding little or no help in my own transition, I decided at that time that my life's work would be the Transition Diet. This was approximately 1970. My health slowly improved, but I was still experiencing dramatic, extremely difficult symptoms of mental and emotional imbalance. My search for peace was fraught with suffering. This eventually led to the discovery of a path of Yoga after which many inner questions were put to rest peacefully.

CAREER ENFOLDMENTS AND UNFOLDINGS

Once on the path to personal health, using my experience and experimentation methods, I spring-boarded from experience to experience, cooking, catering, consulting and teaching, privately and with groups.

MY LUCKY BREAK

I had been cleaning cabins in the Santa Cruz Mountains so I could be home with my children and was asked to clean up at a doctor's seminar. They said I did a beautiful job and asked me to come back the next week. I came back with my

With Dr. Pierre Pannetier at a Polarity Therapy Workshop in Seattle, Washington (1982)

cleaning supplies, and they asked, "What's that?"

I said, "I thought you wanted me to come back."

They said, "We do, but we don't want you to clean, we want you to cook!"

I told them I didn't know how to cook, and they said, "Don't worry we'll teach you." They then went on a break and I don't remember them *ever* coming back!

I ended up cooking for Dr. Pierre Pannetier for two years. It was here I began learning the therapeutic value of natural foods. I began to flourish in this atmosphere, taking note that among doctors and healers in the natural medicine field there was general agreement that greater healing took

---

[10] Eliminating sweets was a temporary healing step and not a permanent change.

place on a vegetarian diet. The dietary recommendations then, were *80% raw and 20% cooked*. Yes, believe it or not, this was in 1974!

By word of mouth (and taste buds), I was fortunate enough to be referred to other doctors who needed a vegetarian chef. These doctors are now noted for their pioneering work in preventative medicine, herbs, natural healing and nutrition: Drs. Michael Tierra, Bernard Jensen, Paavo Airola, and Michael Klaper. Each doctor has lectured, published books and led many workshops. They were teaching about

Dr. Bernard Jensen and Marilyn

specific health conditions and recommending specific foods for those health conditions. I began putting meals together for the seminar students and doctors that reflected the health principles that were being taught. I *loved* what I was learning and teaching.

This photo was taken on Dr. Jensen's 85th birthday. His birthday party had been cancelled because he was not well. He was so happy that I gave him a classic Bible, something he dearly wanted, that he spontaneously kissed me. Dr. Jensen was my family doctor and friend; I had known him since I was 15. We worked together professionally for many years. Photography of a food presentation I made for a TV filming featuring Dr. Jensen is on one of his book covers.

LIBRARY LEGACY

My mother had an extensive health library that she used as reference whenever she was called upon for nutritional advice. One day, to my great surprise and delight, she gave me her entire collection of books. I knew the value she had placed upon these books and when I asked her why she was giving them to me she answered, "I read every book, and they drove me crazy!" I took that to mean she must have found a great deal of controversy and contradiction among the so-called "experts."

I was thrilled to see that she had included Dr. Paavo Airola's books in the gifted collection. He was at the top of the list of respected authors. Because my mom was so impressed with Dr. Airola, and I respected her knowledge about nutrition, I began to seek out ways that I could personally study with him. One day I decided to call him, and to my amazement, through my detective work I found a direct line and reached him personally. I told him that I was interested in his work because I felt that vegetarianism was the wave of the future and morally correct due to my understanding. He asked where I gained my understanding and I explained that I understood this from my meditation. He asked if I would please come to his seminar in Montana as his guest. The seminar was packed with knowledge and facts about vegetarianism, as well as testimonials from doctors and health professionals sharing about their experiences. I was given an A+ on the test.

When I spoke with Paavo at the end of the seminar, I asked about a teacher I could study with when I returned home. He answered, "You don't need any other teachers."

I then said, "You don't understand, I am serious about my work in nutrition."

Marilyn and
Dr. Paavo Airola

He said, "You don't need any other teachers, you study with me."

After the next seminar on the West Coast, I asked Paavo to be my mentor in Nutrition and he said yes.

What impressed me so much about Dr. Airola's work was that medical doctors very heavily endorsed him. I was pleased to note that on the back cover of his book titled *Every Woman's Book*, were endorsements from seven medical doctors.

Dr. Airola gave me certification as a Nutritional Consultant. Among his tenets was the advocacy of juicing for therapeutic conditions and the recommendation of fermented dairy products such as kefir milk for digestion, as well as dairy in general. Most doctors were still recommending dairy products in those days, the years preceding the shocking findings about the harms of dairy.[11]

FORCED SPONTANEITY

In 1974, I was living in the Santa Cruz Mountains at Michael Tierra's *Garden of Sanjivani*, a residential School for Natural Healing and Spiritual Studies. I was asked to teach my first class in food preparation. How did I feel about this? To say I was "anxious and nervous" would have been a *gross* understatement. I was teaching my very first cooking class to a group of doctors, acupuncturists, herbalists, etc., who probably knew more about nutrition than I did. To alleviate my shyness and insecurity, I invested a great deal of time in food and class content preparation. I knew that I had to be highly organized. As I prepped for the dishes that I would teach, I also rehearsed what I would say about the dishes, so that I could feel, if not relaxed, at least well grounded as I stepped into this brand new experience. I carefully labeled all of the prepared dishes and placed them in the refrigerator. This must have made it extra convenient for the midnight refrigerator raider. The next morning, when I went into the kitchen just before class, *EVERYTHING* was gone except the empty, dirty containers in the sink. WOW! I was stunned. This called for instant adjustment. I adapted, immediately swung into a spontaneous cooking style and dazzled the doctors. It was a hit!

---

[11] Please see Chapter Three for facts on the harms of dairy.

In fact, that spur-of-the-moment teaching style worked so well, it is still with me today. *"Look, Ma, no recipes!"*

THE SPA CIRCUIT

My new career as a *Vegan*, then moved on to spas: Alive Polarity at Murrieta Hot Springs, Cal-a-Vie, and consulting for Dr. Deepak Chopra at Mind/Body Center, in San Diego, California.

At Cal-a-Vie, world famous spa resort, Rosie Daley (former Oprah Winfrey chef) hired me. Rosie and I had previously worked together at a restaurant in San Diego called "Basil St. Café." She wanted me to become her sous-chef, but since I was vegan, I could not taste the animal/dairy dishes, and I had to pass on that opportunity. I developed menus and prepared meals at Cal-a-Vie spa for guests with special dietary needs related to allergies and specific health problems. I lectured on the subject of natural foods, and assisted Rosie Daley at weekly spa cuisine cooking classes for their guests. I also created vegetable baskets served daily to guests at Cal-a-Vie; they were frequently photographed.

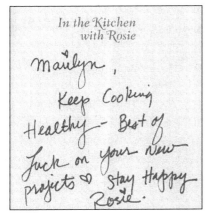

In the Kitchen with Rosie

Marilyn,

Keep Cooking Healthy – Best of luck on your New projects & stay Happy

Rosie.

"Magnificently gorgeous! You do beautiful work!"

(Cal-a-Vie investor)

A WING AND A PRAYER

Around 1996, I came to Los Angeles on a wing, a prayer and my credit card! I longed to be *discovered* as a star in the vegan world and was willing to do whatever it took, money or no! My first client was Vicky, wife of one of the stars of *Victor Victoria*, playing on Broadway, popular actor, Michael Nouri. It was in Los Angeles that I met and catered for Howard Lyman, the former cattle rancher turned vegan who later got sued along with Oprah Winfrey for his exposé about beef that he presented on her show. Julie Cromwell, wife of James Cromwell tasted my catered presentation for Howard Lyman and asked if I would cater her mother's birthday party.

"The only way we would
have a pig for dinner!"
Photo courtesy of Private Chef's Inc.

A BABE WITH "BABE"

I moved to San Diego to work with a client who was referred to me by the nutritionist at Cal-a-Vie. After working with my client for three months, he gave me severance pay of room and board for a month, plus $10,000. As this came to a close, I received a phone call from Julie Cromwell asking me to move in with them as their chef/assistant. Back again to Los Angeles I went, becoming a live-in chef with the Cromwell's for a period of time (until they moved). As a result of this, I was later featured in Christian Paer's book, (not yet published) *Celebrities and Their Chefs*, with James Cromwell, Babe (the movie star pig), and my recipes. While in Los Angeles, I also had the opportunity to consult and cook for Julie Cromwell's mother, Helen Beverly, a famous Jewish actress, wife of Actor, Lee J. Cobb.

WOODY HARRELSON'S RESTAURANT O^2 is where I began to express myself in the art and style of preparing raw foods cuisine. As a consultant, I was asked to create recipes for the menu. As a chef, I would spontaneously create dishes and send them up to the customers for their dining palate pleasure. As a caterer, this opened the door for me to cater a birthday party for Woody's daughter. I loved designing the food with Nature's bounty and awesome array of colors, and I valued the compliments received from the patrons.

Dr. Michael Klaper (known for his work in teaching vegan nutrition to doctors, nurses, and health practitioners) called me from Hawaii to say that he was meeting with an investor in San Diego, whom he wanted to sample vegan food, and asked if I would come out and prepare a meal for them. It was a long commute from Los Angeles, where I was living at the time, but I was up for it! As I was about to serve the meal, in walked the investor's girlfriend, Rue McClanahan. Rue had just come back from visiting her doctor. After the meal, we began a conversation about health, and she asked for my recommendations. After we spoke, she asked for my card. A couple of weeks later she called and hired

With Michael Klaper, MD

me to cook three meals a day, lunch and dinner to go, while she was on a movie set.

Soon after she finished that movie, she moved to New York to do a play. By the way, her favorite breakfast was buckwheat and toasted pumpkin seeds and she loved Kabocha squash, blended very thick, as a dessert. (See: Golden Flower Squash Soup, Chapter Six.)

ZOSA RANCH

A medical doctor and his wife, Nena, owned the Zosa Ranch, a B & B where I was once resident manager.[12] I invited Dr. Benjamin Spock and his wife, Mary Martin, to be my guests for dinner. They graciously accepted. I later heard Dr. Spock speak at a press conference given by Dr. Neal Barnard, saying, "Up until two years of age, a child should be breast-fed. No child, after the age of two, requires any animal or dairy products."

With Benjamin Spock, MD at Zosa Ranch

With Louise Hay

A friend of mine was going to a seminar, and I asked her to give a note to Louise Hay,[13] asking her to call me. I had only met Louise briefly at a presentation given by Deepak Chopra. It was there that I gave her my resume, which later opened the door to my consulting with Deepak. A couple of weeks after the Deepak Chopra event, Louise called me, and I invited her to lunch at Zosa Ranch. She came with a friend and I can remember jumping up and down with excitement when I saw her. She got a big kick out of that.

Consulting with Deepak Chopra[14] was an exciting experience for me. His Ayurvedic menu was being prepared at his new Mind/Body Center by the hotel chefs, who, to me, seemed angry and resentful about having to learn this new food preparation style that was entirely apart from their own consciousness. I pointed out that those vibrations were going into the food and recommended that he seek and hire a trained Ayurvedic chef, someone who loved that way of cooking and would put that love into the food. This would create an all-around healing atmosphere for his clientele. The next thing I suggested was, since this program was in Los Angeles, with many aware, health-conscious people, that he serve *whole* grains, rather than refined grains, as well as *all organic* vegetables and fruits. In the midst of

---

[12] Zosa Ranch owners, Noli Zosa, MD, and his wife Nena often asked me to teach vegetarian nutrition to their doctor friends whenever they visited the ranch.

[13] Noted author of *You Can Heal Your Life* and founder of Hay House publishers.

[14] The only way I feel that he could have heard about my work, was through Louise Hay, as they are very good friends.

our consulting, he called his secretary and told her to see that a video was *immediately* prepared for the staff about food consciousness and also to start looking for an Ayurvedic chef.

Five years after the "wing-and-prayer" flight to Los Angeles, my wish to be *"discovered"* came true; in September 2001 *SPA* Magazine published my photo and a four-page article titled *Vegan Chef of the Rich and Famous* with caption *Marilyn McDonald Heals with Food.*[15] This was a thrill for me to see my dream up in lights so to speak. I had been a busy chef/teacher, as time flew by on golden wings. Then,

SPA Magazine
2001 at age 65

as I looked back, I realized there were *many* other facets, *many* other little lights on the marquee that were part of becoming successful. To me, success means helping to make a positive difference in the world, which includes less suffering for humans and animals.

Today, as I write this book, I am in good health and high spirits. I have an ocean of gratitude for all that I have learned and for all the health benefits this knowledge has brought to me and to others I have shared it with.

Marilyn in 2007
"Gourmet Grandma and her Grand Sous-Chefs"
L to R: Jordan, Ryan and Rachel.

---

[15] Previous married name.

Notes and Quotes
Recommended Reading

PART ONE: A variety of books from my home library, for further study.

Becoming Vegan **by Brenda Davis, RD and Vesanto Melina, MS, RD**
A comprehensive guide to veganism that offers an elaborate, well credited, and well researched expose of the history of the vegan movement, nutritional necessities, and what it takes to maintain a healthy and well balanced vegan lifestyle.

Breaking the Food Seduction **by Neal Barnard, MD**
Dr. Barnard shares his understanding of why we have food cravings, and how to overcome them by explaining which foods "hook" us the most and why, and what to do to break free from them.

Conscious Eating **by Gabriel Cousens, MD**
Aimed toward reasons for transitioning into a more conscious vegetarian lifestyle, this book explores the physical detoxification and psychophysiology of dietary change to promote a gentle open-ended approach to transitioning to a live foods diet, backed by plenty of research and personal experience.

Diet For A New America **by John Robbins**
As one of the major literary works to inspire the modern vegan initiative of the early 90s, Robbins offers an immaculately credible, thoroughly researched, and comprehensive explanation of the nutritional benefits of a plant-based diet, the environmental consequences of consuming animal products, and the socio-economic forces that sustain the Standard American Diet.

Disease-Proof Your Child: Feeding Kids Right by Joel Fuhrman, MD

Dr. Joel Fuhrman presents fascinating scientific research in his book, *Disease-Proof Your Child*, which demonstrates how the current epidemic of adult cancers and other diseases are most closely linked to what we eat in the first quarter of life. He explains how a nutrient-rich diet increases a child's resistance to common childhood illnesses like asthma, or infections, and allergies. Eating Dr. Fuhrman's nutrient-rich diet during childhood is the most powerful weapon against developing cancer, cardiovascular disease and autoimmune disorders. *Disease-Proof Your Child*, provides dietary recommendations for children, and offers guidelines and recipes for the pickiest eaters to enjoy healthy food.

Eat To Live by Joel Fuhrman, MD

Dr. Fuhrman's book offers a healthy, effective, and scientifically proven Six-Week Plan for shedding a radical amount of weight quickly. The key to the program's success is simple: health = the ratio of nutrients to calories. When the ratio of nutrients to calories in the food you eat is high, fat melts away. The more nutrient-dense food you consume, the more you will be satisfied with fewer calories and the less you will crave fat and high-calories. *Eat to Live* will enable you to lose more weight than you ever thought possible.

Fasting Can Save Your Life by Herbert Shelton

Focused on how fasting can be used as a means to lose weight as well as a way to heal your body from common illnesses, Shelton explains the difference between starvation and fasting and allays misperceptions about the unhealthy Nature of fasting.

Fats That Heal, Fats That Kill by Udo Erasmus

This book offers a comprehensive explanation of the difference between healthy fats the body needs and unhealthy fats that do the body harm, some of the vital functions of essential fatty acids, and some of the damaging side effects of improper fats consumed in improper ways. This is a great book to read for extra research on oils.

Life Is Fair by Brian Hines

This book discusses the law of cause and effect: if life is fair, we get exactly what we deserve, and like the law of gravity, karma is an undeniable part of the universe's make up; we may not be able to see it, but we can certainly see its effects. The chapter "Vegetarianism, Meat Eating and Suffering" gives a clear understanding of karma.

Mucusless Diet Healing System by Arnold Ehret

Professor Ehret describes the disastrous clogging effects of mucus foods on the body and the benefits of participating in periodic fasts for cleansing purposes.

Nature's First Law: The Raw Food Diet **by Arlin, Dini and David Wolfe**
For people who are already convinced that raw-foodism is the way to go and are on the transitional path, this book could serve as a perfect guide to help give up cooked foods.

Rational Fasting **by Arnold Ehret**
This book argues all diseases are caused by biologically *unnatural* foods that need to be eliminated from the human diet in order to maintain perfect health. He writes about "building a perfect body through fasting."

RaweSome Recipes: Whole Foods for Vital Nutrition **by Robyn Boyd**
This is an incredibly comprehensive guide to the raw foods diet that describes its advantageous and widespread health benefits, the financial, ecological and ethical considerations, and scientific studies that back up its assertions; a unique component in comparison to most of the other raw food books out there.

The China Study **by T. Colin Campbell, PhD**
Dr. Campbell has succeeded in producing a shockingly relevant and comprehensive study of culturally based dietary patterns and the dangers of the Standard American Diet. He does this by citing countless cutting edge medical research cases that overwhelmingly show the devastating consequences of eating animal products and dairy.

The Food Revolution **by John Robbins**
The thoroughly updated and more-pertinent-than-ever counterpart to Robbins' *Diet For A New America, The Food Revolution* is a must read for anybody who wants an up-to-date and thoroughly well-researched expose on the comprehensive nutritional, environmental and socio-economical benefits of eating vegan.

Vegan Freak **by Bob Torres and Jenna Torres**
The husband and wife authors of *Vegan Freak* wrote the book as a survival guide for vegans in contemporary society, making the transition to veganism as easy as possible by providing support, advice and suggestions to those who are newly vegan or thinking about becoming vegan.

Vegan With a Vengeance **by Isa Chandra Moskowitz**
The author and co-host of *The Post Punk Kitchen* brings her punk, do-it-yourself attitude to this fresh and innovative cookbook which offers a diverse array of animal-free recipes, lots of general cooking tips and advice and ways to keep costs down. More than anything she encourages the reader to be creative and have fun.

PART TWO: Quotes from various subjects that support the transition, for further study.

✓ *Cleanse and Purify Thyself* **by Richard Anderson, MD**
"Raw foods are the perfect food for man and can bring him exceptional health. They keep the body clean and congestion free. Only raw foods have life force and enzymes, which are far more important to your health than vitamins, minerals and amino acids. Vitamins, minerals and amino acids can keep you alive, but life force and enzymes will keep you vibrantly alive. You cannot eat foods without life force and enzymes and not also get vitamins, minerals and protein."

✓ *Colon Health: The Key to a Vibrant Life* **by Norman H. Walker**
"I have referred to milk as being the most mucous-forming food we can use. Raw milk would be bad enough, but to pasteurize or homogenize it is worse. Besides milk, processed cheeses are the frequent cause of excessive mucous. Devitalized starches and sugar are both mucous culprits and when removed from the diet the beneficial results are perceptive. Above all, invariably start with cleansing the colon. During the past four-score years we have seen far too many colds and analogous ailments disappear by removing cow's milk and other mucous-forming foods from the diet and cleansing the body with high enemas and colonic irrigations."

✓ *Dr. Jensen's Guide to Better Bowel Care* **by Bernard Jensen, PhD**
"I want to emphasize that an underactive body burdened with toxic wastes does not have the capability to throw off toxins. As a body becomes increasingly toxic, proper oxygenation cannot take place in the tissues. Without oxygen, the body loses energy, and the tired body continues its downward spiral. A tired body has a reduced ability to throw off toxins, which is why toxic, sick people are always tired people."

✓ *Enzyme Nutrition* **by Edward Howell**
"High temperatures, as in cooking, destroy enzymes in natural foods. But, I can almost hear you say, 'This cannot be, because the human race has been cooking for a long time and is still going strong.' Partly true. We are only half sick. What poses as good health today has been aptly termed by one doctor as 'Pregnant ill-health,' or the absence of symptoms. Good health as we know it is in reality a prolonged incubation period for a variety of killer and intractable diseases. No matter from which angle we view health and disease, we cannot escape from being entangled in the conclusion that intractable disease is as old as cookery. Disease and cookery originated simultaneously. And cookery must be held guilty of assassinating hundreds of food enzymes which, we must be constantly reminded, are the most delicate and precious elements that foods can offer us."

Food Combining Made Easy **by Herbert Shelton**

"More than 60 years spent in feeding the well and the sick, the weak and the strong, the old and the young, have demonstrated that a change to correctly combined meals is followed by an immediate improvement in health as a consequence of lightening the load the digestive organs have to carry, thus assuring better digestion, improved nutrition and less poisoning. I know that such meals are followed by less fermentation and less putrefaction, less gas and discomfort. I do not believe that such experiences are worth much if they cannot be explained by correct principles, but I have explained them in preceding pages, so that they do assume great importance. The rules of food combining herein given are soundly rooted in physiology, thoroughly tested by experience, and are worthy of more than just a passing thought."

Food Enzymes — The Missing Link to Radiant Health **by Humbart Santillo**

"It is important that we preserve the body's enzyme level at all expenses: by eating raw food and by taking enzyme supplements. Supplementing enzymes to our diet and eating a raw food diet are subjects that will be discussed throughout this book. What is important at this time is to understand what happens when we cook our food; the difference between live (raw) and dead enzymatic activity. If you had two seeds and boiled one, which one would grow when placed in soil? There is no question that the un-boiled seed would sprout because it has its enzymes intact. All foods provided by Nature have an abundance of enzymes when in their raw state."

Mad Cowboy **by Howard Lyman**

"A recent Agriculture Department study revealed that more than 99% of broiler carcasses had detectable levels of E.coli. In addition, approximately 30% of chicken consumed in America is contaminated with salmonella, and 70 to 90% with another deadly pathogen, campylobacter.

"In short, the evidence that an animal-based diet is implicated in our soaring cancer rates — our number two killer — begins to rival the evidence of its contribution to our number one killer, coronary heart disease. When meat and dairy products aren't killing us, they're often making us sick and progressively destroying our health and the quality of our lives."

No More Bull! **by Howard Lyman**

"Now I ask you, do you know of anyone who has gotten sick, gone to the hospital, or died from lack of protein? I am quite sure that you don't, whereas I bet you know plenty of people who have become victims of heart disease and cancer. It is remarkable how many people dig their graves with artery-destroying, fatty, animal foods because they are afraid of a condition that scarcely can be found anywhere in America: Protein deficiency."

Quantum Wellness by Kathy Freston

"Sadly, most of the meat, egg and dairy that pretend to be eco- or animal friendly, with packages covered in pictures with pretty red barns, are the same massive corporately owned factory farms. Labels like 'Swine Welfare' and 'UEP Certified' are simply the industry labels. The 'Swine Welfare' label comes from the National Pork Producers Council and the UEP stands for United Egg Producers. Both are trade groups that exist only to maximize profits and their explanations for their labels are filled with grandiose rhetoric, which doesn't do much for the animals. The labels hide what really happens behind closed doors as animals are turned into meat for our tables."

Skinny Bitch In the Kitch by Rory Freedman and Kim Barnouin

"Meat: Hmm…dead, rotting, decomposing flesh of carcasses. Doesn't sound like something you'd want to eat, huh? Not to mention the pesticides, hormones, steroids, and antibiotics. Oops! We almost forgot Mad Cow Disease, bird flu, salmonella, E.coli, trichinosis, and mercury. Well, no wonder Americans are suffering from obesity, cancer; liver, kidney, lung and reproductive disorders; birth defects; miscarriages; and nervous system disorders. **Dairy:** Got osteoporosis? Researchers at Harvard, Yale, Penn State, and the National Institutes of Health have studied the effects of dairy intake on bones. Not one of these studies found dairy to be a deterrent to osteoporosis. On the contrary, a study funded by the National Dairy Council itself revealed that the high protein content of milk actually leeches calcium from the body. These findings are consistent with many others that blame milk not only for osteoporosis, but also acne, anemia, anxiety, ADD, allergies, asthma, obesity, heart disease, diabetes, autism, and multiple cancers."

The Engine 2 Diet by Rip Esselstyn

"There is absolutely no need to combine certain plant proteins at each meal in an attempt to achieve an optimal amino acid balance. Unfortunately, the protein-combination myth continues to be perpetuated by any number of respected organizations. But the American Dietetic Association gets it right. Its position statement reads: 'Plant sources of protein alone can provide adequate amounts of the essential and non-essential amino acids, assuming that dietary protein sources from plants are reasonably varied and that caloric intake is sufficient to meet energy needs. Whole grains, legumes, vegetables, seeds, and nuts all contain essential and non-essential amino acids.' Scream it from the mountaintops: Plant proteins are 100% complete!"

The Kind Diet by Alicia Silverstone

"A varied plant-based diet is packed with calcium-rich foods, including sea vegetables, leafy greens, beans, nuts and seeds. By eating these foods you will get more than enough calcium. Just as importantly, you will be abstaining from foods that steal calcium from your body — namely meat, dairy and white sugar — and it's these foods that play the biggest role in bone loss."

The Nut Gourmet by Zel Allen

"The 10 year Nurses' Health Study at the Harvard School of Public Health, which included more than 86,000 women, who frequently included nuts in their diet, as much as five times a week, lowered their risk of heart attack. Frank Hu, lead researcher on the study, reported: 'Even when we adjusted for factors like smoking, exercise, and consumption of fruits and vegetables, nuts showed up as a powerful defense against heart disease. Monounsaturated and polyunsaturated fats have been shown to lower LDLs or so-called bad cholesterol,' says Dr. Hu in the study published in the November 1998 issue of the *British Medical Journal*. Researchers also learned that those participants who ate nuts actually tended to weigh less than those who didn't eat nuts."

Throwin' Down Vegetarian Style by Martha Theus

"All of our actions, including our choice of food, have karmic consequences. By involving oneself in the cycle of inflicting injury, pain and death, even indirectly by eating other creatures, one must in the future, experience in equal measure the suffering caused. The effects of a flesh diet may not be immediately realized, but this is no evidence that it is not harmful. Few can be made to believe that it is the meat they have eaten which has poisoned their blood and caused their suffering. Many die of diseases wholly due to meat eating, while the real cause is not suspected by themselves or others."

Your Body's Many Cries for Water by F. Batmanghelidj, MD

"It is primitive and simplistic thinking that one could easily lace water with all sorts of pleasure-enhancing chemicals and substitute these fluids for the natural and clean water that the human body needs. Some of these chemicals, caffeine, aspartame, saccharin and alcohol, through their constant lopsided effect on the brain, un-directionally — single mindedly — program the body chemistry with results contrary to the natural design of the body. Very much like the sailboat in the dark that will get beached on uncharted shores if its sailor gives in to the pleasures and exhilaration of fast sailing in place of sticking to the rules of sailing with safety in mind, the intake of wrong fluids will affect the life of anyone who continually consumes them."

RESOURCES

Check out *www.veganbitebybite.com* for delicious, free recipes.

COMPANIES & WEBSITES

Company Name	Company Description	Company Websites
21st Century Vegetarians	Vegetarian transition cookbook	www.21stCenturyVegetarians.com
American Health and Nutrition, Inc.	Organic health and education	Neworganics.com
Before Wisdom	Excellent educational website	http://www.beforewisdom.com/veg/health.html
Creative Citizen	Excellent environmental website	http://creativecitizen.com
Brian Hines	Author – Life is Fair	http://brianhines.com
Dr. Caldwell Esselstyn	*Prevent and Reverse Heart Disease*	http://www.heartattackproof.com
Dr. Joel Fuhrman	Author/Various books/Medical Consultant/Lecturer	www.DrFuhrman.com
Dr. John McDougall	Author/Various books/Medical Consultant/Lecturer	www.drmcdougall.com
Dr. Michael Greger	Director – Public Health Humane Society Excellent educational website	http://www.drgreger.org/
Dr. Pamela Popper	Health-Wellness Forum	www.wellnessforum.com
Dr. Susan Padrad	World United Women	www.worldunitedwomen.com
Go Dairy Free	How to shop dairy free + more	www.godairyfree.org
Green Song Press	80-10-10-Success Guide/Raw foods site	www.GreenSongPress.org
Happy Cow	Vegetarian guide to restaurants, health food stores	www.happycow.net
Lillian Muller	Author – Playboy cover model	www.lillianmuller.com
Mad Cowboy	Howard Lyman's website (Excellent)	www.madcowboy.com
Matt Monarch	Raw Food Advocate/Lecturer	www.rawspirit.org
PCRM	Dr. Neal Barnard's various books/website	http://www.pcrm.org/shop/neal/index.html
Rahel Woldmehin	Vegan Etheopian Restaurant	www.rahelveggiecuisine.com
RAWvolution – Matt Amsden	Raw foods recipe book/Food delivery	www.rawvolution.com
Soy Stache	Raw & Living Restaurants around world	http://www.soystache.com/raw-food-restaurants.htm
Spirits In Transition	Hospice for animals seminars/Education	www.spiritsintransition.org/

Company Name	Company Description	Company Websites
T. Colin Campbell	Impressive, scientific vegan authority/book author	www.tcolincampbell.org/
The Organic Report	Good reasons to buy organic	www.organicitsworthit.org
Veg. Dining	Vegetarian Restaurants around the world	www.vegdining.com
Veg. Family	Magazine/Vegan family living	http://vegfamily.com
Vegetarians in Paradise	Excellent website/Resources	www.vegparadise.com
Vegsource	Excellent website/Resources	http://www.vegsource.com
Vegan	Has a free vegan book download (PDF format)	www.vegan.com
Vegan Athlete	Vegan athlete site – Good information	http://www.veganathlete.com/
Vegan Essentials	Over 1200 vegan items	www.veganessentials.com
Vegan Family	Lifestyle education, health, recipes	www.veganfamilyliving.com
Vegan-Gal	Famous vegetarians and vegans	http://www.vegan-gal.com/famous_vegans.html#
Vegetarian Resource Group	Articles, books, education	www.vrg.org
Vegetarian Times	Magazine, featuring articles and recipes	http://www.vegetariantimes.com/resources/produce_storage_guide/
Will Tuttle	Author – *World Peace Diet*	http://worldpeacediet.org

BOOKS & PRODUCTS

The Tao of Nutrition	Therapeutic plant foods	www.taostar.com 800-772-0222
Vita-Mix Corporation 8615 Usher Road Cleveland, OH 44138	High-powered blender Save $25 US $35 CN (see below) Savings Code 06-003966 to receive Free Standard Shipping	www.vitamix.com/ 1-800-848-2649 Press option 1
Bemer	Promotes blood circulation at the capillary level	www.bemeramerica.com/wendel 323-683-5515
Kangen Water	High quality alkaline water	323-683-5515
DHA	Vegetarian source	http://www.martek.com/
Selfcare4wellness	Excellent well being products	www.selfcare4wellness.com

References

A Report of the Panel on macronutrients, Subcommittees on upper Reference levels of Nutrients and Interpretation and uses of Dietary Reference Intakes, and the Standing Committee on the Scientific Evaluation of Dietary Reference Intakes	*Dietary Reference intakes for Energy, Carbohydrate, Fiber, Fat, Fatty Acids, Cholesterol, Protein, and Amino Acids (macronutrients)*	Washington, D.C.: The National Academies Press http://www.nap.edu/ books/0309085373/html/	2005 Accessed May 5, 2010
Allen, Zel	*The Nut Gourmet: Nourishing nuts for every occasion*	Summertown, TN Book Publishing Co.	2006
Airola, Paavo PhD, ND	*Are You Confused?*	Sherwood, OR: Health Plus Publishers	1974
Anderson, Richard MD	*Cleanse and Purify Thyself: The clean-me-out program*	Self-published	1988
Appleton, Nancy	*Healthy Bones: What you should know about Osteoporosis*	Garden City Park, NY: Avery Pub Group	1991
Barnard, Neal	*News Release: New Study Shows High-Carb Vegan Diet Causes Major Weight Loss*	Physicians Committee for Responsible Medicine http://www.pcrm.org/news/ release050909.html	09-Sept. 2005 Accessed May 5, 2010
Barnard, Neal MD, Scialli, Anthony R.,MD Turner-McGrievy, Gabrielle MD,RD, Lanou, Amy J. PhD. Glass, Jolie MS	*The effects of a low-fat, plant-based dietary intervention on body weight, metabolism, and insulin sensitivity*	American Journal of Medicine	2005 Sept. Vol. 118 No. 9 991-997
Barnard, N.D., Nicholson, A., Howard, J.L.	*The medical costs attributable to meat consumption*	Preventive Medicine	1995 Nov; 24(6):646-55
Barnard, N.D., Scialli, A.R., Bertron, P., Hurlock, D., Edmonds, K., Talev, L.	*Effectiveness of a low-fat, vegetarian diet in altering serum lipids in healthy premenopausal women*	American Journal Cardiology	2000 April 15; 85 (8):969-72

Barnard, Neal MD	*Breaking the Food Seduction: The hidden reasons behind food cravings – and 7 steps to end them naturally*	New York, St. Martin's Press	2003
Batmanghelidj, F. MD	*Your body's Many Cries for Water: You are not sick, you are thirsty: Don't treat thirst with medications*	Falls Church, VA: Global Health Solutions	1995
Berger, Barbara	*Animalia: Thirteen small tales*	Berkeley, CA: Tricycle Press	1999
Beston, Henry	*The Outermost House*	Doubleday and Dorian	1928
Bonne, Rose, Mills, Alan	*I Know an Old Lady Who Swallowed a Fly*	Canada: Peer International Ltd. (used with permission)	1952
Boyd, Robin	*Rawsome Recipes: Whole Foods for Vital Nutrition*	Orem, UT: Essential Science Publishing	2005
Bridges, William	*The Way of Transition: Embracing Life's Most Difficult Moments*	Cambridge, MA: Perseus Pub	2001
Brown, Susan PhD	*Better Bones, Better Body: Beyond Estrogen and Calcium: A comprehensive self-help program for preventing, halting and overcoming osteoporosis*	New Canaan, CT: Keats Pub.	1996
Campbell, T. Colin PhD Campbell, Thomas M.	*The China Study: The Most Comprehensive Study of Nutrition Ever Conducted and the Startling Implications for Diet, Weight Loss, and Long-Term Health*	Dallas, TX: BenBella Books, Inc.	2006
Chittenden, Russell Henry PhD.	*Physiological Economy in Nutrition, with special reference to the minimal protein requirement of the healthy man, an experimental study*	New York: Frederick A. Stokes Company	1904
Cohen, Robert	*Milk A - Z*	NJ: Argus Pub.	2001
Cohen, Robert	*www.notmilk.com*	Self-published website	Accessed May 5, 2007
Cohen, Robert	*Milk: The Deadly Poison*	Englewood Cliffs, NJ: Argus Pub.	1997
Colbin, Annemarie	*Food and Healing*	New York: Ballentine Books	1986
Colbin, Annemarie	*Food and our Bones: The natural way to prevent osteoporosis*	New York: Plume	1998
Cousens, Gabriel MD	*Conscious Eating*	Santa Rosa, CA: Vision Books Int'l.	1992
Cummings, S.R., Nevitt, M.C., Browner, W.S.	*Risk factors for hip fracture in white women. Study of Osteoporotic Fractures Research Group*	New England Journal of Medicine	1995 Mar 23;332 (12):767-73.
Daley, Rosie	*In the Kitchen with Rosie: Oprah's Favorite Recipes*	New York, Alfred A. Knopf	1994
Dass, Ram	*The Only Dance There Is*	Garden City, NY: Anchor Press	1974

Davis, Brenda RD, Melina, Vesanto MS,RD	*Becoming Vegan: The Complete Guide to Adopting a Healthy Plant-Based Diet*	Summertown, TN: Book Publishing Co.	2000
Diego, Pedro	*Letter to the Editor*	Providence Journal	29-Jan-08
Dini, RC, Arlin, Fouad & Wolfe, David	*Nature's First Law: The Raw-Food Diet*	San Diego, CA: Maui Brothers Publishing	1997
Ehret, Arnold	*Mucusless Diet Healing System; A scientific method of eating your way to health*	New York: B. Lust Publications	1970
Ehret, Arnold	*Rational Fasting...for... physical, mental and spiritual rejuvenation*	Beaumont, CA: Ehret Literature Publishing Co.	1965
Elgan, Amira	Research Developments www.vegetarianorganiclife. com/50.htm	Self-published website	Accessed May 5, 2010
Emerson, Ralph Waldo	Essays. Essay III: Compensation	Boston, MA: J. Munroe and Co.	1841
Epstein, Samuel S.	*What's In Your Milk? An expose of industry and government cover-up on the dangers of the genetically engineered (rBGH) milk you're drinking*	Bloomington, IN: Trafford Publishing	2000
Erasmus, Udo	*Fats That Heal, Fats That Kill: The Complete Guide to Fats, Oils, Cholesterol and Human Health*	Summertown, TN: Alive Books	2007
Esselstyn, Caldwell MD	*Prevent and Reverse Heart Disease: The revolutionary, scientifically proven, nutrition-based cure*	New York: Avery	2007
Esselstyn, Rip	*The Engine 2 Diet; The Texas firefighter's 28-day save-your-life plan that lowers cholesterol and burns away the pounds*	New York: Wellness Central	2009
Feskanich, D., Willett, W.C., Stampfer, M.J., Colditz, G.A.	Milk, dietary calcium, and bone fractures in women: a 12-year prospective study	Am J Publ Health – June 1997 Vol. 87, No. 6	1997 Jun; 87 (6):992-7
Fraser, G.E., & Shavlik, D.J.	*Ten years of life: is it a matter of choice?*	Arch Intern Medicine	2001 Jul 9; 161: (13):1645-52
Freedman, Rory & Barnouin, Kim	*Skinny Bitch in the Kitch: Kick-ass recipes for hungry girls who want to stop cooking crap (and start looking hot!)*	Philadelphia, PA: Running Press	2007
Freston, Kathy	*Quantum Wellness: A Practical and Spiritual Guide to Health and Happiness*	NY: Weinstein Books	2008
Fuhrman, Joel MD	*Eat to Live: The Revolutionary Formula for Fast and Sustained Weight Loss*	Boston, Little Brown and Co.	2003
Fuhrman, Joel MD	*Disease-Proof Your Child: Feeding kids right*	New York: St. Martin's Press	2005

Gladwell, Malcolm	*The Tipping Point: How little things can make a big difference*	Boston: Back Bay Books	2002
Greenpeace USA	*True Food Shopping List*	www.greenpeace.org/usa/news/true-food-shopping-list	20-Jul-04 Accessed Jun 2010
Harvard School of Public Health	*Calcium and Milk: What's best for your bones and health?* http://www.hsph.harvard.edu/nutritionsource/what-should-you-eat/calcium-full-story/index.html	Harvard School of Public Health	Accessed May 5, 2010
Heidrich, Ruth PhD	*Senior Fitness; The Diet and Exercise Program for Maximum Health and Longevity*	New York: Lantern Books	2005
Heritage, Ford	*Composition and Facts About Foods: And Their Relationship to the Human Body*	Pomeroy, WA Health Research	1993
Hines, Brian	*Life is Fair: The law of cause and effect*	Punjab, India: Radha Soami Satsang Beas	1999
Howell, Edward	*Enzyme Nutrition: The Food Enzyme Concept*	Wayne, NJ: Avery Pub. Group	1985
Hu, FB, Stampfer, MJ, Manson, JE, Rimm, EB, Colditz, GA, Rosner, BA, Speizer, FE, Hennekens, CH, & Willett, WC	*Frequent Nut Consumption and Risk of Coronary Heart Disease in Women: Prospective Cohort Study (based on the 10 Year Nurses Health Study@ Harvard School Public Health)*	British Medical Journal	1998 Nov; 317:1341-5
Jensen, Bernard PhD	*Dr. Jensen's Guide to Better Bowel Care: A complete program for tissue cleansing through bowel management*	Garden City Park, NY: Avery Publishing Group	1999
Jensen, Bernard PhD	*Foods That Heal: A guide to understanding and using the healing powers of natural foods – various quotes*	Garden City Park, NY: Avery Publishing Group	1988
Jones, Vernon V.S.(translator)	*Aesop's Fables – The North Wind & the Sun*	Barnes & Noble Classics	2003
Klaper, Michael MD	*As quoted in May All Be Fed by John Robbins*	New York, NY: Avon Books	1992
Klaper, Michael MD	*Pregnancy, Children, and the Vegan Diet*	Umatilla, FL.:Gentle World	1987
Kloss, Jethro	*Back to Eden: A human interest story of health and restoration to be found in herb, root, and bark*	New York: Lancer Books Inc.	1971
Klotter, Jule	*The Dangers of Cow's Milk*	Townsend Letter, Issue 142 Page 16	May 1995
Kradjian, Robert MD	*The Milk Letter: A Message to my Patients*	http://www.rense.com/general29/milkt.htm	Accessed May 28, 2010
Kuhne, Louis, & Lust, Benedict	*Neo-Naturopathy: The New Science of Healing or The Doctrine of Unity of Diseases*	Whitefish, MT: Kessinger Publishing	2003

Ladinsky, Daniel	Love Poems from God: 12 sacred voices from the East and West/"Does Every Creature Have a soul?"	New York, NY: Penguin Group, Inc.	2002
Lang, Rich	Marilyn McDonald: Heals with Food; Vegan Chef of the Rich and Famous	Spa Magazine	Sept. 2001
Latson, Deanna	Just About Food	http://www.gotohealth. com/articles/read. cfm?article_id=30	
Lindahl O., Lindwall L., Spangberg, A., Ockerman, P.A.	A vegan regimen with reduced medication in the treatment of hypertension.	Br Journal Nutrition	1984 Jul; 52 (1):11-20
Lyman, Howard and Merzer, Glen	Mad Cowboy: Plain truth from the cattle rancher who won't eat meat	New York, NY: Scribner	1998
Lyman, Howard and Merzer, Glen and Joanna Samorow	No More Bull! The Mad Cowboy Targets America's Worst Enemy: Our Diet	New York, NY: Scribner	2005
McDougall, John MD	McDougall's Medicine: A Challenging Second Opinion	Piscataway, NJ: New Century Publishers	1985
McDougall, John MD	Maximum Weight Loss	www.drmcdougall.com Hot Topics	Accessed May 5, 2010
Moskowitz, Isa Chandra	Vegan With a Vengeance: Over 150 delicious, cheap, animal-free recipes that rock	New York, NY: Marlowe and Company	2005
Mulhall, Douglas Hansen, Katja	The Calcium Bomb: The Nanobacteria Link to Heart Disease & Cancer www. calciumbomb.com	Cranston, RI: Writers' Collective	2005
Muller, Lillian	Feel Great, Be Beautiful Over 40	Toronto, Ontario, Canada Stoddart Publishing Co.	1995
Nicholson, A,S,, Sklar, M., Barnard, N.D., Gore, S., Sullivan, R., Browning, S.	Toward improved management NIDDM: a randomized, controlled, pilot intervention using a low-fat, vegetarian diet.	Preventive Medicine	1999 Aug 29 (2):87-91
Ni, Maoshing PhD, Cathy McNease	The Tao of Nutrition — various quotes	Seventh Star Communications	1987
Noble, Elizabeth PT	Milk Can Kill	http://elizabethnoble.com/ articles.html	1-Mar-08
Noble, Elizabeth PT	Having Twins--and more: A parent's guide to multiple pregnancy, birth, and early childhood	Boston: Houghton Mifflin	2003
North, Rick	Know Your Milk: Does It Have Artificial Hormones?	Physicians for Social Responsibility (PSR) Oregon Chapter — www.oregonpsr. org	Accessed May 5, 2010
Organic Consumer's Assn.	Genetic Engineering and Biotechnology	http://www. organicconsumers.org/ gelink.cfm	Accessed Jun 18 2010
Organic Trade Association	Organic Agriculture and Production	http://www.ota.com/ definition/quickoverview.html	Accessed Jun 18 2010

Ornish, Dean MD	Everyday Cooking with Dr. Dean Ornish: 150 easy, low-fat, high-flavor recipes	New York, NY HarperCollins Publishers, Inc.	1996
Ornish, Dean MD	The Diet War: Low-Fat vs. high-Protein	http://www.Atkinsexposed.org	Accessed Jun 18, 2010
Ornish, D., Brown, S.E., Scherwitz, L.W., Billings, J. H., Armstrong, W. T., Ports, T. A., McLanahan, S. M., Kirkeeide, R. L., Brand, R. J., & Gould, K. L.	Can lifestyle changes reverse coronary heart disease? The Lifestyle Heart Trial	Lancet	1990 Jul 21 336 (8708): 129-133
Oski Jr., Frank MD	Don't Drink Your Milk: Frightening medical facts about the world's most overrated nutrient	Brushton, NY:Teach Services Inc.	2010
Page, Tony Dr. Interview by Vaughn, Claudette	Buddhism and Animal Rights — an Interview with Dr. Tony Page	http://www.purifymind.com/SB37.htm	Accessed Jun 18, 2010
Physicians Committee for Responsible Medicine	Good Medicine	http://www.pcrm.org	Accessed May 5, 2010
Reddy. S.T., Wang, C.Y., Sakhaee, K., Brinkley, L., Pak, C.Y.	Effect of low-carbohydrate high-protein diets on acid-base balance, stone-forming propensity, and calcium metabolism	American Journal Kidney Disease	2002 Aug;40 (2):265-74
Robbins, John	Diet for A New America	Tiburon, CA: H.J. Kramer	1998
Robbins, John	Is Your Favorite Ice Cream Made With Monsanto's 'Cancer Causing' Artificial Hormones?	Huffington Post, August 19, 2010 http://beforeitsnews.com/story/144/652/Is_Your_Favorite_Ice_Cream_Made_With_Monsantos_Cancer_Causing_Artificial_Hormones.html	Accessed September 13, 2010
Robbins, John	The Food Revolution: how your diet can help save your life and our world.	Berkeley, CA: Conari Press 1 edition	2001
Santillo, Humbart	Food Enzymes - The Missing Link to Radiant Health	Prescott Valley, AZ: Hohm Press	1987
Schumacher, E.F.	Small is Beautiful: A Study of Economics as if People Mattered	London: Blond and Briggs	1973
Shelton, Herbert M.	Fasting Can Save Your Life	Chicago, IL: Natural Hygiene Press	1964
Shelton, Herbert M.	Food Combining Made Easy	San Antonio, TX: Willow Publishing	1982
Silverstone, Alicia	The Kind Diet: A simple guide to feeling great, losing weight, and saving the planet	Emmaus, PA: Rodale Books	2009
Singh Ji, Maharaj Charan	The Master Answers; To audiences in America	Beas, India: Radha Soami Satsang	1966
Smith, Jeffrey M.	Genetic Roulette: The documented health risks of Genetically Engineered Foods	Fairfield, IA: Yes! Books	2007

Smith, Jeffrey M.	*Should We GMO or Just Say No?*	LA Yoga Magazine	Volume 9 No. 5 June 2010
Smith, Jeffrey M.	*Seeds of Deception: Exposing industry and government lies about the safety of the genetically engineered foods you're eating*	Fairfield, IA:Yes! Books www.seedsofdeception.com	2003
Spock, Benjamin MD	*Dr. Spock's Baby and Child Care*	New York: Pocket Books	1998
Staffers at the Sacramento Bee	*Seeds of Doubt*	Sacramento Bee www.sacbee.com/static/live/ news/projects/biotech	June 2004 Accessed Jun 18, 2010
Subcommittee on the Tenth Edition of the RDAs Food and Nutrition Board Commission on Life Sciences National Research Council	*Recommended Dietary Allowances January, 1992 edition - edited by Richard Havel, University of California in S.F.*	Washington, D.C.: National Academy Press http://www.nap. edu/openbook. php?isbn=0309046335	1989 Accessed May 5, 2010
Supermarket News	quote from store manager regarding organics	www.supermarketnews.com/	Accessed 8/2/10
Theus, Martha and Theus, Kamaal	*Throwin' Down Vegetarian Style*	Los Angeles, CA: 21st Century Vegetarians	2007
Torres, Bob and Jenna	*Vegan Freak: Being vegan in a non-vegan world*	Tofu Hound Press	2005
Tuttle, Will PhD	*The World Peace Diet: Eating for spiritual health and social harmony*	New York: Lantern Books	2005
USDA Center for Nutrition Policy and Promotion	Food Guide Pyramid	http://www. dietaryguidelines.gov	Accessed May 5, 2010
USDA Food Guide Pyramid	*USDA Food Guide Pyramid (MyPyramid)*	Food and Nutrition Board http://www.diet.com/g/ usda-food-guide-pyramid- mypyramid	Accessed May 5, 2010
USDA National Nutrient Database for Standard Reference	http://www.nal.usda.gov/fnic/ foodcomp	USDA Agricultural Research Service	Accessed 13-Feb-08
Vaughan, Claudette	*Ahimsa, Animal Rights and Spirituality*	New Vegetarian & Natural Health http://veg.ca/content/ view/517/113/	Accessed May 5, 1999
Walker, Norman H.	*Colon Health: The Key to a Vibrant Life*	Norwalk Press; illustrated edition	August 25, 1995
Walsch, Neal Donald	*Conversations with God: An uncommon dialogue*	New York: G.P. Putnam's Sons	1996
Ward, Jack L. MD	*Glucose Tolerance in Schizophrenia*	Journal of Orthomolecular Psychiatry	1972 (1): 137-140.
Wasserman, Deborah (Nutrition section by Mangels, Reed PhD, RD)	*Simply Vegan: Quick Vegetarian Meals; Vitamin B12 in the Diet (Nutrition section)*	Baltimore, MD Vegetarian Resource Group	2006
Watson, Donald	http://en.wikipedia.org/wiki/ Donald_Watson	Wikipedia on-line	Accessed May 5, 2010

Whitaker, Julian MD	*Tomorrow's Medicine Today*	Health and Healing Newsletter	10-98 Vol. 8 No. 10
Wolfe, David and Shazzie	*Naked Chocolate: The Astounding Truth About the Greatest Food*	Sunfood Nutrition	May 2005

Index

Breinigsville, PA USA
22 November 2010
249772BV00002B/95-500/P